Embracing Your
Subconscious

EMBRACING YOUR
SUBCONSCIOUS

Bringing All Parts of You
Into Creative Partnership

Conscious & Subconscious,
Head & Heart, Masculine & Feminine,
Adult & Child, Waking & Dreaming

Jenny Davidow

Contents

Acknowledgments

I gratefully acknowledge all of my teachers, students, friends and family, who helped me directly and indirectly in the writing of this book.

Carl Jung, Fritz Perls and Patricia Garfield have been my most significant teachers. Through their writings, they opened the door that made it possible for me to explore the creative wisdom of the subconscious.

Many other teachers and friends have encouraged and nourished me: Bret Lyon, Jane Stewart, Barbara Rapko, Richard Root, Michael Harner, Ted Falcon, Stan Levy, Frederica Spaeth, and my mother.

My students have contributed greatly to the shaping of this book. Their wholehearted exploration of themselves inspired me to continue developing new material and examples. I especially thank those whose stories I tell in these pages. (All names and some details have been changed to protect their privacy.) Many thanks to my allies in the Senoi Breakfast Club, who participated with me as a dream community for several years.

Special friends have buoyed me up and kept me going throughout this ten-year project. My deepest thanks to James Lewis and Larry Karlin; Evie and Rick Alloy; Jay BloomBecker; Rhoda Erath; and Jeanne Rosen.

My husband, Bret, encouraged me to take each step of this journey, giving tremendous help and support, from the first vision of teaching workshops through every stage of writing, to the final birthing.

*The conflicts between yourself and others
are nothing but the conflicts in your own soul.*

*Overcome this inner conflict
so that you may go out to him and to her
and enter into new, transformed relationships.*

*When you have made peace within yourself
you can make peace in the whole world.*

—Martin Buber

1

Your Subconscious Mind: Friend or Foe?

The Raging Rhinoceros

As though looking through a darkened glass, you can almost see and sense someone inside of you, someone you don't know. This stranger interferes with you every time you try to improve yourself—and you can't figure out why. You've fought with and resisted this person for so long now, it has become a never-ending battle.

Now the other you steps closer. You tense and feel the urge to back away. But without knowing why, you wait. Then something strange happens. Gazing into the eyes of the other, you begin to sense that although you are very different, the differences might be good. The very things that have annoyed and frightened you might even be useful, if you could work together.

Your subconscious is a powerful and mysterious force which can either hold you back or help you move forward. Without its cooperation, your best goals will go unrealized; with its help, you are unbeatable.

You have felt the unavoidable influence of this hidden part of you— sometimes helping you intuitively, but more often getting in your way:

- You are ready to ask for that raise, or that date, or something else you really want. But your heart pounds, your breathing quickens. Something is controlling you—and it doesn't seem to be you. You can't do it.

- You are starting another diet. You are sincere and determined—so why is it that the first thing you do is eat chocolate cake?

- You wake up suddenly from a nightmare, frightened. Even with the lights on, the bad feelings persist. Yet you know that nothing has really happened—or has it?

1

No matter how hard you try, you can't escape your subconscious. But as powerful and mysterious as your subconscious is, it is friendlier than you might think.

Surprisingly, even when it seems to be stopping you, your subconscious is trying to help and protect you. The only reason it fights you is because its perception of what you need is different from that of your conscious mind. When you recognize and accept the help of your other self, the same qualities that made your subconscious a formidable obstacle transform it into a powerful ally.

Through *Embracing Your Subconscious,* you will learn to *understand* what your subconscious is trying to tell you. You are receiving signals and messages from your subconscious twenty-four hours a day—through your body, beliefs, interactions with others, and dreams. These signals and messages, which before were indecipherable, will give you fresh insight and a broader perspective.

The deeper part of your mind knows you better than you know yourself. That is because all of your experiences, both physical and mental, are stored in your subconscious. Most of your beliefs and expectations are based on your childhood experiences, many of which you may not consciously remember. These expectations and beliefs form a subconscious "blueprint" that influences your present behavior and well-being, for better or worse, far more than you realize.

In addition to learning how to decode important messages, *Embracing Your Subconscious* will show you how to *influence* your subconscious with new information and choices. Just as your subconscious remembers everything that you have experienced and felt, so it is also very receptive to *new, empowering images* that will lead to noticeable improvements in the way you feel about yourself. Together, you can create a "blueprint for success" that will be stored in your subconscious, where it will help you to achieve your goals more comfortably and quickly than ever before.

Putting information and ideas together in unconventional, illogical ways, your subconscious will give you the power to solve problems far beyond your conscious ability. Working toward the same goals, as *allies,* your conscious and subconscious will cease pulling in opposite directions. Rather, they will form a cooperative partnership which draws on the strengths of both.

Liberating the creative wisdom of all parts of you—conscious and subconscious, known and unknown, heart and head—leads to *lucid living.* You will experience heightened awareness, wonder and enjoyment, as you bring all of who you are into your relationships. Your life will become a high adventure, rich with new possibilities.

The other you is smiling now, and you wonder why it seemed so scary before. You see it with new eyes, hear its message with open ears and deeper understanding. The other you, your subconscious self, has a gift to give you. As you take the gift into your hands, you realize that your other self has always wanted to be your ally. What seemed like interference before was really its attempt to help you. A warm feeling spreads through you, as you think about the ways this alliance will help you to feel stronger and more fully who you are. With wonder, you are drawn toward your new ally—into a loving embrace.

This book offers all the tools you need to penetrate the mysterious veil of the subconscious: to *understand why* it tries to stop you; to *negotiate* a way to resolve inner conflict; and to *work together* toward a common goal—your well-being and happiness. You will learn how to embrace your subconscious and receive its rich resources as a gift that will revitalize every area of your life.

THE INNER BATTLE

As a child, I was fascinated by my dreams. Although I had some pleasant dream adventures, I was also plagued by a recurring nightmare that both frightened and puzzled me:

> In my nightmare, I am a soldier on a battlefield. Nearby, I can see cannons and guns firing and hear their explosions shattering the air. The enemy is advancing toward me. I feel a terrible foreboding. The forces on my side are about to be overrun and defeated.

Intuitively, I sensed there must be a reason why this particular dream repeated over and over again. It seemed that if I could understand what the dream was trying to tell me, I might no longer need to have this troubling experience.

As a teenager, I started keeping a record of my dreams. I delved into the psychology and literature on dreams, searching for ways to decode my subconscious messages. Finally, after several years, the key to unlocking the puzzle came when I learned from Gestalt psychology that all symbols in dreams represent *aspects of yourself.*

Drawing on the Gestalt idea that you can enter into a dialogue with subconscious parts of yourself, I began to create a series of practical steps, which evolved into what I call **Inner Dialogue.**

At first, my only goal was to get rid of nightmares and have more pleasant dreams. But before long, as I experimented and developed the steps for Inner Dialogue, I noticed that not only were my dreams changing for the better— my self-esteem and self-image were improving as well.

In later chapters, I will share the surprising and wonderful ways in which Inner Dialogue changed my waking life—and how it can do the same for you.

HEALING MESSAGES

Everything that happens to you, inside and out, real and imaginary, can be explored as a communication from your subconscious:

- A person you are having difficulty with
- A significant event in the present or the past
- A place or an object that is important to you
- A part of your body that is uncomfortable or in pain
- The "child" inside of you
- Two sides of yourself: head & heart, public & private, adult & child, responsible & irresponsible, masculine & feminine, independent & dependent, confident & afraid
- A symbol in a dream or visualization

Every symbol offers you a chance to discover and reclaim parts of yourself— inner resources you have lost track of and are no longer using consciously. Even a difficult situation or a frightening dream can provide you with a helpful message.

Through Inner Dialogue, you will discover the helpful and healing messages your subconscious sends you every day to help balance and improve your life. Once you understand the messages and recognize their value, your subconscious will support you in making necessary changes.

Inner Dialogue enables you to shift from your normal conscious perspective into a state of mind that *includes the awareness of your subconscious.* You begin by playing the part of any symbol, and *speaking as that symbol.* For example, you can speak as a person, place, object, or feeling. This allows you to shift out of your normal awareness and to step into your symbol, experiencing its identity and purpose.

Inner Dialogue lets you give a voice to any character, symbol, place or feeling that you wish to explore. It is different from Gestalt and other dialogue techniques in that it provides a specific set of steps which will help you:

- Discover and understand the message your subconscious is sending
- Identify subconscious conflicts that have held you back from achieving goals, feeling confident and comfortable, or accomplishing what you want in life
- Negotiate an agreement that lets your conscious mind work in partnership with your subconscious
- Appreciate and integrate the unique ability and perspective of your symbol by applying its message to a specific area of your life

THE RAGING RHINOCEROS

In the following Inner Dialogue session, you will witness the step by step transformation of fear into strength as Joe dialogues with his rhinoceros symbol. Joe's encounter with his rhinoceros is a remarkable metaphor for the way many people experience the subconscious.

> "I see a rhinoceros. It is bolting out of what looks like a zoo compound. He charges out through an open gate. Once outside, he wheels about and charges back. He is coming right at me.
>
> A little boy is standing near the gate, wearing a black and white striped shirt. I yell to him, 'Close the gate! Close the gate!' The boy runs to the gate and tries to slam it shut, but it swings open.
>
> I am afraid the Rhino is going to attack him, but he passes right by the boy. He charges back into the compound, wheels around, and heads toward me. I am frozen with fear. Just before he hits me, I wake up."

In this dream, the rhinoceros represents powerful subconscious energies at work in Joe. So long as Joe tries to keep this aggressive, raging part of him closed off or caged in, the rhinoceros remains scary and potentially destructive. By using Inner Dialogue, Joe will come to recognize some positive qualities in the rhinoceros.

Joe was very disturbed by the helplessness and paralysis he felt in his dream; it was one of his worst nightmares. The charging attack of the rhinoceros filled him with dread. It was difficult for him to imagine that he might find a helpful message from his subconscious in his dream—but he was willing to try.

I guided Joe through each step of Inner Dialogue:

- **Recall the dream** *(Step 1)*. Described above.

• **Speak as the symbol** *(Step 2)*. I asked Joe to shift his awareness so that he could imagine being the rhinoceros. Speaking as his symbol, he described himself:

> "I am the Rhino. I am big and powerful. I am covered with thick plates of armor. I have sharp horns on my snout."

• **As the symbol, describe your qualities** *(Step 3)*. I asked Joe's Rhino to tell me about itself—its function, its personality, its unique qualities, and how it is different from the other animals in the zoo.

> "As the Rhino, my function is to be here in this zoo so people can come and look at me.
>
> "I am basically a quiet rhino, and I don't ask for much. But I can be very mean if I'm crossed. Then I can do a lot of damage because of the way I am built.
>
> "Also, I can barely see anything, because rhinos have terrible eyesight. That makes it hard for me to figure out what's going on or where I'm going.
>
> "I am *different from* the other animals in the zoo because I am much larger and tougher than they are."

• **Describe what is happening from your point of view** *(Step 4)*. Now the Inner Dialogue has progressed far enough to begin to uncover some of the subconscious feelings and motivations in Joe's dream. I asked Joe to continue speaking as the Rhino and to describe what is happening from the Rhino's point of view.

> "What is happening from my point of view is: I'm in this zoo and I don't like being held here. I charge out of my compound and I'm trying to get free.
>
> "The trouble is, I can't see very well, and I keep losing track of what direction I want to go in. Joe is standing nearby, but I barely take notice of him. Then he shouts to the boy to close the gate to keep me in. That's when I get really angry. I charge toward Joe because he's trying to keep me from being free."

• **Express how you feel as this is happening** *(Step 5)*.

> "I'm really angry! I'm tired of being confined in this zoo. I should be free to roam where I want to. And I'm even angrier that Joe is trying to lock me inside by closing the gate. I want to be free!"

Inner Dialogue

Rather than trying to analyze or interpret the Rhino, Joe has used Inner Dialogue to quickly discover what his symbol has to say. Joe now understands that the Rhino wants to be free. But Joe's conscious mind still views the Rhino as dangerous and wild. At this point, he is not willing to let the Rhino out.

Joe's conscious mind is being confronted by the raw power of his subconscious—the raging rhinoceros. Joe wants to keep the rhinoceros part of him tethered, reined in, and penned up. But Joe's Rhino—his subconscious—needs to be free.

To resolve this powerful inner conflict, Joe will need to use Inner Dialogue to negotiate a way for both his conscious and subconscious needs to be respected.

• **As the dreamer, describe what is happening from your point of view** *(Step 6)*. The rhinoceros, who is angry and aggressively charging back and forth, is having a very different experience from "Joe in the dream," who is afraid and paralyzed. To acknowledge this contrast, I asked Joe to review what "Joe in the dream" is like, what is happening from his point of view, and how he feels.

> "I am alone. I do most things alone. I am walking near a fence, and I see a big rhinoceros trying to get out. He seems dangerous. I don't want him anywhere near me, so I tell the boy to close the gate. I seem rather cowardly, because I am willing to have the boy risk getting hurt by the Rhino, but I am not going to go any closer. Maybe I sense the Rhino won't hurt the boy; I don't know. But when the Rhino turns and charges toward me, I am paralyzed with fear."

• **Let your symbol speak directly to you** *(Step 7)*. Now Joe and the Rhino can begin to communicate directly, exchanging points of view. Beginning with the Rhino, each will tell the other, "How I feel about you is...; My gripes toward you are...; and What I want to say to you is..."

> Rhino: How I feel about you, Joe, is...I am angry at you! I should be free.
>
> My gripes toward you are...You don't have any right to keep me caged up here! This is no kind of life for me. How can you expect me to be happy in this zoo when I was meant to be free in the wild?
>
> What I want to say to you is...You're such a wimp to send the boy to close the gate for you. You're so scared—all I can feel for you is contempt.

• **Speak directly to your symbol** *(Step 8).*

> Joe: How I feel about you, Rhino, is...You really scare me! You're charging all over, then right at me. You look very dangerous.
>
> My gripes toward you are...I don't feel safe while you're running around loose. You are really overpowering. You're out of control.
>
> What I want to say to you is...I'm not trying to hurt you, but I don't want you to hurt me, either. I just want to be safe, and I can't be safe if you're running around loose.

Now Joe can continue his Inner Dialogue, speaking as both the Rhino and himself, to further define the subconscious conflict, negotiate an alliance, and resolve the conflict *(Step 9).*

• **Identify the conflict** *(Step 9 - a).*

> Rhino: If it weren't for you, I could...be free. I could get out of this horrible zoo and go back to the wild where I can be myself.
>
> Joe: If it weren't for you, I could...be safe. I wouldn't have to be terrified and get attacked by you. I wouldn't feel so overwhelmed.

• **Negotiate an alliance** *(Step 9 - b).*

> Rhino: It would be easier to trust you and accept you if...you didn't act afraid; if you didn't reject me; if you'd let me run free.
>
> Joe: It would be easier to let you come closer to me if...you didn't act so scary; if I knew you wouldn't hurt me; if you'd calm down.
>
> Rhino: If you could be less wimpy and paralyzed, I could be more respectful of you. If you could be less controlling of me, trying to keep me in here, I could be more friendly toward you.
>
> Joe: If you could be less overpowering, I could be more confident and friendly to you.

• **Define the terms of your alliance** *(Step 9 - c).*

> Rhino: Let's make a deal. I will not charge and attack you if you will not try to cage me. I will be friendlier and respect your need for safety if you will be friendlier and respect my freedom. Okay?
>
> Joe: Okay.

• **Resolve the conflict and integrate** *(Step 9 - d).*

> Rhino: What I like or value about you, Joe, is...your ability as a human to think and to plan. Also, you can see a lot better than I can, and you have a better sense of direction than I do.
>
> I need you, Joe, in order to...have a clearer sense of where I'm going. You could help me see more clearly. You could help me find a better place to live, so I won't be charging around all over the place with no focus.
>
> Joe: What I like or value about you, Rhino, is...your raw animal strength. I also like how much you want to be free. I value your ability to move, to powerfully put your desires in motion. I also value your ability to protect yourself when you need to.
>
> I need you, Rhino, in order to...feel strong inside myself, so I am more connected to my own power and instincts. You could help me be more aware of my feelings, especially my anger when I don't like something. With you I'd be able to move freely and confidently. I'd also know I could protect myself when I had to.
>
> If we could be allies and work together, Rhino, we could...have both power and direction in our lives. We would both be free to do what we want, and we would also feel safe because we would be helping each other.
>
> By joining forces with you, Rhino, and using your strength and power in my life, I can...face difficulties at work and in my relationships without feeling paralyzed. I can express my feelings, especially my anger. I'll be able to protect myself and create both safety and freedom for myself. Feeling both safer and freer, I can be closer to the important people in my life. I'll also have more energy to be creative and more productive at work.

To his surprise, Joe began to appreciate the strength and energy his Rhino could offer. For the first time, he came to understand that the Rhino was a subconscious part of him. Now he could envision a *cooperative relationship* between two polarized aspects of himself: the part that wanted to be safe and the part that wanted to be free.

• **Apply your insights to specific situations and feelings** *(Step 10).*
I asked Joe to think about how the Rhino's feelings and perceptions might connect to feelings and situations he experienced in his waking life.

> Joe said that the Rhino expressed a part of him that felt trapped and unable to express its natural way of being. Like the Rhino,

Joe now realized he had pent-up feelings of aggression, a tough appearance, and the determination to be free.

The Rhino part of Joe had been scary to his conscious self—because he saw his anger and aggression as a danger to himself and others. In his waking life, Joe tended to keep his feelings hidden from others and had a lot of fear of going out of control.

Keeping a part of him locked up was costing Joe energy, confidence, and the ability to have honest and healthy relationships. Now Joe was excited that he could set his Rhino free.

Although at first Joe feared that using his "rhinoceros energy" in his daily life would lead him to act like a raging rhinoceros, in fact the reverse was true. The "raging rhinoceros" had the power to act destructively in Joe's relationships *because* his conscious mind rejected that part of himself. When Joe dialogued with the Rhino, an important shift took place: Joe discovered that the Rhino really wasn't so terrible after all, if it was given respect and consideration. Joe was sympathetic about the Rhino's sense of being trapped and rejected. Most importantly, Joe made the connection between the Rhino and himself, realizing that the Rhino represented powerful subconscious needs and feelings *in him*. Joe was now willing to consciously use a little bit of the rhinoceros energy, and as a result, he would be more in control of his life.

Negotiating with his rhinoceros opened up the way for Joe to choose an attitude of strength instead of paralysis in his life. By speaking as the Rhino, Joe got a gut feeling of his symbol's strength and naturalness. This new strength would be carried into Joe's relationships with others as an ability to express his needs more clearly and, when necessary, to take steps to preserve his freedom.

A POWERFUL METAPHOR

How do *you* deal with a raging rhinoceros? The rhinoceros is a useful metaphor for the subconscious: if you try to keep it penned up and don't listen to it, it gets more and more aggressive. But the powerful energies that might at first appear to be destructive or scary are really subconscious forces which can be used constructively, in partnership with your conscious mind, to achieve your goals and get what you want out of life.

Can you identify the "rhinoceros" part of you? Most of us have feelings we're afraid to let out, feelings we fear would make us too vulnerable, or that might be seen as unacceptable. "The Rhinoceros Dream" often touches people because, in life, each of us is doing a balancing act between safety and freedom, vulnerability and power.

Take a moment now and imagine yourself as the rhinoceros. Notice how you feel. Imagine what it would be like, as the rhinoceros, to meet yourself, the dreamer. Observe the dreamer who is here with you now. How do you feel about the dreamer? What would you like to say to him or her?

When you are done, think about your relationship with the rhinoceros part of you. How comfortable was it for you to "be" the rhinoceros? How comfortable was it for the dreamer (yourself) to meet the rhinoceros? Take a few minutes and do an Inner Dialogue to explore your personal version of "The Rhinoceros Dream."

(See Exercise 1 in this chapter for the Inner Dialogue steps.)

YOUR SUBCONSCIOUS MOVIE

Your symbols and dreams are like movies: fast-moving images that flash by in seconds. Each image in your movie is a symbol, made of highly condensed energy and feeling.

I like to compare how Inner Dialogue works to a scene in Woody Allen's movie, *Annie Hall.* Allen is talking to his love interest, played by Diane Keaton. On the screen, he is trying to appear very suave and certain of himself. As he talks, *subtitles* suddenly appear at the bottom of the screen, reflecting his uncensored *inner dialogue.* The contrast between his actions on screen and the feelings revealed in the subtitles is very comical because, in spite of his "cool" behavior, he is saying to himself: "Oh, no! I can't believe I just said that! Now she's going to think I'm a jerk!"

The movie's *subtitles* reveal feelings, doubts, and motives in Allen's movie character. They underscore the contradiction between his outward behavior and his inner lack of confidence. Another kind of inner-outer contradiction was revealed in Joe's dream between Joe's conscious fear and his subconscious frustration, embodied in the Rhino.

Taking a clue from Allen's film, you can think of Inner Dialogue as the appearance of subtitles in your subconscious movie. Through Inner Dialogue, you are slowing down the action of your movie so that you have a chance to explore each part of it, read the subtitles, and sort out all the information.

The Inner Dialogue gives your symbols a chance to talk and reveal their true feelings—something they probably didn't get a chance to do the first time around.

What To Do With
A RAGING RHINOCEROS

If you try to keep me penned up,
I will break loose.
If you try to close me out,
I will break in.
If you reject me,
I will be angry and attack you.
But if you trust me and let the gate swing wide,
I will be a powerful ally.

GET TO KNOW THE UNKNOWN

When we look for answers, we have a natural tendency to focus on what we already know or on the parts of ourselves that we can readily accept. However, much of the healing power of Inner Dialogue can be found in the symbols that represent the unknown in you.

Certain subconscious parts of you, like the Rhino symbol, may not appear to be very valuable or attractive at first; but every symbol and subconscious aspect of you has value and needs to be recognized and accepted. As you have seen in "The Rhinoceros Dream," your Inner Dialogue makes it possible for you to establish a cooperative relationship with symbols that represent unknown parts of you. By consciously accepting and valuing these symbols as allies, you release vast subconscious resources to serve you.

Inner Dialogue conveys information on many levels at once. Unlike the conscious mind, which tends to limit an interpretation to "It's either one thing or the other," your subconscious mind's message is most complete when it applies on as many levels as possible. If, for example, the main issue is "to trust the Rhino part of me—to trust the instinctive, powerful part of me so that I can create movement, freedom, and safety in my life," you can explore that message as it applies to:

- your energy level
- your creativity
- your spirituality

- your physical health
- your relationships
- your productivity

When you note as many levels of meaning as you can, you are inviting more information and insight to come through.

Symbols always give you helpful information about your relationship with yourself. They let you know how comfortable or uncomfortable you are with your power, creativity, needs, vulnerability, and many other aspects of your conscious experience.

If your relationship with a certain symbol is distant or distrusting, as it was between Joe and the rhinoceros, Inner Dialogue will show you how to develop more communication and cooperation. This positive shift improves your relationship with subconscious aspects of yourself. As a result, your subconscious messages will become more enjoyable and empowering, and your conscious experience of yourself will become more comfortable and satisfying.

Subconscious symbols become angry and destructive because they have been ignored. When you recognize that the power of a difficult symbol is yours, you can begin to reclaim that subconscious part of you *as an ally*.

LIFE IS BUT A DREAM

Your subconscious is very much like a guidance system that is designed to help you stay on a healthy track in your life. While it may have faulty blueprints that hold you back in certain areas, its main function is to help you.

Your subconscious sends you information through your thoughts, your emotions, your five senses, your dreams, and your interactions with others. You don't have to be dreaming to have a "dream"—because your subconscious uses real events and imagination equally well to convey information that can help you.

In Chapters 2 and 3, you will discover more specifically how your subconscious is always at work, sending you messages through *waking dreams*—events that you experience every day.

DECODING THE MESSAGE

At first, subconscious messages seem to be in a different language, as though they are in code. It often seems just about impossible to understand them. This is because your *normal* awareness is only a small part of your *total* awareness.

Your subconscious follows its own special logic, which, when understood, can be amazingly helpful. "The Rhinoceros Dream" was initially disturbing and puzzling to Joe. But when he used Inner Dialogue to communicate with his subconscious, the Rhino's needs, feelings and abilities became very real to him. Joe was able to understand the Rhino's value as an important part of himself.

To read a map well, you have to know the territory. And in the same way, you need to know the territory of the mind in order to translate subconscious code into understandable language.

Your brain has two hemispheres, and these two halves have different ways of operating. One hemisphere is analytical and is good with *words*. The other hemisphere is intuitive and expresses itself with *images and feelings*.

Inner Dialogue takes you beyond your normal (left brain) awareness so you can *understand the unique code* of your subconscious. Inner Dialogue gives both hemispheres of your brain a chance to communicate—linking conscious and subconscious, rational and intuitive, words and feelings.

Your brain hemispheres are designed to be complementary. The information flows back and forth from one hemisphere to the other through a thick bundle of connecting pathways called the corpus callosum. Each can do the job of the other, but prefers to concentrate on its own specialized assignments. And like a company that works with a particular technology, each hemisphere also has its own language and way of organizing information.

You are probably most aware of your left brain hemisphere. When you plan your day, keep to a schedule, talk, and analyze, you are drawing on this part of your brain.

The left-brain is rational and logical. It does well with observing individual parts and following a sequence of linear events. But when it comes to finding the meaning in subconscious messages, the left-brain tends to be too linear and literal. It assumes an event or symbol means only what it appears to mean.

You cannot understand symbols and dreams with the left brain alone. It simply does not speak the symbolic, feeling language of the subconscious. If the left brain tries to break the code in which symbols and dreams communicate, at best it will arrive at an interpretation that is a dull rehash of what you already know.

Sometimes, in desperation to decode their symbols, people turn to books that claim to explain what these symbols mean. But symbols are very individualistic and personal. Standard meanings or interpretations are of very limited value, since they reduce your subconscious messages to an impersonal formula. Relying on such books, you do not gain access to your subconscious.

Embracing Your Subconscious gives you the tools to use both your right brain and left brain, so you can discover for yourself the rich creativity and brilliant intelligence at work in your subconscious.

RIGHT-BRAIN LANGUAGE

The right-brain hemisphere has a very different way of organizing and communicating information. Unlike the left brain, which likes to analyze and observe, the right brain likes to feel and experience. Where the left brain evaluates individual parts, the right brain embraces the whole pattern or larger perspective.

The language of the right brain is the language of the subconscious and dreams. Rather than using words, which the left brain does so well, the right brain prefers to communicate with images and feelings. The left brain follows a form of linear logic that leads to one "right" answer; whereas the right brain uses a holographic approach that leads to many "right" answers.

The secret code used by the right brain and the subconscious is that *the message is always sent in images and feelings,* rather than in words—and the symbols always mean more than they appear to mean. (For instance, Joe's rhinoceros was much more than just a wild animal.) Moreover, your subconscious gives you information on many levels at once, enabling you to solve problems and recognize patterns in a way your conscious mind cannot.

A RESPECTFUL PARTNERSHIP

Left Brain	*Right Brain*
words	images & feelings
literal meaning	symbols & metaphors
rational & analytic	intuitive & creative
thinking & observing	experiencing & feeling
individual parts	whole pattern
linear logic: one answer	holographic logic: many answers
critical messages	nurturing messages
normal consciousness	broader perspective
linear time	timelessness
what you already know	new information
structure	spontaneity
how to get where you're going	where you want to go & why

A TREE IS JUST A TREE—OR IS IT?

Imagine you have dreamed of a tree. It's not just any tree. The sensory details of your symbol have a direct bearing on the message your subconscious is sending you.

> The tree might be losing its leaves or be damaged in some way. Or the tree might be thriving and healthy—covered with lovely blossoms, or its leaves turning beautiful colors. The tree's bark might be rough or smooth. You might be able to hear the sound of the wind whispering in the leaves.

If your tree looks wilted or damaged, it is probably there to alert you that some part of you feels weak, wilted or damaged. If your tree is thriving, your subconscious is probably confirming that you are doing well. If your tree is blossoming, your subconscious may be congratulating you on how *you* are blossoming, bearing fruit or branching out.

If your tree is undergoing a seasonal change, like having its leaves turn color and fall, your subconscious may be reminding you that even a change or loss is part of a natural cycle and can be beautiful or positive. Your tree is still standing, ready to revive in the spring, symbolizing your own strength and resiliency.

Your subconscious creates symbols that are filled with personal meanings. Every symbol has something to say to you. Look beyond their literal appearance—such as people you know or situations you encounter in everyday life. Instead, explore these symbols as meaning-holders or energy-containers that represent a valuable part of you.

HOW THIS BOOK WILL HELP YOU

Embracing Your Subconscious will help you to increase your awareness on all levels: awake and dreaming, conscious and subconscious, rational and intuitive, intellectual and emotional, physical and spiritual.

The methods you will learn from this book can be applied to all areas of your life, including your relationships, career, creativity, health, and self-esteem. Your subconscious is always at work, influencing your feelings and behavior much more than you realize.

As you read this book and do the suggested exercises, you will gain a deep appreciation of how your subconscious can help you every day. You will also develop a rewarding relationship with the deeper part of your mind.

In the next chapter, you will learn how to explore real-life situations to discover the ways your subconscious is influencing you all the time.

Exercises for
Your Subconscious

EXERCISE 1
Inner Dialogue

Any image or symbol, whether from real life or fantasy, can be used for an Inner Dialogue. An animal, person, place, feeling, or quality can be treated *as if* it were a symbol. You can do Inner Dialogue on anything—a day dream, a real event *(waking dream)*, a fantasy, or a dream.

Every symbol has something to tell you. No matter how small, how silly, or how strange your symbol may be, your Inner Dialogue will reveal helpful messages.

Through Inner Dialogue, you are strengthening the bridge between your conscious mind and your subconscious, your waking and dreaming experiences, and your rational and intuitive abilities. As a result, your awareness of your subconscious will increase, and you will more easily remember your dreams.

WHAT TO DO: Choose a symbol from a recent dream or waking dream on which to do Inner Dialogue. If you want a quick symbol to use, you may close your eyes and wait until an animal pops into your mind. You can then use the symbol of the animal in your Inner Dialogue.

Write out the steps of the Inner Dialogue (pp. 21-22) one at a time on a piece of paper or in your journal. Allow yourself to relax, close your eyes and see your symbol. Let the answer to each question come to you. Write down each answer in your journal before going on to the next question. This process will help you to record and remember what happens, so you can get more insight and benefit from your Inner Dialogue.

While doing Inner Dialogue, allow yourself to be in a meditative, right brain state. Suspend rational judgment and experience the unexpected, distinct perspectives of each symbol.

INNER DIALOGUE STEPS

1. Choose a dream, waking dream, or individual symbol *(one that inspires, puzzles or haunts you)*. We'll call this your "dream."
   a. Write the dream in your journal, in the present tense.
   b. List the main symbols, as well as unusual symbols.
   c. List the contrasts you notice: i.e., dark-light, big-small, confident-afraid, masculine-feminine, child-adult, etc. *(See Exercise 2.)*

2. Speak as the first symbol. (Begin with a symbol that is not you, the dreamer.) Say: "I am...(name of the symbol)" and describe yourself physically.

3. As the first symbol, complete these phrases:
   a. **"My job or function is..."**
   b. **"My unique qualities are..."**
   c. **"I am different from _____** *(another person, animal, object of the same category)* in that..."

Remember that in dreams, real people whom you know in waking life often symbolize aspects of your consciousness. If your symbol is a person, speak as that person in your Inner Dialogue. In addition, ask: **How do I characterize myself as a person? What is my personality like?** For example, "I'm the kind of person that never gives up," "I'm a terrific business person," "I'm very artistic," "I thrive on adventure," etc.

4. As the first symbol, **"What is happening from my point of view is..."**

5. As the first symbol, **"How I feel as this is happening is..."**

6. Repeat Steps 2 - 5 for another symbol in the dream. *(If you choose yourself as the second symbol, and if you are your "usual self" in the dream, skip this step and go on to Steps 7 & 8.)*

7. & 8. Let each symbol say, in turn, to the other symbol:
   a. **"How I feel about you is..."**
   b. **"My gripes toward you are..."**
   c. **"What I want to say to you is..."**

9. Develop a spontaneous dialogue between the symbols. Some suggestions:

a. *Identify the Conflict:*
>   **"What I don't like about you is..."**
>   **"If it weren't for you I could..."**

b. *Negotiate an Alliance:*
>   **"It would be easier to trust you/accept you if..."**
>   **"It would be easier for me to get closer to you if..."**
>   **"It would be easier to let you come closer to me if..."**
>   **"If you could be less _____(overpowering, etc.),**
>   **I could be more _____(friendly, etc.)"**

c. *Define the Terms of Your Alliance:*
>   **"Let's make a deal: I will...**(*do something specific for you*) **if you will...**(*do something specific for me*)." Now check in with the other symbol to see if the "deal" is acceptable. Make certain the deal benefits *both* symbols.

Keep negotiating until you get specific agreement. If it is difficult to imagine a symbol's energy as valuable, try negotiating to *accept one molecule at a time*; i.e., **"By using one molecule of your energy or strength, I will be able to..."**
When you do not know how to begin to make a deal with a difficult symbol, or if you reach an impasse in your negotiations, it is helpful to go on to step 9-d before finishing with the "let's make a deal" step.

d. *Resolution and Integration:*
>   **"What I like or value about you is..."**
>   **"I need you in order to..."**
>   **"If we could be allies and work together, we could..."**
>   **"By joining forces and using your _____(special quality or strength) in my life, I can..."**

10. At this point or earlier, think about the ways in which your negotiation and alliance with your symbol can help you to resolve an inner conflict and be more effective with others. Notice in what ways your symbol(s) may picture, give voice to, or give you a grasp of specific situations and feelings in your waking life.

Think about the message or insight you have received on as many levels as possible, such as relationships, career, creativity, spirituality, health, and inner child.

(A process developed by Jenny Davidow, M.A. © 1982)

EXERCISE 2
Using Contrasts to Decode Subconscious Messages

When you look at the contrasting qualities of your symbols, you are looking at the stuff of which your inner conflicts, struggles, healing, and creativity are made. Dreams and waking dreams give you a spontaneous, unedited version of all that you feel and know, both consciously and subconsciously.

Contrasts like *light and dark, big and small, strong and helpless* serve an important function in decoding your subconscious messages. Noting the contrasts or polarities in your symbols is one of the first steps of Inner Dialogue *(Step 1-c)*. The contrasts you notice may be dramatic or subtle, implied or obvious. Concentrate on the key areas identified in your contrasts when doing your Inner Dialogue—so that your insights will be as specific and helpful as possible.

For example, your dream might have a key contrast similar to the "Rhino Dream," such as *trapped-free*. You can explore this contrast in Step 9 of the Inner Dialogue as follows: In step 9-b, the Rhino symbol could say:

"It would be easier for me, the Rhino, to be *free* if...
...I could see more clearly where I am going.
...I could plan what to do with my freedom.
...you (the dreamer) would help me and support me."

As the Dreamer, you can also explore *the other side of the contrast* by saying,

"It would be easier for me, the dreamer, to *let you be free*
(and not keep you trapped or penned up) if...
...I knew I could trust you.
...I knew you wouldn't go out of control.
...you would listen to me and respect me.
...I were sure I would benefit from having you around."

In step 9-c, you can "make a deal" with your symbol that specifically centers on resolving the polarization between *free* and *trapped*:

The Rhino could say: "Let's make a deal: I will not attack you,
if you will not try to keep me trapped and will let me be free."

In step 9-d, the two symbols and their contrasting qualities can resolve their conflict and integrate their energies:

The Dreamer could say: "By joining forces with you, Rhino, and using your strength and power in my life, we can both feel less *trapped*; we can both enjoy more *freedom* to be our natural selves."

Contrasts point out the difference between what you feel or know consciously and what you feel or know in your subconscious. Inner Dialogue helps you to free the polarized energy that is represented by your contrasts, so that the alliance of conscious and subconscious aspects of you can benefit you in your conscious life.

Which contrasts are particularly strong for you in your dream? Are there any you noticed that are not among the ones listed on the next page? Every person, if presented with the same experience, will pick out different contrasts that seem important or relevant. While some contrasts are so obvious that many people would tend to notice them—like big-small, free-trapped—the ways in which we phrase those contrasts, or combine them with other contrasts, vary from individual to individual.

Notice also that sometimes the contrasts are *implied*. For example, the opposite of *fear* may not be present in the dream, but you will benefit greatly by listing the positive side of the contrast anyway, to help focus your energy in that direction. If, for example, you felt fear in a dream, you can list the contrast as *fear-strength* or *fear-confidence*. This practice helps you to recognize the feelings and actions which you might need to express more in your life.

In your dreams and waking dreams, you react most powerfully to the people and details that represent what you need to learn about yourself This is a good reason why it is important to explore your own symbols. Having another person interpret your symbols for you does not really benefit you, since someone else cannot possibly experience the same meanings or reactions as you.

WHAT TO DO: In your journal, write down a dream or waking dream and underline all the words or symbols that represent or imply a contrast. (Although contrasts or polarities travel in pairs, only half of the pair may be clearly present in your dream.)

Next, write down *both parts* of each contrast that you have underlined.

Pick the most obvious or strongest contrast, or pair of opposites, that you notice. Do an Inner Dialogue, incorporating the suggestions for Step 9 given above.

Feel free to add to and embellish the following list of contrasts as you discover the contrasts in your own dreams and waking dreams.

COMMON CONTRASTS

powerful-helpless	protected-vulnerable
male-female	trapped-free
big-small	light-dark
deep-surface	natural - man-made
fast-slow	young-old
beautiful-ugly	empty-full
friend-foe	scary-attractive
inside-outside	healthy-sick
nourished-hungry	light-dark
alone-with people	child-adult
nurturing-critical	open-closed
confident-afraid	accepting-rejecting
wild-tame	hopeful-despairing
heart-head	body-spirit
awake-asleep	rational-intuitive

EXERCISE 3
Mapping Your Contrasts

Your contrasts or polarities can serve as a personal map that gives you a clear guide to your subconscious conflicts and issues, as well as subconscious strengths that are ready to emerge.

Both sides of a contrast have value to you. Their energy has been polarized or split apart, making each aspect seem exaggerated. By using Inner Dialogue, the energy locked in polarized symbols will become more balanced and accessible, so that you can express it constructively in your waking life.

WHAT TO DO: After you have recorded a dream or waking dream in your journal, go on to note the strong symbols or "stars" of your dream.

Next, look for contrasts in your dream *(Step 1-c)*. Note both *physical* contrasts (like big-small or black-white) and *emotional or qualitative* contrasts (like afraid-confident or trapped-free). Make a list in your journal of as many contrasts as you can for this particular dream. When you are finished, put a check or asterisk by the two or three contrasts that seem to be the most important; you can focus on these when you do Inner Dialogue.

Now, dedicate a few pages in your journal to map your contrasts over a period of time. List the contrasts for three or more dreams (and include the date of each dream). Notice if there are any similarities among these contrasts.

When similarities occur over a period of time, your subconscious is telling you to pay attention to these contrasts. Do an Inner Dialogue that explores both sides of the contrast, relating it to two parts of you that need to be brought into balance.

Do this exercise again in two or three weeks, listing additional contrasts from three or more dreams. Do another Inner Dialogue on a contrast that seems to appear repeatedly.

When you continue to track your symbols and contrasts over time, you will gain a deeper appreciation of the logic of your subconscious. Your contrasts will become important points on your subconscious "map," helping you to set a straighter course in your life.

EXERCISE 4
Creating A Journal

Creating a journal is a way of saying to your subconscious that you value it and are ready to receive its help and wisdom. Buy a special notebook, if you don't already have one, in which to keep your journal.

Your journal is the ideal place to record the insight and wisdom you receive from subconscious messages. These messages may come in many forms: through dreams, strong emotions or reactions to any situation, your body, visualizations, and Inner Dialogue.

Even if you find it difficult at first to remember a nighttime dream, you can still write in your journal every day. Record your feelings and first thoughts when you awaken or just before you go to bed. Write as little as a sentence or two, or as much as you feel inspired to write. You can also record contrasts you notice while awake, day dreams, fleeting images, memories or thoughts. Just having a place to write your thoughts and experiences will increase your awareness of subconscious messages.

You may want to embellish your journal by making drawings of your symbols or by pasting in photographs or magazine images that relate to your dreams.

Any attention you give to symbols from dreams, day dreams, waking dreams, or fantasies will increase the activity of your right brain and enhance your ability to recall dreams. Recording your dreams, drawing pictures of symbols, writing poems, or seeking out tangible versions of symbols (for example, finding a picture of a rhinoceros) all serve to make you more aware of your subconscious messages.

EXERCISE 5
Suggestions For Recording Your Dreams

Always write down the date of your journal entry.

When recording a dream or waking dream, note the date of the dream as well as today's date. Write the dream while it is fresh in your mind. The longer you wait, the more details you will tend to forget, thereby losing important information that makes your subconscious messages especially clear. Try taking ten minutes in the morning or evening to write in your journal.

Record your dreams and waking dreams in the *present tense*. For example, "I am back at my childhood home..." Using the present tense when you record your dreams keeps the experience vivid and encourages you to continue feeling involved as you explore it. For the same reason, use the present tense when doing Inner Dialogue, also.

Spend fifteen to thirty minutes writing in your journal, once or twice a week. I suggest that you take an additional hour once a week to do an Inner Dialogue.

Set aside a time during the day that is most conducive for you to do Inner Dialogue or review your journal. This might be in the morning over tea, at night just before bed, or when you go to the park or mountains to be alone. This can be your special time—when you stretch beyond your normal awareness to become aware of your subconscious messages.

After you do an Inner Dialogue, summarize it in your journal. Record the key message your Inner Dialogue gave you, and write down a summary of what each symbol had to say (including you).

Also, write down the images or symbols that stand out to you. Include any important associations you may have to them, from waking life or other dreams.

When you write your dreams or waking dreams (or speak them into a tape recorder), let the images flow spontaneously. Fill in details as they come to you, as long as they are in keeping with the dream. For example, in writing down a car dream, you might remember that the car is a Camaro and then recall that its color is blue. These details may serve as valuable clues to the meaning of the dream when doing Inner Dialogue.

Do not listen to your inner critic! Ignore the internal voice that says a dream, symbol, thought, or feeling isn't worth recording—because it was too short, too mundane, too silly, too embarrassing, or any other excuse. This voice can keep you from the helpful and empowering messages of your subconscious, and it tends to speak the loudest when your subconscious needs your attention.

Whenever there is a change of scene or action in the dream or waking dream, you can indicate this as *a new scene or episode*. Place a number 1, 2 or 3 in front of each episode to indicate its order. (If you are unsure of the order, make a guess or put a question mark.) When you do Inner Dialogue, you will need to limit your focus to *one episode or scene at a time* in order to get the maximum benefits.

Rereading your journal before you go to sleep can attune your subconscious to special questions and issues you want to dream about. It is as though your subconscious needs less time to sift through impressions and choose messages. Even the first dreams of the night can give a clear and helpful picture of present concerns.

Remember that every detail of a dream or waking dream is there for a reason. You can ask yourself, "Why this place, and not another? Why this person, and not some other? Why this time period, and not another? Why this particular clothing, etc." Your Inner Dialogue will reveal to you the significance of these symbols as subconscious parts of you. Further, as you record your dreams and do Inner Dialogue, you will find that your ability to record and remember details will become easier and more enjoyable.

Even the smallest recollection of a feeling or a single image is worth recording. Inner Dialogue can be done on the smallest dream fragment or on a single symbol or image.

EXERCISE 6
Suggestions for Recalling Your Dreams

You change the position of your body at the conclusion of every dream. This is because you tend to lie very still while dreaming, and then you need to move again to keep your circulation going. During the night, whenever you turn over, you can use this as a cue to review the dream that went before. (I recommend that this review only take a few seconds, so you don't wake up fully.)

When you wake up in the morning, try to wake up to your own suggestion: for example, "I will wake up at 6:30 a.m." You can use the alarm clock to back you up, just in case. Since the last dream of the night often conveys most clearly what all of your dreams of that night have been exploring, this practice allows your personal rhythm to naturally bring this valuable dream to a close, rather than have it disrupted by an alarm. You are also more likely to remember the dream if you are not jarred out of it.

If you do use an alarm clock, try waking up to soothing music rather than to a buzzer. This also allows your consciousness to make a gradual shift to waking, which is more conducive to remembering your dreams. As much as possible, avoid buzzers and rushing around first thing in the morning, as they jar your consciousness and yank you away from the recollection of your dreams. Try to create a smooth transition, an easy flow, from your dreaming to your waking activities.

I recommend you allow five to ten minutes in the morning to awaken gradually in bed. Don't "snap to" and immediately review your plans for the day. Instead, allow yourself to linger on the border between dreaming and waking for a few minutes, remembering the dreams you have had. Notice your feelings as you do this.

As you lie in bed, you might try slowly changing positions in order to evoke dream recall. Certain studies have suggested that dreams are encoded in the brain according to the position we were in when we dreamed them. Reassuming that position can trigger the memory of the dream.

EXERCISE 7
Incubating A Dream

Dream incubation is a helpful way to gather more material for your Inner Dialogues. When you incubate a dream, you are planting a seed—an image or idea—that will grow into a dream experience. For thousands of years, people all over the world have used this technique in seeking answers to their questions.

Just before you fall asleep is a valuable time to incubate or suggest certain activities to your subconscious. For example:

> "Tonight I will remember my dreams."
>
> "Tonight my dreams will show me what I need to know about...(a problem or concern)."
>
> "Tonight I will fly in my dreams."
>
> "Tonight I will be lucid in my dreams."

Along with saying the words, it is essential to visualize what you incubate, since imagery is more in keeping with the language of the subconscious and right brain. For example, *see and feel* yourself awakening and remembering your dreams; *see and feel* yourself flying, and so on.

WHAT TO DO: In your journal, write down a subject that you would like to dream about. Write out any details that you would like to have happen, such as meeting a special person or performing a certain task with ease and confidence.

Now close your eyes, relax, and visualize what you just wrote. Imagine yourself with that special person, or imagine yourself performing that task. *See and feel* this experience in as much detail as possible. If you're with a special person, *hear* his or her voice; hear your own voice; hear the sounds around you. If you're performing a task, *see* yourself perform with ease; *feel* the confidence and strength inside you.

Be creative and embellish your idea as much as you want, as this will also enhance the power of your dream incubation.

Through incubation, you can influence your dreams to some extent, but you cannot rule them. There is really no danger that your conscious mind can interfere with a subconscious process. The relationship between your conscious mind and your subconscious is a partnership—a respectful exchange that enlarges your conscious perspective, giving you access to more of your total self.

EXERCISE 8
Fishing for a Dream

If remembering dreams is difficult for you, these suggestions may help you "catch" a dream.

When you go to sleep, set your alarm clock to go off in ninety minutes. Since you have a dream approximately every ninety minutes, this practice enables you to remember a dream at the end of a ninety-minute period. (Be sure to write down the dream in your journal right away, so you have a record of it.)

Another way to fish for a dream is to lie in bed and prop your arm up so that your forearm is perpendicular to the bed. In this position, you can begin to doze. When you fall into a light sleep, your arm will drop down and wake you up. At this point, you can catch the images and feelings of your dream.

2

You are Dreaming All the Time

Amazon Woman Meets Inner Child

Your subconscious is always influencing you, in ways ranging from subtle to dramatic. Even real events that appear to be outside of your control—like losing your house keys, having your car break down, an argument with someone, or a physical pain—can serve as communications from your subconscious. I call such events *waking dreams* because, while they are very real, they also convey a subconscious message.

Like a detective, you will learn how to identify waking dreams and decode the valuable messages they contain. In this chapter, you will use Inner Dialogue to discover and heal the unresolved issues and conflicts which are often hidden within real events.

The main clues that alert you to a waking dream are:

- *Intense Reaction.* You respond to a person or a situation with intense anger, sadness, love or attraction. Something happens that is annoying, for instance, but you react as if it's the end of the world.

- *Repetition.* A situation keeps happening: you lose your keys; you show up at several appointments, but the other person doesn't; you have arguments with different people; you injure yourself or experience physical problems repeatedly. On the positive side, you meet several friends by chance on the same day.

- *Unusual Event.* Something about a situation puzzles you or seems unusual. For instance, an old high school friend has the room next to yours at a remote vacation resort. You may feel as though an event is happening in slow motion, or so fast that you hardly remember it happening at all.

THE 90/10 SPLIT

When you react intensely to a situation, it is because your subconscious has remembered one or more other times when you felt annoyed, frustrated, angry, or worse. Instead of reacting to the one simple incident of annoyance in the present, you are reacting to *everything that has ever gone wrong like this in the past.* It is as if only 10% of your emotional response is to the present incident; 90% is fueled by your subconscious remembering similar events from the past. Some psychologists call this the 90/10 Split.

It is like having a dream while awake: your subconscious feelings have erupted into a real-life situation. Your reaction may surprise you or seem exaggerated, possibly beyond your control. The strength of your reaction serves as a signal that your subconscious has become a key player in this drama.

When you react very strongly to a person or situation, your subconscious is using this waking dream to get your attention. Whether your overreaction is one of anger or love, this is an ideal opportunity to take some time to do Inner Dialogue. Inner Dialogue will help you to sort out what part of your waking dream is *about your relationship with yourself,* and what part is *about your relationship with another person or a present situation.*

You can apply Inner Dialogue to *any experience* in your life—whether it is a real event, emotion, physical symptom, or belief.

If you feel blocked in a certain area of your life or unable to achieve a goal, you can treat that block or obstacle as a *waking dream.* Inner Dialogue will help you to change your subconscious blueprint from "No, I can't/won't do it" to "Yes, I can/will do it." Although you may not be able to change the real events that happen to you, you *can* change the way you react so that you can experience the best possible results.

A + B = C

Your feelings and beliefs greatly influence your ability to achieve goals, have relationships, and feel comfortable. Like a filter or camera lens, your subconscious selects what you will experience: hope or pessimism, trust or suspicion, confidence or insecurity, communication or isolation.

A+B=C is a simple equation that explains how your subconscious can either help you or hold you back.

"A" is *any event that happens to you,* any situation you find yourself in. "B" is *how you react inside:* whether you feel strong or weak, what you say to yourself, and whether you expect to fail or succeed. By changing "B," *your reaction,* you change "C", your *outcome.*

A	+ B	= C
Any event that happens to you:	**How you react inside,** *your beliefs and attitudes:*	**Your outcome, positive or not:**
• A real event • A memory or fantasy • A dream	• How you feel • What you say to yourself • Expecting to succeed or fail	• Stress or comfort • Failure or success in achieving a goal

You will learn how to identify what is going on in "B" which might be getting in the way of the comfort and success you want to achieve. Further, you will learn how to use Inner Dialogue to *improve* "B"—and clear the way for the positive outcome you want.

Certain situations seem to be more "loaded" than others in terms of the "B" part of this equation. Relationships, food, money, your health, your car, and your home are all situations that generally have strong associations, conscious and subconscious, attached to them. When strong feelings occur in any of these areas of your life, it is useful to pay close attention to them *not only as a response to a real event, but also as a waking dream* that can tell you more about yourself and how to improve your partnership with your subconscious.

For instance, one of my clients, Sally, lost her house keys. This accident prevented her from getting into her own home. Although the inconvenience was only temporary *(10%)*, Sally was very upset at being locked out *(90%)*. She had also misplaced her keys two weeks before. Both her upset and the repeating pattern were clues that she was having a waking dream.

To reveal the subconscious message intertwined with this real experience (and to explain her waking dream), Sally followed the steps for Inner Dialogue and began by *speaking as* the lost house keys.

> KEYS: I am the keys that open the door. I give you passage to the place that you call home.
> What is happening from my point of view is...I don't know where I am. I'm not where I belong. I can't do what I'm supposed to do. How I feel as this is happening is...I feel lost and confused. I feel abandoned.

My gripes toward you are...you are not taking care of me.

What I want to say to you, Sally, is... you've been careless with me. I don't feel valued.

If it weren't for you, Sally, I could...be where I belong. I could do my job.

If you could be less...careless, I could be more available. I could open the door and let you come home.

In dialoguing with the keys, Sally discovered that she had lost "the key" to taking care of herself. She had become careless and confused because she wasn't taking enough time to rest and nurture herself. Sally realized that she needed to value and protect her time alone.

INNER DIALOGUE ON WAKING DREAMS

You can decode the message of any waking dream. Whether it involves a real event or an internal conflict, Inner Dialogue will help you turn your waking dream into an opportunity to learn about yourself and enlist the support of your subconscious.

1. *A Real Event, Person or Place.* There are an unlimited number of real-life experiences to explore as waking dreams:

- an argument or problem with someone
- a strong attraction to someone or something
- an accident, injury, or illness
- a rite of passage, either your own or someone else's—an engagement, marriage, birth, promotion, graduation, etc.
- the process of moving out of or into a new home or office
- a favorite place or a mysterious place
- losing or finding something important to you

2. *Two Contrasting Parts of You.* When you experience inner conflict, there are two parts of you that want very different things. Your feelings or goals alternate from one extreme to the other, with the very real result of making decisions difficult or impairing your enjoyment of the moment.

You can speak as each of these contrasts:

- heart and head; body and mind
- creative and stuck; social and shy; powerful and powerless

- child and adult; present and past; public and private
- accepting and critical; confident and insecure; responsible and wild
- any part of your body and yourself; a health problem and yourself

When you have a problem with a particular part of your body, such as a backache or an infection, these health concerns can also be viewed as a waking dream. Many of my clients and students have reported that their physical symptoms improved after doing Inner Dialogue on a certain part of their body. This is because Inner Dialogue helped them to uncover how their subconscious might have been contributing to the problem and slowing their recovery.

Inner Dialogue on a waking dream serves a dual purpose: providing insight, and changing a limiting blueprint into a Blueprint for Success. Inner Dialogue also activates the power of your subconscious to support the immune system's efforts to heal the body.

The possibilities are endless. What contrasting parts of yourself might you want to explore as symbols in an Inner Dialogue?

See Exercise 3 for full guidelines on doing Inner Dialogue on Contrasting Parts. Much more will be said about the relationship of your subconscious to your health in Chapters 3 and 5.

YOUR TWO MINDS

Many of us experience a waking dream when we have difficulty making a decision and say, "I'm of two minds about this." Or, "My heart (or gut) says one thing, and my head another."

Depending on the situation, many people alternate between making "mature, logical decisions" and "following their gut." You may embrace both your rational left brain and intuitive right brain as valuable and complementary in varying degrees. Or you may find it hard to accept one or the other, choosing instead to express only the one you view as useful.

Nature designed all of your parts to be useful. There is a price that you pay when you overuse one part and ignore or reject another. For instance, many business people who put great value on being logical and analytical *all the time* frequently feel creatively blocked, suffer from chronic physical tension, and have difficulty being spontaneous and having fun. Similarly, people who try to express the intuitive or creative aspect *all the time* often feel handicapped by a lack of organizational skills and the focus necessary to bring their creative vision into practical reality.

Inevitably, when you try to reject or ignore a part of yourself, it will find a way to get your attention. Whether in business or personal relationships, whenever you respond with strong like or dislike to a person, a place, or even an idea, you are experiencing a waking dream. Usually you do not realize that much of your attraction—or dislike—is based on something you have subconsciously rejected or lost touch with in yourself. Waking dreams are signposts that remind you to reclaim valuable subconscious parts of yourself. By paying attention to waking dreams, you strengthen your relationship with your subconscious. As a result, you will enjoy increased self-acceptance and more ease in accomplishing your goals in every aspect of life.

INNER BALANCE

We experience inner conflict and imbalance in many forms. Like the two hemispheres of your brain, it seems there are *two basic, complementary qualities* that every person needs to bring into balance, but they are known by many different names:

logical - intuitive

rational and structured - creative and spontaneous

intellectual - emotional

observing - experiencing

masculine - feminine

yang - yin

assertive - receptive

conscious - subconscious

Both sides of your brain are valuable and have qualities necessary to maintain your inner balance. Each has its time and place to be useful.

There is another group of complementary qualities, related to those noted above. When out of balance, these paired qualities can cause unpleasant waking dreams:

adult - child

serious - playful

responsible - irresponsible

worldly - innocent

tough - vulnerable

critical - accepting

skeptical - trusting

YOUR INNER CHILD—A WAKING DREAM

Your inner child is the part of you that likes to play. Like a real child, your inner child is naturally spontaneous, trusting, innocent and childlike in its simplicity and joy.

Carl Jung, a pioneer in his exploration of the spiritual and self-actualizing aspects of symbols, regarded the child as a symbol of the divine in each of us. The child is an expression of potentials and abilities that, when developed, can give us inner balance and fulfillment. Jung recognized the inner child's qualities as potent catalysts for emotional healing, as well as creativity and success.

When we experience a dullness, boredom or lack of purpose in our lives, we have generally given too much attention to our adult responsibilities and not enough to our need to let loose and play. Studies of work stress have shown that unless time is allowed to get away from work, and play at a pleasurable activity, you will eventually suffer job burnout or emotional difficulties.

Most of us spend our lives trying to juggle our adult responsibilities with our need to have fun. In the stress of everyday living, we often forget the importance of having a play time where we can shed our adult cares and worries for awhile. We have trouble scheduling a break in the work routine so that we can get away and relax, whether for only a few minutes, or for that needed and deserved vacation.

Some of us feel guilty taking time for ourselves. Time for a hobby, time to walk, time to do something creative, time to meditate, or time just to goof off and have fun. Often we have a strong desire for relaxation, as though the child in us is saying, "I want to play." But we may override this desire, as though the adult part of us is saying, "You can't afford to waste time when you should be working and making money." Further, we may override our feelings, telling ourselves, "You're being immature. It's a tough world and you have to keep your nose to the grindstone." When the adult and child parts of you are in disagreement, the conscious and subconscious parts of you are in conflict—and you are experiencing a waking dream.

MAKING PEACE WITH YOUR INNER CHILD

Your inner child is probably the most revitalizing subconscious resource you have. As a symbol, your inner child can tell you much you need to know about both yourself and your relationships with others.

Not surprisingly, the energies and qualities of the inner child encompass many of the same qualities as the right brain and subconscious. Studies of people whose right-brain hemispheres were impaired have shown that although they may retain an ability to deal with facts, their ability to enjoy life is missing.

Oliver Sacks, a prominent clinical neurologist and author of *Awakenings*, has written that it is the right brain that enables us to experience states of transcendence of time and space, oneness with the universe and with nature, deep inner motivation, and the sacred dimension. Access to these transcendent states opens us to experiences of awe, inspiration, and spiritual bliss. Through the right brain we are able to view our lives from a grander perspective and feel satisfied that we are part of a greater pattern or whole.

In sessions with people who complain of job burnout, a sense of dullness and boredom, or the lack of purpose and meaning in their lives, I have found it very useful to have them imagine and visualize the child part of them and dialogue with it. Inner Dialogue with the child part of you opens up the energy and wisdom of the right brain, renewing the joy, motivation and meaning that make life worthwhile.

Making peace with your inner child can help you to resolve inner conflict and gain access to the spontaneity, gusto, simplicity and joy of the childlike part of you. In fact, your inner child holds the key to understanding your subconscious feelings and conflicts.

Beginning an Inner Dialogue with your inner child may at first seem difficult—your inner child may be distant or distrustful of you. Or, sometimes the adult part of you finds the child part too demanding or needy.

If you have difficulty making loving contact with your inner child, or if your inner child is frightened or hurting, be patient, take your time, and keep trying. Your Inner Dialogue will begin a powerful and needed healing process. *(See Exercise 4 for more details.)*

A TIME TO WORK, A TIME TO PLAY

Dave began sessions with me because his life seemed dull and monotonous. When I asked him to tell me about his life, he told me about his work. Dave had a good job and was well-paid, but he did not enjoy or take pride in his talents and achievements. When I asked him what he did for relaxation and fun, he looked at me blankly.

Dave had experienced a lot of neglect as a child. After several sessions doing Inner Dialogue on various symbols, I asked Dave to imagine his inner child.

> *Dave saw a sad little boy of about four years old.*
> *When he spoke as the boy, he said he was lonely.*

I asked Little Davey to tell me about his life at home. As the child, Dave was able to recall details of his childhood that he had not remembered before. Little Davey told me how his mother was sick in bed a lot and could not take care of him.

Next, I asked Little Davey if it would be okay for Big Dave (his adult self) to come and visit him. This adult, I told him, was someone who cared about him and who wanted to be his friend.

> Little Davey saw Big Dave coming over to visit with him. Little Davey was very interested in Big Dave, but also wary—he had been let down too many times.

I encouraged Dave to speak to his inner child. At first, unaware of what he was doing, he started to lecture his inner child about how he should be. Dave was showing a tendency many people have—to do to ourselves what our parents did to us. In this case, Dave's adult self was *lecturing and critical* toward his inner child, duplicating the lack of sympathy with which his parents had treated him as a child.

To help him move past this barrier, I explained to Dave that his inner child was only four years old and could not understand adult, rational language. Instead, I suggested that Dave gear his communication to the simple words and feelings of a four-year-old, so Little Davey could understand. He could also use a friendly, soothing tone of voice, so Little Davey would relax and feel less wary.

Big Dave took a breath, and in a gentle voice said,

> "Little Davey, I want to be your friend. I want you to know that I will be here for you to play with. And I'll be here to listen to your feelings and help you, too."

Little Davey liked this idea, but found it hard to believe, since his parents had left him alone much of the time, seldom playing with him or helping him. Little Davey wasn't ready yet to let Big Dave get too close.

Dave's inner child still needed the loving attention and help that were missed in his childhood. I suggested to Dave that he could tell Little Davey,

> "I know you have been hurt, and you have good reason to be suspicious. I want to be your friend, and I will be patient and give you the time you need to let your trust for me grow.
>
> "I will keep coming back to visit you, so you will see that I mean what I say.

> I will keep coming back for as long as it takes to earn your trust. Your thoughts and feelings are important to me. I care about you and love you, Little Davey, and I want to be your friend."

Little Davey liked Big Dave's acknowledgment of his fears and hurts. Even though Little Davey could not fully trust Big Dave immediately, this first session was a very important step to establishing a relationship between Dave and his inner child.

After the session, Dave told me that he felt stronger. By nurturing his inner child, he had begun to resolve the conflict between the adult and child parts of him—gaining an opportunity to trust again.

At his next session, I asked Dave to allow himself to get a fresh image of his inner child.

> This time, Little Davey looked happy and was dressed in a cowboy outfit. He was standing by a corral. After he and Dave talked for awhile, he told Big Dave that he would like to play, but he didn't know how. To help him, Big Dave got into a cowboy outfit too, and asked Little Davey if he'd like to go for a ride.
>
> Taking a big step in trusting Big Dave, Little Davey said yes, as long as they stayed inside the corral and went slowly. Big Dave gently led Little Davey on a pony around the corral. After awhile, Big Dave got on a horse, too, and they rode together.

GIFTS OF HEALING

By exploring and strengthening your relationship with your inner child, you can give yourself powerful healing messages. Many people who have had difficult or traumatic childhoods have used Inner Dialogue to heal and re-parent their inner child. You, too, can dialogue with your inner child, *in the present*, and give him or her the love and encouragement that perhaps was lacking in the past.

Inner Dialogue is a potent tool, since your subconscious perceives your dialogue as *a real event* that can influence your waking feelings and behavior just as much as a real event of the past.

As adults, we are usually very good at reasoning things out. But we need to use the wisdom of our subconscious in order to discover the feelings and unique perspective of our inner child. Our conscious, rational, adult mind is simply not able to give us that experience.

To discover the healing message of your inner child, or any symbol, it is vital to *let the symbol talk* in the Inner Dialogue. This right-brain exploration will give you new insights and information that your conscious mind cannot come to by trying to "figure it out."

In his sessions, Dave discovered that Little Davey carried much of his emotional energy—his love, vulnerability, spontaneity, and, as became apparent later, his joy in being alive. Learning to be patient and loving with Little Davey showed him that he could also be more patient and loving with himself. As Dave encouraged Little Davey to be playful, he also learned how to be more playful himself. Dave had begun to heal his inner child and, in the process, he was also reclaiming the gusto he had been missing in his life.

Over the next several months, Dave continued to have dialogues with his inner child. His relationship with Little Davey strengthened and became a joyful alliance.

Dave's earlier feeling of boredom vanished and a host of new interests and pleasures appeared. He was more able to trust and accept his feelings of vulnerability, passion, and even anger. As his trust of himself grew, it became easier for him to trust others—and to enjoy being playful.

In Chapter 4, you will find out how Dave was able to take his relationship with his inner child even further. You will learn how to use the Lucid Fantasy technique in combination with Inner Dialogue.

THE INNER CRITIC

After attending one of my workshops, Sheila told me she didn't think she had an inner child. All that she was aware of was an internal voice that was constantly judging and criticizing her.

Sheila could not think, feel, or do anything without this inner critic having its say.

When we had a chance to discuss it, Sheila told me that she had a strong reaction to "The Rhinoceros Dream" discussion in class. For her, the strongest contrast between the aggressive rhinoceros and the paralyzed dreamer was one of *powerful-powerless.*

I asked Sheila if her response to "The Rhinoceros Dream" might be *a waking dream.* Perhaps it pointed up powerful and powerless parts of her of which she needed to be more aware. Somehow, these contrasting parts of her had something to teach her about both her inner critic and her inner child.

Sheila became very excited that she could use her waking dream in such an immediate way to discover something that had eluded her conscious understanding. She decided to do an Inner Dialogue on the powerful and powerless parts of her.

As you read through her dialogue, notice how quickly Sheila gained increased awareness of her inner child. You may want to do your own Inner Dialogue later, to experience the powerful and powerless aspects of you.

Sheila began her Inner Dialogue by saying, *"I am the powerful part of Sheila."* Next, following the guidelines for Inner Dialogue on Contrasting Parts *(see Exercise 3)*, she allowed herself a *spontaneous image* for the symbol of Powerful Sheila. This image would give form, feeling and energy to the powerful side. Sheila began to describe herself as the symbol:

> **I am the powerful part of Sheila.** I am an Amazon woman. I am big and very strong. I'm dressed in a Tarzan outfit. I live in the jungle.

Sheila continued to do Steps 2 through 4, asking, "As Powerful Sheila, what are my specific qualities? What is life like for me?" Powerful Sheila described herself as strong and independent. She thrived on being challenged and relished each day as an exciting adventure.

Next, Sheila paused to get an image for the powerless part of her (Step 5):

> **I am the powerless part of Sheila.** I am curled up in the corner, in the shadows. I am about five years old.

As Powerless Sheila, she explored: "What are my specific qualities? What is life like for me?" (Step 6) Powerless Sheila described herself as a shy young child, afraid of being disapproved of, afraid of failing, lacking in confidence.

Now Powerful Sheila, the Amazon-adult, was ready to meet and have a dialogue with Powerless Sheila, the child (Steps 7 - 9). The highlights:

> **Powerful Sheila, as the Amazon Woman:** Child, you're not so different from me. You just need to believe it. What is keeping you from being as powerful as I am?
>
> **Powerless Sheila, as the Child:** I'm afraid that if I venture out and express some power...I might fail. You'll criticize me. I'll look silly. I'll be hurt. I'll be rejected.
>
> It would be easier for me, the Child, to venture out and to be more powerful, like you, if...
>
> ...if you would help me at first.
>
> ...if I knew that you cared about me.
>
> ...if I knew you would help me, protect me with your power.
>
> ...if you didn't criticize me or look upon me as a failure.
>
> ...if you didn't make fun of me being curled up in the corner.
>
> ...if you accepted me.

Powerful Sheila: I could relax and not have to be powerful all the time if...
   ...if you would be strong some of the time, too.
   ...if you would trust me more.
   ...if you were with me to remind me.
   ...if you would come out and play with me.

Next, I reminded Sheila that *both* of these symbols were parts of her. Although it might not seem apparent at first, these two parts needed each other in order to function well; while they were in conflict, neither could be fully satisfied or effective. Sheila's powerful and powerless parts needed to be brought together into a friendly relationship.

> At this point in her Inner Dialogue, Sheila said she felt that her Amazon-adult had all the power, and her Child had no power at all. This polarization was being played out in her life by her inner critic having all the say and her inner child remaining silent and invisible.

Every symbol has value. Contrasts like *powerful-powerless* express energy that has become polarized and stuck in two extremes—one conscious, the other subconscious; one acceptable, the other unacceptable. What Sheila needed now was a way to bring her powerful and powerless parts into a cooperative relationship, replacing the extreme contrast of powerful-powerless with an accessible, empowering middle ground.

I suggested to Sheila that the qualities and energies of two contrasting parts are usually *complementary.* One part appears to be strong, perhaps dominant; this part may seem either good or bad, but almost always lacks something essential. On the other hand, the weak or unacceptable part often has hidden abilities or strengths that the dominant part is missing.

In her Inner Dialogue, Sheila could ask:

> "Is there anything that I, Powerless Sheila/the Child have that Powerful Sheila/Amazon Woman doesn't? Is there some kind of an exchange or combining of energies that can happen here?"

In the next part of her Inner Dialogue, Sheila would be surprised at how many valuable qualities her powerless or child part possessed. She discovered the complementary relationship between her Amazon-Adult and her Child:

The Child: I have more sensitivity than you, Amazon Woman. I have more receptivity, more inner life. I am the creative source of your power and direction. I provide you with the raw material of your power, which you can then act on.

I need you, Powerful Sheila, in order to...

...feel safe and cared for.

...have more energy and be more active.

...put my creativity and desires into action in the world.

Powerful Sheila/Amazon Woman: I need you, Child, in order to...

...be complete.

...relax and not have to be strong all the time.

...let myself just experience life, rather than always trying to make something happen or judge what happens.

...be in touch with my inner life and feelings.

...feel an inner purpose that helps guide me.

...experience times of stillness as well as action.

In the final stages of her Inner Dialogue, Sheila was able to *make a deal,* negotiating trust and cooperation between these two parts of herself.

The Child: Let's make a deal. I will come out of the shadows and be with you more, if you will slow down and include me in your activities. I will also support you by giving you more connection to your inner life, if you will support me by giving me more connection to the world.

Is that okay with you? *(Powerful Sheila/Amazon Woman says yes.)*

By joining forces and working together, we can...

...have a meaningful connection to our inner life and the world.

...enjoy the simple joys of life as well as worldly achievements.

...choose the times when we want to be vulnerable and open, and also choose the times when we want to be strong and decisive—knowing we don't have to be either one all the time.

Reading this Inner Dialogue, you may become aware of what the powerless-powerful parts of you would say. Take a few minutes now and allow your subconscious to suggest an image for each of these contrasting parts. Allow your powerful and powerless symbols to dialogue with each other, following the steps for Inner Dialogue on Contrasting Parts. *(Exercise 3 in this chapter.)*

DREAM OR WAKING DREAM?

> I am a soldier on a battlefield. Nearby, I see cannons and guns firing and hear their explosions shattering the air. The enemy is advancing toward me. My anxiety becomes a terrible foreboding. The forces on my side are about to be overrun and defeated.

This dream, shared in Chapter 1, motivated me to search for a way to understand my dreams and subconscious. Even as a child, I sensed there must be a reason for having this particular dream over and over again. The dream was trying to tell me something, and if I could figure out the message, I wouldn't need to dream it anymore.

For many years, I could not figure out why I was dreaming of war. The dream came and went in countless variations—sometimes on historic battlefields with antiquated weapons, sometimes in a futuristic land with deadly laser beams.

The daily journal and record of my dreams which I began as a teenager proved to be not only a mirror for my thoughts and feelings, but in later years also became a map of my own subconscious. Over time, I noticed that my dream symbols and themes changed and evolved in ways that paralleled my own evolving awareness. But my nightmares persisted into my twenties. Only now, instead of battlefields, I was trying to escape a terrible danger that lurked around my childhood home. Sometimes it was a person, sometimes a deadly fog, sometimes a tidal wave.

I pondered what my nightmares meant, but the message kept eluding me. I also wondered if my latest nightmare themes were in any way connected to the battlefield dreams I had as a child.

When I developed Inner Dialogue in my late twenties, I finally was able to communicate with the subconscious parts of myself represented in my dreams. After so many years, I was eager to decode the recurring dreams I had as a child, as well as those I was experiencing as an adult. With great anticipation, I talked to my symbols and listened to what they had to say.

THE BATTLE, REVISITED

The battlefields of my childhood dreams were a poignant and revealing metaphor. At the time of those dreams, my life was troubled by my parents' divorce. Their unresolved conflict with each other seemed like an ongoing battle, a war zone. *Their conflict was a waking dream for me.*

As a child, there wasn't much I could do to protect myself or change what was happening around me. I was afraid and discouraged, and my dreams pictured my reaction with perfect symbolism: I was a soldier, and I was losing the battle. I was afraid, overrun and defeated.

On the outside, in real life, I was acting the part of the "good little soldier," bravely facing the realities I had to deal with. But looking back now on those dreams, I realize how devastating my parents' conflicts must have been for me. Shuttled back and forth between the two "opposing forces" for weekend visits had caught me in the middle of their battle.

But the battleground on which I bravely tried to cope as a young child became more than a disturbing real-life event. As I struggled with feelings of insecurity and being torn in two directions, the battlefield also became a symbol of my *relationship with myself*. Consciously and subconsciously, I was battling with my own anger and hurt. My battlefield, which had begun as a real situation, became a symbol or waking dream for feelings I could not resolve. Worst of all, my subconscious battle continued to follow me long after the real-life battle was over.

A CHANCE TO MOVE ON

Through recurring dreams, my subconscious continued for many years to direct my attention to the battle of emotions inside of me. I had acquired a self-limiting blueprint, one that predisposed me to feel defeated when faced with a conflict situation. By repeating the dream over and over, my subconscious was bringing this blueprint to my attention, giving me a chance to correct it and move on.

Using Inner Dialogue and Lucid Fantasy *(described in Chapter 4)*, I finally freed myself and my inner child from the "losing battle" and introduced my subconscious to some positive, life-enhancing alternatives:

> At first, I became more assertive and determined to survive. No longer the fatalistic and passive good soldier, I spoke up, held my ground, defended myself, and fought back when necessary.
>
> After awhile, I went further. I began to negotiate with the opposing forces. I looked into their eyes. I was no longer afraid of them.
>
> Then, something happened that I never expected. The opposing forces backed down and stopped their attack. They agreed to negotiate a peace. The long-endured battle was over.

Inner Dialogue on my battlefield dreams, as well as other frightening and disturbing dreams, caused a profound change. Recurring dream symbols, like an overpowering tidal wave or a scary attacker, now became friendly. Instead of crashing over me, a tidal wave lifted me up and propelled me forward on an exciting and enjoyable ride. Instead of attacking me, shady pursuers now stepped into the light and took my hand as new friends and guides. Inner Dialogue helped me to envision a more powerful and satisfying way of being. My subconscious responded with new allies and new feelings of confidence and comfort—both dreaming and awake.

THE STAFF OF WISDOM

Not all waking dreams are upsetting. Waking dreams can also be joyful and inspirational. Several years ago I experienced a very inspiring waking dream which still gives me warm tingles when I think about it:

> I am walking on Bell Rock in Sedona, Arizona. Suddenly I look down and see a beautiful walking stick lying on the ground. It seems to be waiting for me, a gift from the mountain.
>
> As I bend down to pick up the staff, I flash back to many years ago, when I had a dream in which I saw someone on a mountain top, holding a staff like this one. I sensed a special power and vision in that mysterious person. That dream came at a turning point in my life and touched something deep inside of me. I knew that I wanted to be in that special place of wisdom and vision.
>
> The clarity of that long-ago dream had inspired me to choose a new direction. For the first time, I began sharing my knowledge of dreams and the subconscious with others, showing them how to discover the wisdom and vision within. Through sharing, I grew, too.
>
> As I stand on the mountain remembering, my heart pumps faster and a warm shiver goes through me. More than a coincidence, the staff brings a powerful dream symbol into tangible form.
>
> I feel the staff's smooth surface in my hand, and I am filled with wonder. Suddenly I realize that *I am* the mysterious person on the mountain, pictured in my dream many years ago.

RITES OF PASSAGE

My experience on Bell Rock could be regarded as a waking dream *rite of passage.*

Rites of passage mark an important transition from one stage of life to another. Such transitions often have a strong charge attached to them: consciously or subconsciously, they evoke powerful emotions—whether it is pleasure or anxiety, fear or pride.

Occasions such as graduations, reunions, promotions, engagements and marriage, are rites of passage. These socially-recognized transitions are opportunities for positive waking dreams. In each of these experiences, you receive recognition for knowledge you have gained, as well as for achievement or commitment at a new stage in life. As waking dreams, these events can also reflect a "graduation" to a new level of awareness, a "reunion" with aspects of yourself, a "promotion" to a new point of view or feeling of personal power, and an inner "marriage"—a balanced integration of the masculine and feminine, rational and intuitive.

BIRTH AND DEATH

I am often asked what dreams and symbols about death mean. Frequently, we dream about death, or notice conscious thoughts about death, when we are in the process of changing and "letting go." At such times, we may be undergoing a difficult change or transition —another kind of rite of passage. We may be experiencing the end of a relationship; or we may be letting go of a familiar way of being, as when we change careers, homes, or points of view.

Death is not an easy thing to think about or dream about. But whether it is encountered as a symbol or as a waking dream, death can alert you to a change that is taking place inside you. It is natural to be uneasy when dealing with such a loaded symbol or issue. But surprisingly, when you use Inner Dialogue to speak as the symbol (such as a person or animal that is dying or dead), your outlook will probably change. You will discover the helpful, often liberating, message behind your symbol.

Death symbols, like all other symbols, communicate an important message. Symbolically, death is tied to letting go of the familiar. Most of us are at first afraid that letting go of something or someone will leave us empty or alone. But on a deeper level, letting go is necessary to make room for something new to come in. When we can trust the natural, universal cycle of life and death, we feel more comfortable letting go. We surrender to change and experience a new cycle of growth and awareness: Birth.

Birth is a symbol for opening, emerging, and participating more fully in life. A *death to birth* progression often occurs when you resolve a subconscious conflict using Inner Dialogue. The energy that was tied up in the subconscious conflict is now free to move on and do something else. Having let go of an old way of being or thinking, you can now experience the birth of a new way of being.

For many of my clients, birth symbols (both in dreams and waking dreams) follow closely after death symbols. Women often dream about giving birth;

both men and women dream about finding a baby and caring for him or her. As symbols, babies and giving birth express *new life, new energy and vitality.*

Birth dreams often communicate a subconscious acknowledgment of the self-confidence and awareness that has been gained through doing Inner Dialogue regularly. Birth dreams also reveal a new relationship—between your conscious self and a subconscious part of you that is small, but full of potential.

Birth symbols, in waking dreams and dreams, may involve a human baby, a young child, a kitten, puppy or other young animal. When you are in a happy relationship with such a baby-symbol, your relationship with your subconscious is prospering. All baby-symbols represent new potential in specific areas of your life—areas which also need to be cared for, valued and nurtured.

Gain full benefit from a birth symbol by speaking as that symbol in Inner Dialogue. For example, speak as the beautiful baby you encountered in a dream or in real life. Identify the specific ways in which this symbol applies to your life by dialoguing with it and noting contrasts.

But what happens if you don't follow through on your new way of being? You may forget about the valuable part of yourself that you have discovered; you may lose the awareness you have gained. Then your subconscious alerts you: by giving you a dream, for example, in which you are still with a baby, but now you are wondering,

> "Where's that baby? I've forgotten where she is."

Another variation on this theme would be suddenly realizing that you haven't seen the baby in a while. In a rush of panic, you might say,

> "Oh my gosh, I've completely forgotten about the baby!
> I haven't fed her for weeks!"

These kinds of dreams offer a warning and a helpful reminder—that you need to keep encouraging and nurturing the partnership between your conscious and subconscious.

Inner Dialogue will help you to work through an inner conflict so that your symbols (subconscious parts of you) will become more cooperative. Self-limiting blueprints will change into blueprints that support and empower you. To come to a full resolution, you usually need to do Inner Dialogue several times on the same issue. Each time, there will be degrees of improvement, using a subconscious part of you in a more positive way.

When a disturbing symbol or a conflict that you have been working on with Inner Dialogue reappears in either a dream or waking dream, your subconscious is alerting you: more Inner Dialogue is necessary. If you do not pay attention, this signal will become more dramatic:

> Your lighthearted birth dreams may change to troublesome birth dreams, where something is going wrong. Or, you may return to the preceding step in your growth cycle and experience death dreams again. It is like learning a valuable lesson, then forgetting it, and having to learn it again. If you lose enough awareness, your subconscious returns you to the beginning of the process and seems to say: start again.

ENCOURAGING YOUR GROWING EDGE

Luckily, it is easy to keep your growth cycle moving forward. Your symbols provide a valuable window into your subconscious. Through them, you can view *and influence* your level of confidence and motivation.

All change and personal growth begins on a subconscious level, outside your conscious awareness. In your subconscious, new feelings and attitudes take form over a period of time. The improvement appears first in your dreams and subconscious; then manifests more noticeably in your daily life.

Doing Inner Dialogue on symbols or events that are powerful, healing or inspirational is just as important as doing it on symbols or events that trouble you. For example, you can speak as the beautiful baby you encountered in a dream or waking dream. Inner Dialogue will help you experience that symbol as a part of you and to better integrate its empowering energy into your conscious life.

Even a good dream or waking dream can be made better. By reinforcing the positive trends in your symbols, you can play an active part in maintaining your growing edge.

Simply by keeping track of your symbols in dreams and waking dreams, and by doing Inner Dialogue, you will gain increased awareness and confidence. Further, when you pay attention to recurring symbols, such as death or birth, and recurring waking dreams, such as conflicts with others, you will have fewer unpleasant surprises and be more in charge of your life.

Exercises For
Your Subconscious

EXERCISE 1
Inner Dialogue on a Real Person, Place or Event

Experiences of frustration, fear, loss, irritation, argument or embarrassment can be viewed as waking dreams. Inner Dialogue will help you to discover the subconscious message hidden in a real experience. With Inner Dialogue, you can turn a rather unpleasant occurrence into an opportunity to learn about yourself and enlist the support of your subconscious.

There are an unlimited number of experiences to explore as waking dreams: an argument or problem with someone; an accident, injury, or infection; the process of moving out of or into a new home or office; losing or finding something important to you; or experiencing a rite of passage, either your own or someone else's—an engagement, marriage, birth, promotion, graduation, and so on.

WHAT TO DO: In your journal, write down a waking dream. Write it the same way you would if it were a dream, i.e., "I am at the market and realize I have lost my keys..." Do Inner Dialogue on two or three of the prominent symbols, including yourself. (Speak as a person, an object, an accident, an injury, an event, a feeling, etc.) Also, remember to list the contrasts which stand out to you.

EXERCISE 2
Positive Waking Dreams

When we think of waking dreams, we tend to focus on the unpleasant or unhappy events that seem to intrude on our lives. For this reason, I have set this exercise apart from the one above. If you have not yet done Inner Dialogue on a *positive* waking dream, here is a good opportunity to give yourself a big boost of support and encouragement.

Positive waking dreams are real-life events that are also reflections of your subconscious feelings. In this case, though, your waking dream reflects the *comfort and well-being* you feel when your subconscious is working in partnership with you.

Graduations, promotions, reunions, engagements and marriage are opportunities for powerful and positive waking dreams. Rites of passage, in which you receive recognition for your new awareness or achievement, can often be experienced as waking dreams.

On another level, unexpectedly finding something of value can become a positive waking dream when it takes on subconscious meaning. For instance, you may find something you lost or meet an old friend unexpectedly. You may discover beautiful flowers blooming in your garden, or suddenly understand the solution to a problem you have been thinking about.

WHAT TO DO: In your journal, write down a positive waking dream. Write it down in the same way you would if it were a dream, i.e., "I am at Bell Rock and discover a staff..." Do Inner Dialogue on two or three of the prominent symbols, including yourself. List the prominent contrasts.

EXERCISE 3
Inner Dialogue on Contrasting Parts

The contrasts in your symbols—such as light- dark, child- adult, and good-bad—can help you pinpoint what symbols to choose for your Inner Dialogue. Your contrasts usually clarify what you need to know about a subconscious conflict. For Sheila, the powerful-powerless dialogue immediately clarified the relationship between her adult and child parts, as well as between her self-critical and nurturing parts. Like Sheila, you can use your contrasts and Inner Dialogue as powerful and creative tools.

Keep track of your contrasts and review them periodically. Inner Dialogue on your contrasts can help you identify and correct a self-limiting blueprint *before* it has an adverse effect— either by holding you back subconsciously or by undermining your achievements and relationships.

WHAT TO DO: Choose a waking dream. In your journal, write down all the contrasts you notice. Now put a star by the most obvious or strongest contrasts.

Follow the steps below to create an Inner Dialogue on Contrasting Parts— to explore contrasting parts of yourself—i.e., the child and adult parts of you, or your heart and your head. Or, you can create an Inner Dialogue between a particular part of your body and yourself, i.e., between an infection (or another physical problem) and yourself. Allow half an hour to an hour in a quiet place to do an Inner Dialogue. *(See the list of contrasts in Chapter 1, Exercise 2.)*

INNER DIALOGUE ON CONTRASTING PARTS

1. First, choose the contrasting parts with which you will be working:
    - heart and head; safety and freedom; powerful and powerless
    - confident and self-critical; creative and stuck; social and shy
    - child and adult; present and past; public and private
    - any part of your body and yourself; a health problem and yourself

2. Next, close your eyes and wait to get a spontaneous image for **one part of the contrast** you are addressing (*i.e., "the powerful part of me"*).
As the new symbol, say: "I am..." and describe yourself physically as the symbol. (*I.e., "I am the powerful part of Sheila. I am like an Amazon woman, strong and tall, etc."*)

3. As the symbol, say:
    a. "My job or function is...
    b. "My unique qualities are...
    c. "I am different from...(the other symbol or contrast) in that...

4. As the symbol, say:
    a. "What is happening from my point of view is..."
    b. "How I feel as this is happening is..."

5. Next, close your eyes and wait to get another spontaneous image for **the other side of your contrast** (*i.e., the powerless part of you*).
As the new symbol, say: "I am..." and describe yourself physically as the symbol: i.e., "I am the powerless part of Sheila. I am a child curled up in the corner, about five years old, etc."

6. Repeat Inner Dialogue Steps 2 - 4 for your *second* spontaneous symbol.

7. & 8. Let each symbol say, in turn, to the other symbol:
    "How I feel about you is..."
    "My gripes toward you are..."
    "What I want to say to you is..."

9. Develop a spontaneous dialogue between the symbols. Some suggestions:
    a. "What I don't like about you is..."
        "If it weren't for you, I could..."

    b. "It would be easier to trust you/accept you if..."
       "It would be easier for me to get closer to you if..."
       "It would be easier to let you come closer to me if..."
       "If you could be less _____(overpowering, etc.),
          I could be more _____(comfortable, friendly, etc.)"
    c. **"Let's make a deal: I will...**(do something specific for you),
       if you will...(do something specific for me)." Check in with other
       symbol to see if the deal is acceptable. Keep negotiating until
       you get specific agreement.
    d. "What I like or value about you is..."
       "I need you in order to..."
       "If we could be allies and work together, we could..."
       "By joining forces with you and using your _____ (special quality
         or strength) in my life, I can..."

10. Encourage your insights from this Inner Dialogue to be even more specific by doing the following:

- Let your symbols give each other a *gift*. Trust what comes to mind spontaneously. It doesn't have to make sense. For example, Sheila's Amazon or powerful part gave the Child a red power ring. Then the Child gave the Amazon a crystal heart necklace. (*This gift-giving step will be included in the Lucid Fantasy in Chapter 4.*)

- At this point or earlier, think about ways in which the negotiation and alliance between your two contrasting parts can help you to resolve an inner conflict and be more effective with others. Notice in what ways your symbols may picture, give voice to or give you a grasp of specific situations and feelings that you are experiencing.

- Think about the message or insight you have received on as many levels as possible: relationships, career, creativity, spirituality, health, inner child, etc.

EXERCISE 4
Discovering and Healing Your Inner Child

To begin an Inner Dialogue with your inner child, you can close your eyes and allow an image of a child to come into your mind. Then you can speak as the child and follow the Inner Dialogue steps, dialoguing between your child self and adult self. This is a very powerful technique for helping you to heal childhood hurts and reclaim the joyful qualities of your inner child.

In dialoguing with your inner child, remember that children generally have strong likes and dislikes about some things. When given enough support and safety, your inner child may express strong feelings that relate to the past (your childhood) or the present (for instance, your inner child's reaction to a present situation or relationship).

Remember that your inner child's feelings and views will probably be different from your conscious, adult perspective; notice the contrasts or polarities between your inner child's feelings and needs and your adult self's point of view.

Your inner child's reactions may not always make "rational" sense, but it is important to accept and respect them. Taking your inner child's experiences into consideration will aid you in balancing and integrating your child and adult parts, giving you more vitality and motivation to achieve your goals.

When you follow the steps for Inner Dialogue, see, hear and sense this child in as much detail as possible. Try to determine the child's age, the place or location where he or she is, the clothes he or she is wearing, and his or her facial expression and body language. Noticing these details will make your interaction with the child symbol much more vivid and memorable.

Imagine that you can feel your inner child's energy inside of you, when you speak as the child during your Inner Dialogue. Imagine the special qualities and strengths of your inner child inside of you now.

EXERCISE 5
Inner Dialogue on Strong Feelings

If you cannot imagine your inner child or have difficulty beginning a dialogue with this part of you, this exercise will help.

Feelings that are *playful, creative, innocent, trusting, full of vitality,* or on the other hand, *hurting, frightened, powerless or vulnerable,* may be linked to your inner child. Such feelings often accompany waking dreams.

WHAT TO DO: Choose one of the strong feelings listed above. Follow the steps for doing Inner Dialogue on Contrasting Parts (*See Exercise 3* to get a spontaneous image for the *strong feeling* you are going to explore. This will be your *first symbol* in the Inner Dialogue.

Continue follow the steps for Inner Dialogue on Contrasting Parts.

For the *second symbol* in your Inner Dialogue, you have a choice:

1. You can speak as yourself, then have a dialogue with the symbol representing your strong feeling, or

2. You can speak as the *contrast or opposite* of the strong feeling. If, for instance, you began with the feeling of being full of vitality, the contrast might be numb, lifeless, or drained of vitality. If, on

the other hand, you began with the feeling of being frightened,
the contrast would be calm, at peace, powerful, or confident.

If you choose to speak as the contrast, you will need to get another
spontaneous image for your second symbol. Speaking as this second symbol
will give you additional insight on the contrasts you have chosen.

If you find one of your symbols difficult to accept as a part of you, use Inner
Dialogue to discover its value so you can enter into a more accepting and
cooperative relationship with it. This phrase can be useful:

> "By expressing more of the _____ (*child/feminine/vulnerable, etc.*)
> part of me in my life, I can, specifically...

An answer might include:

> ...feel more in touch with my inner life
> ...be more open or vulnerable in my intimate relationships
> ...tune into more of my spiritual powers

As you can see, it is important to pinpoint the specific areas of your life to
which you want to direct the energy of your symbols and the power of your
new inner alliance. You can pinpoint *several areas* at a time. For instance: to feel
more connection with your inner life, relationships, creativity, confidence,
spirituality, etc. The more specific you are in your negotiation with a symbol,
the more precisely your subconscious abilities can be put into action in your
life.

Being specific is vital; it connects your Inner Dialogues and symbols to
practical reality. Being specific also creates a valuable bridge between your
right-brain insights and your left-brain ability to use information in practical
ways.

EXERCISE 6
Movies as Waking Dreams

Any waking event that affects you strongly can be viewed as a waking
dream—even a movie. For example, the film *Amadeus*, about composer
Wolfgang Amadeus Mozart, is to many people a powerful metaphor of the
self-doubt and inner conflict that is often a part of artistic creation.

To begin your Inner Dialogue, first list the key symbols and some of the contrasts
you see in this movie or story. Note them the same way you would if it were a
dream:

Symbols: Mozart and Salieri

Contrasts:
> gifted—average talent
> childlike spontaneity—adult reserve
> irresponsible—responsible
> wild—conventional
> fear of wasting one's genius or gift—
> > fear of failing or of mediocrity

Next, following the Inner Dialogue steps, the symbols of Mozart and Salieri would each speak. This particular Inner Dialogue would probably point up the distinct differences in the two composers' personalities and musical styles.

As depicted in the film, Salieri had a reserved, responsible, "adult" approach to life, as well as to music. Mozart, in contrast, was unconventional in both his life and his music. His personality seems to have been the polar opposite of Salieri's reserve in that he was full of childlike spontaneity, which probably was a part of his musical gift, but also contributed to his mismanaged finances.

You might want to try this Inner Dialogue yourself, viewing the story *Amadeus* as a waking dream and the symbols of Mozart and Salieri as parts of you. Use Inner Dialogue to *negotiate an alliance* between these very different but complementary parts.

WHAT TO DO: Choose a movie whose characters are exciting or moving to you, or a film or story that affects you strongly. List some of the contrasts you see in this movie, as though it were a dream.

Now, do the Inner Dialogue steps *(see Exercise 1, Chapter 1)* on two of the characters in the movie, preferably two that were interacting or had contrasting motivations and abilities. Be sure to negotiate an alliance between the two symbols. Remember that accepting and expressing even a little bit of a symbol's energy can create a significant change in your life.

After your symbols negotiate an alliance, you can expand your Inner Dialogue to have each symbol or character (i.e., Mozart and Salieri) *speak to you directly and give you helpful advice*. Think about how you might benefit from the qualities and guidance of each of these symbols.

There is never a shortage of symbols to work on. Other popular movies to treat as waking dreams are: *Camelot* (dialogue as Guinevere, Arthur and Lancelot), *Superman* (dialogue as Superman, Clark Kent and Lois Lane), and *Batman* (dialogue as Batman, Bruce Wayne, the Cat Woman, or the Joker).

Think of some of your favorite films, especially the ones that excited or moved you, for more ideas. For future reference, write down the names of these movies and the movie characters that were most memorable to you.

List as well the *contrasts* that portray a conflict and give these stories their drama and meaning.

You can also do an Inner Dialogue on a real person, historical or contemporary; a fictional person; a book, a poem, a song, a place, or an event. *(See Exercises 1 and 3 in this chapter.)*

Inner Dialogue on waking dreams will give you a satisfying, creative connection with your subconscious. Through your Inner Dialogue, you will be convinced that your subconscious is influencing you all the time.

EXERCISE 7
Inner Dialogue With A Partner

In many cultures, both past and present, telling dreams and visions to each other is a cornerstone of social activity. Sharing the symbols of one's inner life brings special rewards, whether it is done in a tribal circle or in a living room.

Inner Dialogue gives many people their first experience of sharing their symbols, dreams, and waking dreams with another person. In my classes, many students tell me that after doing the Inner Dialogue with someone they just met, they feel surprisingly well-acquainted and even close. Sharing symbols is an exciting way to feel more connected with others, as well as more connected with your deeper self.

Your partner is there to support you, read the Inner Dialogue steps to you, and be attentive while you answer each step aloud. But you are in charge of your own session. A great advantage of this approach is that you can go at your own pace and reach your own conclusions about your dream or waking dream.

When you take your turn as the one helping, try to resist the temptation to interpret your partner's dream. You may have an impression of what *you think* it means. Likewise, you may react strongly to your partner's dream or waking dream if it reminds you of events in your life or similar dreams you have had. Remember, though, that what you react to in your partner's dream is *your* *"dream."* Your interpretation of the dream is always true for you. It is not necessarily true for your partner.

As the one helping the dreamer, simply read the Inner Dialogue steps one at a time; listen to the answer without interrupting, then read the next step when your partner is ready. If the dreamer gets sidetracked or confused, you can help by asking the question again or clarifying it.

WHAT TO DO: When working with a partner, make certain you allow enough time for both people to have an Inner Dialogue session. Choose who will be the dreamer and who will be the helper for the first session. Set a time limit; usually, thirty to forty-five minutes is sufficient to get through all the

Inner Dialogue steps for *each person*. After doing one session this way, the person who has completed an Inner Dialogue becomes the helper, and the other person now takes his or her turn doing Inner Dialogue for the time agreed upon.

Some tips for helpers: When you reach Step 10 of the Inner Dialogue, listen to the dreamer as she shares her insights and connects the dream to her life in as many ways as possible. Once she has done this, you can then ask your partner if she would like to hear your impressions and what you noticed during her session.

When you share your impressions or intuitions about another person's dream, *go gently*. Dreams and symbols touch us in the deepest way possible; this is sensitive territory. Try to phrase your comments *as questions* rather than as statements, so they do not sound like a fixed interpretation. For instance, "I had a feeling this dream could be about *(whatever your impression is)*. Does that seem possible?" Or, "When you said *(whatever was said)*, I sensed you were sad/angry about that situation. Does that fit?"

Give the dreamer plenty of room to discover and experience his or her own insights. The dreamer should always have the last word on what the dream or waking dream means.

3

The Key to Loving:
Your Inner Marriage

Hungry for More

What you feel and do in a relationship may not always make sense, even to you. With the unnerving sensation of not being in control, you may amaze yourself, and your partner, by the strength of your reactions. Even a seemingly insignificant issue may get blown out of proportion when your subconscious is involved—such as when you and your spouse fight over who takes out the trash.

Although you may find yourself in the grip of a waking dream, you don't have to stay there. Before you wonder what to do about your relationship with another, take the time to understand your waking dream's message about *you*. You can use Inner Dialogue to learn about how your relationship with yourself influences your relationships with others.

When you speak *as* the other person, you will become aware of the subconscious thoughts and feelings that have caused your waking dream. You will understand your interaction with the real-life person much better once you explore him or her as a symbol for a hidden part of you. By using Inner Dialogue regularly, you will find that your interactions with others become less puzzling and more satisfying.

Let me give you an example of how your subconscious influences your real-life relationships, from one of my dreams:

> I am with my husband. We are in a restaurant, eating. Without asking me, he reaches over and eats all the food off my plate. Now my plate is empty and I am still hungry. I get upset and angry at him.

When I spoke as the husband-symbol in my dream, and then as myself, this is part of the Inner Dialogue that occurred:

HUSBAND: I have a huge appetite. I've eaten everything on my plate, and now I've reached over and eaten everything on yours.

WIFE: I didn't have a chance to eat my food! You didn't even ask me if you could have it all. I'm hungry and you ate everything!

HUSBAND: I'm sorry. I guess I got carried away. You were so quiet, you didn't tell me not to eat your food. Of course I don't want you to be hungry. I want both of us to have enough to eat.

WIFE: What I need from you is to remember that I have needs too. I need to eat. I need nourishment, nurturing. Just because I'm quiet, don't assume I don't have needs.

HUSBAND: I didn't really forget. But I am going to be more careful about giving you room to express your needs. What I need from you is to speak up more. Tell me what you need. Tell me if I'm taking too much or doing something that upsets you. I need to have you tell me where I stand.

WIFE: Yes, I see that I should speak up more. If I don't communicate how I feel or make sure I get your attention when I need to, that's my fault. I'll make more of an effort to tell you what I need.

If I had interpreted my husband-symbol literally, I would have blamed my husband for doing something wrong. Instead, my Inner Dialogue helped me discover a very different, and more helpful, subconscious message:

There were ways in which I wasn't protecting and nurturing myself.

Through my Inner Dialogue, I discovered that one part of me (*my husband-symbol*) had gotten carried away and was taking too much, while another part of me (*my conscious self*) felt deprived and "hungry for more."

FOOD AS A SYMBOL

My subconscious mind's choice of my husband as a symbol was not a coincidence. In reality, he eats off my plate occasionally. (But he usually does not eat everything!) He likes to share food, so our mealtime custom often involves swapping portions of food or eating off each other's plates. I have grown to appreciate and enjoy this custom of sharing food; but there are still times when I feel more comfortable keeping my plate to myself.

Truthfully, once in a while his eating off my plate has upset me, creating a waking dream. Now I wondered if my "hungry for more" dream was pointing out an imbalance in my relationship with him or in my relationship with myself. Only after doing an Inner Dialogue with my husband and the food as *subconscious symbols* would I be able to sort out how much of the dream was about my relationship with myself, and how much was about my relationship with him.

Food as a symbol often represents getting emotional nurturing. The manner in which we give ourselves food, how we may withhold it, and even how we share it, can convey much about how well we are nurturing ourselves. Eating disorders and food-related problems also express this subconscious symbolism and can be explored as waking dreams. For example, when people give themselves food "treats" as a reward, food becomes a symbol or substitute for love, rather than a source of physical nourishment. This confusion about food may indicate that more beneficial and healthy ways of getting emotional nurturing are not available or are not being sought, either in relationships or from oneself. Using food as a substitute for love does not lead to more love; usually it results in weight problems.

On a literal level, the dream could be interpreted as a message about how well my husband was or wasn't nurturing me. Based on our customs at mealtime and our attitudes about food, my dream presented a sensitive area in our relationship. While it was possible there was a message in the dream about my real-life relationship, there was more to it than that. On a symbolic level, the symbols of my husband and the food were also offering me an important message about myself.

Feeling dissatisfied, distant from or distrusting of certain symbols (in this instance, my husband-symbol), indicates trouble accepting a *part of oneself.* Even in cases where a dream or waking dream is about a real-life relationship, it is very helpful to explore the person you are involved with as a symbol representing a part of you. Once you discover the subconscious message— something your subconscious is telling you about yourself—then you are in a much better position to evaluate and solve problems in your relationship with the real-life person.

THE INNER MARRIAGE

As I thought about how my dream might apply to my life, it became clear to me that lately I had been making my career my highest priority. This in itself was not bad, but something had gotten out of balance. Before my career move, I had spent a lot more time being in nature, gardening, meditating, journaling, and reflecting on my symbols. In other words, I used to give myself plenty of "feeding time," with specific activities that helped me to feel balanced and replenished.

In Eastern philosophy, life energy is made up of two complementary parts: yin and yang, or feminine and masculine. Feminine energy is associated with receptivity and inner-directed activities, such as meditation and intuition. Masculine energy is associated with outer-directed activities, such as competing, completing a task and asserting yourself with others. (You may notice from this description that masculine energies usually correspond to left-brain hemisphere abilities, and feminine energies to the abilities of the right brain.)

In addition to reflecting my real relationship or marriage, my dream conveyed an important message about my *inner marriage*—how I balanced my feminine and masculine energies. I needed to recognize value in both.

My dream was reminding me that I'd lost track of the power of my feminine. This part of me had become too quiet for its own good. The healing message was:

> *I need to nurture both parts of me equally: my career self (masculine, left brain) and my intuitive self (feminine, right brain) need to join in a marriage that balances, nurtures and supports all of me.*

If I had taken this dream literally, I would have put blame on my husband—and I would have missed learning something valuable about myself. On the other hand, if a real problem with my husband had come up—concerning eating styles, food, emotional nurturing, or anything else—I was in a much better position to discuss it with him objectively after my Inner Dialogue with the husband-symbol. I would be more aware of what part of the problem was in *my relationship with myself,* and what part was in *my relationship with him.*

Inner Dialogue helped me to sort out how I could be more nurturing to myself, as well as how I could ask for and receive more nurturing from my husband.

Exercise 3 in this chapter gives more information about masculine and feminine energies and their balance in the inner marriage.

INNER AND OUTER RELATIONSHIPS

Consider for a moment how your subconscious may be at work right now, influencing your relationships.

For instance, if I had forgotten or ignored the message my dream offered, the imbalance between my career self and intuitive self would have continued and probably worsened. I would have been primed to have an unpleasant waking dream. I would have been more likely to get angry at someone over a small annoyance; I might have blamed my husband for not being attentive or supportive enough. My subconscious conflict would have influenced my attitudes toward my husband and others and, as a result, a real conflict might have erupted.

Inner Dialogue will help you recognize *your part* in an interaction with another person. But this does not mean that you should take all the responsibility for what happens in a relationship; you and your partner share that responsibility fifty-fifty. While Inner Dialogue is not a cure-all for real problems that exist in a relationship, doing Inner Dialogue can lead to more understanding of your part in the difficulty and, therefore, a more productive discussion of any problem.

There are many relationship issues that make it important for you and your partner to share your feelings and thoughts with each other. Inner Dialogue and other methods presented in this book can help you to be more aware of what you feel and need, but they are not a substitute for communication with a partner, friend or relative. Communication is necessary in order to help you and another person resolve your differences.

If you are unsure how to negotiate with another person to get what you need, the steps for Inner Dialogue can serve as guidelines. They are remarkably similar to steps taken in conflict-resolution: describe the situation from each person's point of view; express feelings clearly; identify the conflict; negotiate a solution that involves action from both people; appreciate each other's differences as complementary qualities that make the relationship stronger.

When there is physical or emotional abuse in a relationship, both people need to learn how to change their behavior so the destructive interaction can end. Many times you cannot achieve these changes on your own, without the help of a trained professional.

In the following example, my client was experiencing severe problems, both with her health and her relationship. Our sessions involved using Inner Dialogue as well as discussing her very real interpersonal problems and suggesting ways in which she could change her behavior for better results.

A WAKING DREAM NIGHTMARE

Sarah had colitis, and her condition was so severe it was affecting every part of her life, making her afraid to go out of the house. She was referred to me by her doctor, who recognized that she needed additional help in learning to reduce stress.

When I asked her what might be contributing to her stress, Sarah told me she was not getting the love she needed from her husband, either emotionally or physically. In fact, she had kept her colitis a secret from him because she was afraid he would be critical that her illness made her a bad wife and mother.

Sarah's health and home life were a waking dream nightmare.

Initially, she laid the blame on her weak physical constitution and on her husband—and there was good reason for her to be concerned in both areas. But there was much more going on than met the eye. Sarah's subconscious was sending her an urgent message—through her stress-related health problem—in a last-resort effort to get her attention.

I talked to Sarah about the symbolism of her colitis—an inflammation of the large intestine that can cause painful colon spasms and sudden diarrhea. Her body seemed out of control, and Sarah feared "making a mess." Then she might become constipated, and "nothing would come out." In terms of her emotions, I asked her if she felt comfortable letting her feelings out and sharing them with her husband. She said she did not, and frequently she'd hold onto her emotions until she lost control and exploded at him.

The parallel between her body and her emotions was not lost on Sarah. In her Inner Dialogue, when she spoke as her colon, this (subconscious) part of her said, "I feel squeezed and pressured, as though I don't have enough room to breathe." At the same time, Sarah also got a spontaneous image of herself as a child, being criticized and having her childish interests and enthusiasm "squeezed" out of her.

Sarah understood that her colitis was giving her an important opportunity. Although her illness was a very distressing waking dream, it also gave her valuable information that could help her get well—both physically and emotionally. She may have been prevented from learning how to express herself in a healthy way when she was a child. But now, as an adult, she could choose to learn a more balanced way to express her emotions and thoughts with her husband and with others. The first step was to *give herself more love and support.*

Sarah had been focusing on needing her husband to pay more attention to her; but in fact she paid very little attention to herself. She needed to take the time to care for herself—by taking a walk in the park or going to a lecture with a friend. By improving her relationship with herself, she would feel less "squeezed" by her responsibilities as wife and mother.

It was time for Sarah to realize that her individual needs were important; her ability to care for her husband and children depended on her feeling good about herself. By giving herself "room to breathe" and learning to express her thoughts and feelings in a more direct and healthy way, she had the power to rid herself of the stress that had debilitated her.

Sarah benefited greatly from her Inner Dialogues. She felt more sympathy for both her colon and her inner child, and she wanted to give them the attention they needed so they could feel protected and comfortable. She liked talking to these subconscious parts of her every day, telling them she was their friend and imagining that she could hold them and comfort them when they were tense. Sarah's sympathy for her colon and inner child also gave her the impetus she needed to begin to assert herself more and to set more realistic limits about how much she could do for her husband and children each day.

In a short time, Sarah experienced a noticeable improvement in her physical health. As she experienced less stress, her colitis symptoms became infrequent and then disappeared. She found that she could handle stressful situations more confidently and was expressing more of her thoughts and feelings to her husband. Eventually, she told him that she had been suffering from colitis. She was surprised that he was very concerned and sympathetic.

In addition, Sarah noticed that as she valued herself more and paid more attention to her personal needs, her husband became more considerate and attentive also. Significantly, Sarah and her husband regained a closeness and intimacy, both physical and emotional, that they had not had since the early stages of their relationship. When Sarah valued and nurtured the subconscious parts of her that needed healing, she also experienced her real-life relationship as more satisfying and loving.

THE DIFFERENCE BETWEEN THINKING AND DOING

Instead of doing Inner Dialogue, many people are tempted to take a mental shortcut; they assume that if they can figure out what a symbol means, or what part of them the symbol represents, that is enough. It isn't. For instance, when Sarah understood that her colon was expressing a subconscious part of her, or when I recognized that my husband-symbol represented the "masculine" energy in me, those insights were helpful—but without Inner Dialogue, this awareness could not resolve a subconscious conflict.

The healing power of your subconscious is released by *doing* Inner Dialogue. Inner Dialogue takes you beyond your conscious thought-process; your emotional and physical *experience* while doing an Inner Dialogue is what helps you to understand and resolve problems on a subconscious level. Just *thinking* about the meaning of your symbols does not enable you to resolve a subconscious conflict. In order to change a pattern of limitation into an experience of self-discovery and empowerment, you need to *do* Inner Dialogue.

SYMBOLIC WRAPPING

When you dream of someone you know, or when you keep thinking about a symbol that *looks like* someone you know, you are experiencing a message from your subconscious. Pay attention to the *quality or energy* this person represents—and get to know it and value it as a subconscious part of you.

Symbols are *energy-holders*, and like any container, they give a particular *look and shape* to the energy they hold. Your symbols may appear as dreams, spontaneous images, or waking dreams. Awake or dreaming, your subconscious uses whatever means is available to tell you about your relationships—both with yourself and with others.

The symbolic wrapping has, perhaps, *someone else's face on it* (like a lover, friend, relative or celebrity); or it may take the form of *an object* (like a body part or a car) or *a place* (like your childhood home). By doing Inner Dialogue, you gain awareness of the subconscious part of your personality which is under this symbolic wrapping. Through Inner Dialogue, you will find out how much your conscious and your subconscious agree or disagree about a certain area of your life. In addition, you will discover how nurturing and expressing this subconscious part will benefit you in your conscious activities.

Viewed in a right-brained way, even symbols that at first seem negative— such as Sarah's spastic colon or her difficult relationship—are *potential allies*, because they carry valuable energy. Even a little of that symbol's strength, power, or persistence will probably be very useful to you—when you consciously direct that energy where you want it.

For instance, Sarah's colon (and subconscious) was resorting to extremes of constipation and diarrhea. Emotionally, Sarah was holding on to her anger and hurt, aggravating her physical condition. When she couldn't hold her feelings in any further, she would explode. Instead of this destructive cycle, Sarah learned to use the body's natural rhythm of holding on and letting go *as her ally*. Providing more for her own needs, as well as asking for what she needed from her husband and others, helped Sarah let go of her anger and resentment. She also learned that she could hold on to her good feelings, generated by taking more time for herself, nurturing herself, and receiving attention from her husband.

DEFUSING ANGER

When you are experiencing a difficult relationship, often it is just about impossible to let go of anger toward the other person. For example, Sarah couldn't let go of her resentment toward her husband. Likewise, someone whose lover has been unfaithful has trouble letting go of the anger and hurt of betrayal. When you experience a strong reaction of anger, resentment, betrayal, rejection, or abandonment, you are experiencing a waking dream—and you need to *defuse* the subconscious charge by doing Inner Dialogue.

Through speaking as the symbol that represents the person(s) you resent, you can actually de-intensify your emotional reaction to that person. Inner Dialogue is an excellent way to regain your balance and perspective for the next time you communicate with the real person.

THE OTHER WOMAN

Infidelity in a relationship is always a loaded issue—so it is a prime opportunity for a waking dream.

The *other woman* or the *other man* often seems more attractive and desirable than you are. Many times, people are afraid of being rejected and left for such a person. In some cases, people fear that "the other" will cause them to be unfaithful or to leave their partner.

There are very real consequences to infidelity. Many times, however, infidelity is anticipated before it happens, by thinking about it consciously or in dreams.

In a dream, you have *carte blanche* to go ahead and embrace your dream lover. On a symbolic level, you are really embracing yourself. Making love to a dream lover also has a healthy and positive symbolic meaning: your blissful union symbolizes that you have brought your masculine and feminine energies into a creative and dynamic balance.

However, if in reality you find yourself attracted to someone who is not your partner, be very careful. Your attraction could be a waking dream for a part of you that you urgently need to bring into balance. In this case, acting out your attraction or having an affair is *not the answer.*

Use Inner Dialogue to defuse some of the subconscious charge that could cause an unpleasant waking dream (although it might be pleasant at first). The other woman or the other man may reflect a part of you which you need to know and enjoy more fully—perhaps a part that is more sensual, playful, and desirable than your conscious view of yourself allows.

By the same token, when you worry or dream that your lover or partner is unfaithful, exploring your partner as a part of you can also defuse a potential waking dream. Instead, you may get to know a part of yourself that asserts its needs more openly, seeks excitement and challenge, and is willing to take risks.

Men and women in my classes have found, after doing Inner Dialogue, that their anxiety over possible infidelity by either their partner or themselves was greatly reduced. Inner Dialogue helped them to recognize and reclaim the sensuality and excitement in themselves. They felt more attractive and desirable, and as a result, they were also more attractive and exciting to their partners.

(See Exercise 5 for more on "Dream Lovers and Other Loaded Situations.")

A WAKING DREAM IN THE WORK PLACE

Ted was a successful engineer who enjoyed his work. But, he told me, he hated his boss, who was critical and demanding. The situation at work had deteriorated, the enjoyment had gone out of it, and Ted was always on edge.

I suggested to Ted that it might help to work on his real-life problem as a waking dream. In his Inner Dialogue, Ted *spoke as* his unreasonable boss, repeating many of the things his boss had actually said to him. Now, though, Ted could use his Inner Dialogue to tell his boss how he honestly felt—something he could not do so freely at work.

Ted's Inner Dialogue took an unexpected turn when his boss-symbol had a chance to say *what he needed*. To Ted's surprise, his boss said he felt insecure, and that was why he tended to push himself, and others, too hard. This made Ted think about his own insecurities and how much he criticized himself and made demands on himself to perform better.

> Ted realized that when his boss criticized him and was demanding, this waking dream mirrored Ted's tendency to be self-critical and overly demanding of himself.

When Ted went back to work the day after his Inner Dialogue, he looked at his boss as though through new eyes. He could now sense that his boss was insecure and even felt some sympathy for him. Ted was amazed that he was less affected by his boss's comments and demands, even though they continued to be somewhat unreasonable. Inner Dialogue had helped him defuse the subconscious charge that had created his waking dream.

THE ADULT AND CHILD BALANCING ACT

Every relationship might be seen as a balancing act between the *adult and child parts* of you and another person: responsible and playful; rational and emotional; planned and spontaneous.

Sarah, whose colitis became a waking dream, found that her inner child felt "squeezed" and helpless. In her childhood, she remembered feeling as though she had no room to have a life of her own; now she was having the same feelings in her adulthood and in her marriage. When she identified with her "child" feelings, she tended to react to her husband by being fearful and secretive, the same way a child would react to an unfair or punitive parent.

Not surprisingly, Sarah's husband also had child and adult parts that needed to be brought into balance. Since this was something only he could do for himself, I suggested to Sarah that she concentrate on giving her own inner child the love and protection she needed, but had never gotten before. By doing this for herself, she would gradually be able to understand her husband's confused and needy inner child. She would then be able to deal more effectively, and more sympathetically, with the difficulties that arose between them when either his inner child or hers created a waking dream in their relationship.

Sarah learned a valuable lesson about the subconscious forces influencing her health and marriage through Inner Dialogue. She realized that her waking dream conflicts with her husband were a good opportunity for her to change her behavior and self-image from that of being squeezed out of existence to that of empowering herself in the relationship.

Through Inner Dialogue, Sarah discovered that her inner child's interests and simple pleasures could bring healing into her life. She began painting again and also greatly enjoyed reading stories to her two young children. As her inner child received attention and acknowledgment, the adult and child parts of her came into a comfortable balance. Sarah felt calmer and more accepting of her vulnerability. She was now comfortable setting aside time for herself, as well as special time to be with her husband and children.

RECOGNIZING PATTERNS

Many people wonder why they have had unsuccessful relationships over and over again. They may not notice any similarity or pattern among these unfortunate experiences. Many times the pattern is subconscious, making it elusive to your conscious, rational probing. Inner Dialogue will reveal any subconscious pattern in a safe and helpful way.

By doing Inner Dialogue on two or more relationships, you will find the *subconscious link* that these experiences have in common. You will also be able to bring subconscious parts of you into balance, so that you are freed from an unhappy repeating pattern and the way is cleared for healthier and more positive experiences.

The ability to recognize patterns is valuable in every area of life. Inner Dialogue helps you to use this ability to solve problems and gain a broader perspective, so that you can avoid repeating past mistakes.

In a short time, you will start to notice patterns among your symbols. You will discover how your waking dreams are part of a message designed to help you. Recognizing patterns, where previously you noticed only seemingly unrelated elements, is an exciting part of discovering the wisdom and creativity of your subconscious.

(See Exercise 3 in Chapter 7 for guidelines on identifying the patterns and repeating messages in your symbols and dreams.)

ENJOY THE RIDE

Inner Dialogue can show you how you may be stopping yourself from fully enjoying or entering into a relationship with someone. By exploring your relationship with yourself first, you can discover ways in which you can improve your relationships with others.

One of my clients, Louise, had a scary dream which seemed, at first, totally unrelated to her real-life relationships:

> I get into the elevator of an office building. I push the button for my floor, #7. The elevator goes up, but instead of stopping at my floor, it gathers speed at an alarming rate. Now I'm frightened. I try to stop the elevator, but the buttons don't respond. The elevator goes faster and faster, then shoots out of the top of the building and goes into outer space! By now I am hysterical. I don't believe there is a way for me to return to Earth. I am trapped in this runaway elevator.

To Louise, this was a horrible dream and the elevator was a very upsetting symbol. She could see no redeeming value in this dream. She could not even make a guess as to why she would have such a dream.

I guided Louise through the Inner Dialogue steps so that she could arrive at her own understanding of the message her subconscious was sending her. I began by asking her to imagine her dream again *(Step 1)*, and then shift her awareness so she could imagine being the elevator. Then I asked, "As the elevator, please describe yourself. What do you look like?" *(Step 2)*

LOUISE: I am the Elevator. I am a large metal box. I have doors and a control panel inside.

Next, I asked, "Now, as the Elevator, just tell me what elevators *normally* do." *(Step 3)*

LOUISE (As the Elevator): I take people up and down. Up and down in the building.

To fill out as much detail as possible, I asked, "Elevator, please tell me about yourself—what is unique about you, and how you are different from other elevators." *(Step 3, continued)*

LOUISE (As the Elevator): My unique qualities are...my walls are a golden color, inside me, where people ride. I'm a gold-plated elevator! I have unusual powers. I can shoot through the top of the building and go into outer space. I am different from other elevators because I have a much wider range of where I can go. Also, I'm gold-plated. That makes me more valuable and special.

Now we could begin to find out what Louise's subconscious was trying to tell her. I asked the Elevator, "What is happening from your—the Elevator's—point of view?" *(Step 4)*

LOUISE (As the Elevator): What is happening from my point of view is...I am going up in the building, and I just keep going up. I shoot out of the top of the building and start travelling in outer space. Louise is inside of me. She's going nuts, she's so scared—but *I'm having a wonderful time!* She thinks something is wrong, but this is what I do naturally!

Already Louise looked surprised at how different the Elevator's personality was from her conscious personality. I asked the Elevator, "How do you feel as this is happening?" *(Step 5)*

LOUISE (As the Elevator): How I feel as this is happening is...I feel great. *I like not having any limits on where I can go.*

While speaking as the Elevator, there was a dramatic change in Louise. Her voice and body language became bolder and more zestful than they were before. These changes were also a marked contrast to the fear and powerlessness that Louise previously felt as the dreamer.

The Elevator's different point of view represented a valuable subconscious part of Louise. Speaking as the Elevator has shed some light on the subconscious, unused abilities which the Elevator represents: a zest for life that encourages adventure and a desire to push beyond the normal limits which Louise assumed her life must have.

Now Louise was ready to continue her Inner Dialogue and clarify the source of the conflict between herself and the Elevator:

> THERAPIST (T): Louise, I'd like you to imagine and feel yourself the way you were in your dream. Visualize the Elevator in front of you now. You can talk to it. This is your chance to tell this runaway Elevator how you feel about it. *(Step 6)*
>
> LOUISE: Elevator, what I feel about you is...You scare me to death! I don't like what you're doing to me! I don't like where you're taking me.
>
> T: Now I will give you some phrases that I'd like you to complete, still speaking as Louise. Tell the Elevator, "What I don't like about you is..."
>
> LOUISE: What I don't like about you is...I just wanted to go to the seventh floor, not into outer space! You didn't give me a clue where you were going, and I'm not ready for this!
>
> T: "What I want to say to you is..."
>
> LOUISE: What I want to say to you is...I want to go home! I don't want to be here! This isn't fair!
>
> T: Now I'd like you to shift your perspective and speak again as the Elevator. I'd like you to complete these phrases. *(Step 7)* As the Elevator, tell Louise, "What I feel about you is..."
>
> LOUISE (As the Elevator): What I feel about you is...You're not giving me a chance! I'm really not so dangerous.
>
> T: "What I don't like about you is..."
>
> LOUISE (As the Elevator): What I don't like about you is...You're not letting me have any fun! I am a special elevator and I was made for more than just going up and down in an office building.
>
> T: "What I want to say to you is..."
>
> LOUISE (As the Elevator): What I want to say to you is...Give me the benefit of the doubt. Loosen up and have some fun with me! *Trust me and enjoy the ride!* Let's go have an adventure, and then I'll bring you back.

At this point, Louise's face melted into an expression of wonder. Suddenly, she could feel the confidence and power of her Elevator. Inner Dialogue had transformed her earlier perception of the Elevator as out of control and holding her hostage into an appreciation of it as something valuable. She had difficulty putting it into words, but Louise could sense that the Elevator was a part of her that she needed.

By now in the session, Louise realized she had misunderstood the Elevator. In fact, she said, this was not really a scary symbol at all. Once she recognized the adventurous intentions of her Elevator through Inner Dialogue, she understood that her subconscious was encouraging her to have more fun and take more risks. In fact, her fear and reluctance to "enjoy the ride" now seemed humorous to her.

Next, I wanted to help Louise understand more fully the message her subconscious was sending her. I translated the action of the "elevator propelling Louise into outer space" into a metaphor for her life. I asked,

> ...Are you at a time in your life when you feel like you're being propelled into something you are not ready for?

The Elevator reflected something significant about a subconscious part of Louise. The Elevator wanted to "go beyond normal limits" and have an adventure—and more importantly, it was quite capable of doing so. But the Elevator's boldness and enthusiasm was in sharp contrast to Louise's fear and need to be safe. I asked,

> ...Is there a way in which you might be limiting yourself, when your abilities could take you much further?

As Louise and I explored these subconscious metaphors, I gave her room to discover her own meanings and apply them to specific areas of her life.

Louise realized that her subconscious was pointing out that she needed to reclaim the very capable, confident adventurer in her. Up until now, she had been afraid to use the valuable "gold-plated elevator" part of her—the part that wanted to take risks and meet challenges. Because of her Inner Dialogue, Louise was willing to begin to change the safe and habitual limits she had set for herself, so she could really use—and enjoy—her abilities.

Next, I asked Louise,

> ...To what areas of your life might you want to apply this subconscious message to take more risks and use more of your abilities?

Louise said she was in a good relationship, but she was confused about it. She liked her boyfriend's self-confidence, and at the same time she didn't like feeling pressured to keep up with him in areas where she wasn't as confident as he was. For instance, when they went skiing, he liked to go fast and take chances; she didn't. She said she preferred to ski safely, which meant going more slowly and staying on easier slopes.

I asked Louise if her Elevator might also represent the adventurous energy in her boyfriend that was pulling her toward taking more risks.

As she thought about her responses to the Elevator, and then to her boyfriend, Louise's eyes widened. After we talked about it, she said she was convinced that her relationship was a waking dream. Her subconscious was sending her the same message, both in her dream and in her relationship: *Take more chances and enjoy the ride.* In fact, she told me, it was her boyfriend's ability to enjoy himself which had attracted her to him in the first place. Now it was time for her to learn how to more fully enjoy herself, too.

A similar pattern could now be seen in both Louise's Elevator Dream and in her waking dream: Louise was struggling with a part of her that wanted to stay in a predictable but safe routine (conscious), and a part of her that wanted to push beyond the normal limits and have an exciting adventure (subconscious).

Further, the *contrasts* present in Louise's dream and waking dream were the same: safe-risky, limited-unlimited, slow-fast, dull-exciting.

A new appreciation of how her subconscious conflicts influenced her reactions to her boyfriend and her expectations of herself began to dawn on Louise. Now it became apparent to her that her subconscious conflict was also making her reluctant to get married.

Louise had been in the relationship for three years and considered it a good one. But now that she and her boyfriend were talking about getting married, she felt apprehensive; she didn't want to give up the safe limits of the relationship they had been having or risk a change.

Marriage would feel scary, she said—like going faster and further than she was used to, as with the Elevator in her dream. The prospect was exciting, but also risky. She wasn't sure if she was ready for the challenge of marriage. Unlike her Elevator, she doubted that she could experience marriage as an adventure or trust herself enough to "enjoy the ride."

For the first time, Louise recognized the part of her that wanted to break out of her safe but limiting routine. While it would take more than one session to be fully comfortable with the adventurous part of her, Louise could use the elevator symbol as a helpful reminder on a daily basis. For instance, in considering the possibility of marriage, she could now consciously weigh her desire for maintaining a safe status quo with her desire for enjoyment and personal growth.

During the year, Louise used Inner Dialogue to discover the value of many more symbols as subconscious aspects of herself. She regularly noticed the theme of "needing to take more risks and have more fun" in her symbols and dreams. Gradually, Louise became more comfortable with the adventurer in her, more confident of her strengths and abilities, and more willing to test them in her relationship and in other areas of her life.

Louise's explorations became a catalyst, inspiring in an increased appreciation of her abilities and the rewards that risk-taking could bring her. She used Inner Dialogue to learn how to embrace and accept even the troublesome symbols—as she had done with her Elevator. Symbols representing subconscious parts of her became powerful allies. Louise was in the process of developing an exciting partnership between the conscious and subconscious parts of her.

A transformation was taking place that manifested as beneficial changes in Louise's life. Now Louise enjoyed the challenge of new situations that were outside her old, safe routine. The resolution of conflicts in her subconscious had set her on a different path, moving toward a more fulfilling outcome. Louise was now using her subconscious in a new and more empowering way.

Later that year, Louise told me that she had experienced a breakthrough in her skiing, and now she had fun going faster on steeper slopes. Her new confidence gradually rippled out into other areas of her life—including her relationship. Significantly, a year later, she made the decision to get married. She was ready to enjoy the ride.

LIFE IS A JUGGLING ACT

No one can always be in perfect balance—either with oneself or with others. In a way, we are all like jugglers, trying to keep several balls in the air at once. We juggle different needs while trying to bring the creative and the practical aspects of our lives into an integrated and dynamic balance.

Sometimes we do a great job keeping all the balls in the air at once—staying in balance with ourselves and others. Like a skilled juggler, we may even be able to create an attractive configuration with the juggled balls, bringing them into a special relationship with each other.

At other times, one or two balls fly off and we lose track of them for awhile. The balls are not lost—in a strange way, they follow us. As if they are connected to us by invisible strings, they may even drag behind us and slow us down a little. Then, another cycle begins. We turn around and recognize these lost balls and pick them up. We may hold them for awhile and wonder how they got there. When we throw them into the air again to juggle again, we consciously put their energy back into motion—as essential parts of the configuration.

Your relationship with your subconscious needs regular doses of loving attention in order to thrive. And the more you strengthen this bond, the more vitality and clarity you will enjoy both consciously and subconsciously. It is important to keep strengthening and appreciating the partnership between your conscious and subconscious, even when everything is going well.

The philosopher Martin Buber has said that the conflicts between yourself and others are really the conflicts in your own soul. Through Inner Dialogue, you will heal inner conflicts and create loving alliances with subconscious parts of you. When you make peace within yourself, you can build more caring and cooperative relationships with others—and make peace in your world.

Exercises for
Your Subconscious

EXERCISE 1
Exploring Inner and Outer Relationships

When exploring relationships, your most powerful starting place is with yourself. No matter how realistic the person in your dream or waking dream is, no matter how much the situation may resemble reality (or your fear of what may happen), explore the person that is represented *as a symbol* first.

WHAT TO DO: Choose a waking dream or dream that involves someone you know. Use Inner Dialogue to explore this person as a symbol.

Through your Inner Dialogue, you will discover and recognize ways in which this symbol represents a part of you. After doing Inner Dialogue, you will be able to tell more accurately if this symbol also gives you information about your relationship with its real-life counterpart.

Remember, just thinking about your symbol from a left-brain or conscious point of view will not let you accurately judge if this symbol is telling you about your inner relationship or your real-life relationship. Instead of trying to take a mental shortcut, do Inner Dialogue and increase your right-brain awareness of subconscious parts of you, in order to arrive at a useful insight.

Also, keep in mind that a person you know, including yourself, may appear as a symbol—but perhaps with important differences from the person you know in reality. Give yourself room to explore this possibility before your rational mind jumps to conclusions.

EXERCISE 2
Masculine and Feminine

Feminine and masculine energies are inside each of us, regardless of our gender. In this century, the pioneer psychiatrist Carl Jung described these energies as *anima* (feminine) and *animus* (masculine). For thousands of years in the Far East, the same energies have been described as *yin* (feminine) and *yang* (masculine).

In Taoist philosophy, yin and yang are two complementary sides of our life force, which need to be in dynamic balance in order to achieve harmony of mind, body and spirit. Dialoguing with your symbols will reveal the health and balance of the masculine and feminine energies in you.

Masculine energies, like left-brain hemisphere abilities, tend to be rational, logical, practical, and assertive. *Yang* energy enables you to go out into the world, explore, and achieve.

Feminine energies, on the other hand, mirror right-brain hemisphere abilities: intuitive, emotional, vulnerable, nurturing and accepting. *Yin* energy allows you to be receptive and go inward to experience yourself.

Both masculine and feminine energies are indispensable. Many times, though, because of cultural conditioning, the masculine traits are overdeveloped in men and the feminine traits are overdeveloped in women.

I've experienced an endless variety of symbols for my inner masculine: my husband, my father, old boyfriends, teachers, famous male comedians and actors; aggressive, powerful, or frightening animals (such as gorillas and lions); men I don't know, male babies, and even myself (being assertive; performing creatively; solving a problem).

Similarly, the symbols for my inner feminine have been diverse: my mother, my sisters, critical or nurturing women, gentle male and female teachers and guides, children, nature, blooming flowers, water (either calm and inviting or turbulent), butterflies, playful or dangerous animals (such as panthers, mountain lions, horses), and myself (being gentle, loving, or humorous; reaching a new insight or understanding; helping to heal myself or others).

WHAT TO DO: In your journal, list as many of your *masculine symbols* as you can. This will be easier if you write one or two descriptive words beside the symbol, i.e., "Gorilla—aggressive, strong." After you have made your "masculine symbol" list, make another list for your *feminine symbols*.

If you are not sure whether or not a particular symbol is masculine or feminine, do Inner Dialogue and have a conversation with it. Do not forget that *you* are also a symbol in your dreams and waking dreams! Your qualities and expressiveness may vary—from assertive and adventuresome in one experience (masculine) to receptive and affectionate in another (feminine).

Symbols may not appear to be masculine or feminine in an obvious way. If you have trouble identifying your symbols as masculine or feminine, try to pinpoint some of the general qualities or energies which I've described for masculine or feminine. Also, keep in mind that each person brings their own individual history, cultural orientation and self-expression to their masculine and feminine symbols, so your symbols might be masculine or feminine for different reasons than I have stated. Be on the lookout for unusual symbols.

Lastly, review your lists of masculine and feminine symbols. Notice the symbols, qualities and feelings that seem to repeat in your dreams and waking dreams. Also, notice if any of your masculine and feminine symbols interact with each other on a repeated basis.

Do an Inner Dialogue on a masculine or feminine symbol that appears frequently in your dreams. Or, choose a symbol that represents a *quality or feeling* that repeats often in your dreams and do Inner Dialogue on it.

EXERCISE 3
Enhancing Your Inner Marriage

You can use Inner Dialogue to balance and enhance your masculine and feminine energies. As you improve the cooperation between your masculine and feminine symbols, you are also strengthening your *inner marriage.*

When you have generally positive and cooperative relationships with your feminine and masculine symbols, as shown in your dreams and waking dreams, this indicates that you are in a good position to attract and develop satisfying relationships with others. A cooperative inner marriage also reflects that the abilities of your left and right brain hemispheres are being used in a mutually-enhancing way.

WHAT TO DO: Review some of your recent dreams and waking dreams. Notice how much cooperation, satisfaction and loving are present between you and your symbols right now.

Choose a dream or waking dream in which your relationship to another person-symbol can be improved. Do Inner Dialogue, writing it out in your journal. As part of your Dialogue, in Steps 2 and 3, *note the qualities in you and the other symbol which may indicate masculine or feminine energy.* (You may see a complementary kind of relationship here, with one symbol having primarily feminine qualities, and the other having primarily masculine qualities. Or, both qualities may be present in a symbol.)

As you continue your Inner Dialogue, use steps 7, 8 and 9 to improve the communication, acceptance, and understanding between you and the other symbol. After you have finished, imagine what it would be like to have an ongoing relationship with the other symbol, an alliance which allows an exchange of energies and strengths that benefits both of you. Imagine becoming close friends or allies with the symbol and giving the symbol an embrace. *(See the Lucid Fantasy guidelines in Chapter 4 for more ideas.)*

EXERCISE 4
Waking Dreams In A Relationship

When you experience a real-life problem or waking dream with someone, I suggest that you *first explore that person as a symbol for a part of you,* using Inner Dialogue. Your Inner Dialogue will also give you more clarity to deal effectively with the real-life counterpart of your symbol.

WHAT TO DO: Select a real-life person you are having a strong response to, either positively or negatively. Do Inner Dialogue, speaking *as* that person, and then as yourself. You will discover the subconscious part of you that is influencing your relationship.

EXERCISE 5
Dream Lovers and Other Loaded Situations

Many people get very worried if they have a dream or a waking dream in which they are attracted to someone other than the person with whom they are in a relationship. In a dream, if they make love with an exciting new partner (who may or may not resemble someone they actually know), these people may feel guilty, as though they have been unfaithful to their partner. Or they may take their attraction as clear evidence that they are no longer interested in staying in their relationship. *None of these interpretations may be true.* Your new attraction may be a symbol for a valuable part of you that is seeking expression.

Before you do anything else, do an Inner Dialogue. Speak as the person you are attracted to, as yourself, and as your partner. As yourself, speak to each of them about what you like and don't like about them. Let them respond. You will learn how they are different, and you will also begin to recognize the subconscious reasons why this situation became loaded.

Wait until you have finished your Inner Dialogue before you consider what to do about your real-life relationship and your attraction to another person. If your subconscious is bringing a problem in your real-life relationship to your attention, you will be in a better position to deal with it after you have done your Inner Dialogue.

Dreams and waking dreams in which you are attracted to or sexually involved with someone other than your partner have much to say about *the subconscious influences* at work in your relationship with yourself and with others.

Many times we are attracted to another person for the exact qualities we need to express, but which we either subconsciously or consciously reject in ourselves. This pattern of attraction and rejection can get people into frustrating interactions: sometimes they end up criticizing and blaming their partner for exactly the quality that attracted them in the first place; or, worse, they reject their partner for the quality that initially attracted them, then choose another partner who has the same quality and repeat the pattern. Louise, for example, was able to avoid this kind of repeating pattern or waking dream: through Inner Dialogue, she identified the part of her that wanted to enjoy herself more (represented by the Elevator), and used Inner Dialogue to resolve her attraction/rejection pattern with her real-life boyfriend.

WHAT TO DO: Choose a dream or waking dream in which you are attracted to someone who is not your partner. You will be using Inner Dialogue to explore *three symbols:* the person you are attracted to, your partner, and yourself. Speak as each person, following the Inner Dialogue steps. In doing this process, you may discover attractive aspects of yourself that you can reclaim. You are also likely to gain insight as to how your inner marriage influences your feelings of attraction to certain people in your life.

Following the guidelines below, explore why a real-life situation has become loaded by doing Inner Dialogue and:

- Speak as *the person you are attracted to,* describing yourself as him or her.

- Speak as your *partner,* describing yourself as him or her.

- Speak as *yourself:* Dialogue with the one you are attracted to, and then with your partner.

- Tell the person you are attracted to, and then your partner, what you like and don't like about each of them. Let each of them respond.

- Notice in what ways the two people are different, and in what ways they are the same.

- Think about the qualities of both people as *qualities you need to be more aware of in yourself*—both positive and negative.

- Negotiate an alliance between you and your partner, as well as between you and the one you are attracted to.

- Think of some ways in which you could benefit from using the qualities each person represents (even to a small degree). Imagine expressing those qualities with good results in a particular situation in your life.

4

Lucid Fantasy:
Blueprint for Success

Riding the Whale

Imagine that you have accomplished your greatest goal. You feel excited, energized and strong. Your eyes are shining with joy. You look taller, more relaxed and confident. You say to yourself, "I've finally done it! It's really happened."

What you can imagine, can happen. By using your imagination and all of your senses to experience success, you give your subconscious a "real" experience on which to build. As a result, your dreams are much more likely to become reality.

When you do anything well, it is because you have done the same or a similar task before. Repeated practice has conditioned you to do it more effectively. Like an athlete who has trained for peak performance, you can *condition your subconscious* to respond to the challenges of everyday living with more creativity and vigor.

In this chapter, you will learn Lucid Fantasy, a method I developed to help you gently guide your subconscious toward achieving a goal. When used with Inner Dialogue, Lucid Fantasy produces powerful results—because it goes beyond your conscious awareness to utilize all the resources of your subconscious.

Lucid Fantasy will provide your subconscious with the *experience of success*, creating a blueprint that enhances your confidence, creativity, playfulness, or whatever qualities you need in order to achieve your goal.

Through Lucid Fantasy you can mentally improve upon any experience. Once you can clearly imagine a successful, satisfying outcome, you are much more likely to make it happen in reality.

WHAT YOU SEE, HEAR AND FEEL

Building a Blueprint for Success requires a strategy. You need to know what success really looks like, feels like and sounds like for you.

Olympic athletes know very well the importance of creating a mental Blueprint for Success. During their training and preparation for competition, they condition their minds as well as their bodies. Often, an athlete's mental preparation involves challenging a belief that he or she can't win or does not deserve to win. If a self-defeating belief is left unchallenged, the athlete suffers from performance anxiety and may sabotage his or her success.

When outstanding athletes are interviewed during the Olympics, they are asked, "How did you win? What was your strategy?" Usually these winning athletes answer, "I have given a lot of attention to preparing mentally as well as physically. Mental preparation is as important as physical preparation—maybe even more important."

Athletes condition their minds by mentally rehearsing every movement they need to make. These athletes *see* themselves doing their moves with great confidence, accuracy and ease. They *feel* energized, comfortable and relaxed while doing their routine. They imagine completing their moves, still relaxed and with energy to spare. They say to themselves, "I *can* win. I *will* win," and they *hear* the audience respond to their performance with enthusiastic applause.

Mental rehearsal has been shown to reduce performance anxiety and even transform a stressful situation into one of freedom and enjoyment, enabling Olympian athletes to deliver their personal best. *(For more about mental rehearsal, see Chapter 5, Exercise 3.)*

Like mental rehearsal, Lucid Fantasy enables you to *imagine how your success will look, feel, and sound.* As a result of your Lucid Fantasies, your subconscious will be primed for success in real-life situations.

GO FOR THE GOLD

Lucid Fantasy is similar to mental rehearsal because it encourages you to use *all of your senses* to fully imagine and experience the best possible outcome. The difference between Lucid Fantasy and mental rehearsal is that your Lucid Fantasy *can be geared either to a realistic situation or to a symbolic situation.* Surprisingly, when you let your Lucid Fantasy take on a magical or illogical quality, it often provides you with even more benefits.

Lucid Fantasy lets you experience an enjoyable and empowering outcome to any experience. Not only does it condition your mind to expect success, it also opens doors to your subconscious potential.

A little-known fact about the subconscious is that it stores the memory of a *fantasy* in the same way it stores the memory of *a real event.* This means that

Lucid Fantasy provides an empowering *memory* which can transform a faulty blueprint and increase your confidence and self-esteem.

Lucid Fantasy follows a simple formula:

1. Imagine a positive, pleasurable outcome to your dream or waking dream. See, feel and hear yourself actively resolving any problem or conflict and bringing about an enjoyable or positive outcome.

2. Utilize the symbols in your dream or waking dream. Turn adversaries into allies, fear into confidence, conflict into cooperation, crisis into opportunity.

3. Have an adventure that is fantasy-like and pleasurable, in which you enjoy a new level of cooperation with your allies, as well as increased strength, confidence and creativity.

4. Receive a gift from each ally. Feel the power of the gift, and the energy of your ally, inside of you.

Take a moment now to think about a recent dream or waking dream. Notice where you may have missed an opportunity to be active, assertive, confident and creative, or playful—an opportunity that could have made your experience more satisfying in some way.

Lucid Fantasy Meditation

You can start your Lucid Fantasy at the beginning, middle or end of your original dream or waking dream. Close your eyes. See, hear and feel yourself there again. Only now, you can take advantage of the opportunities you missed before. Your purpose is to make the experience as satisfying as you can. There are no limits or rules. In your Lucid Fantasy, you have the power to do whatever you want. You can even have magical powers.

Trust whatever comes. Let your subconscious give you spontaneous images that show you an unexpected, maybe illogical way of creating a more satisfying outcome for this experience.

If you had a problem or conflict in the original experience, imagine resolving that situation now—be assertive, confident, creative, and compassionate in your solution. You may have physical powers, magical powers, or clarity of understanding in your Lucid Fantasy that you did not have before.

Look into the other person's or symbol's eyes; try to see that symbol with compassion and love. Feel your connection: sense how your qualities are complementary.

While in your Lucid Fantasy, let yourself spontaneously try out ways to be even more creative, confident, active and expressive. Communicate more clearly than you ever did before.

Let your new ally give you a gift. Hold the gift in your hand and notice what it is. Sense the special qualities or magical powers this gift gives you.

Now imagine that you can place the power or quality of your gift somewhere inside your body. Feel its special energy inside you, filling you. Notice where in your body you feel this energy. Breathe into that area now and enjoy the way it feels.

LUCIDITY WHILE AWAKE

I developed Lucid Fantasy many years ago when I began to use a simple formula attributed to the Senoi Tribe of Malaysia: confront your dream enemies, rather than run away in fear, and transform them into friends and allies. The Senoi, a dream-centered culture, reportedly applied these techniques *while still dreaming.* They are said to regularly practice a state of heightened dream consciousness known as lucid dreaming. *(Lucid dreaming will be explained more fully in Chapter 6.)*

I was not yet a lucid dreamer. The idea that I could recognize that I was dreaming, while still in a dream, was brand-new to me. Yet I wanted to improve my relationship with my subconscious. Out of necessity, I began to use lucid dreaming techniques *while awake*—visualizing the changes I desired in myself, in my symbols and in my dreams.

After years of struggle, I began to experience a new sense of personal power. As a result of my Lucid Fantasies, my symbols began to express fresh vitality and creativity. New themes emerged as my subconscious conflicts were resolved. Fear was replaced by confidence; loss by abundance; uncertainty by achievement. With surprise and joy, I was discovering the beauty and value in previously unknown parts of myself.

By visualizing a satisfying outcome to any dream or waking dream, I was *consciously* suggesting new choices and possibilities to my subconscious. The results amazed me. The positive changes I had visualized were being incorporated. Both dreaming and awake, the empowering suggestions were paying off.

Inner Dialogue provided a way to explore my symbols and enter into a cooperative relationship with them. Lucid Fantasy gave me a way to suggest new, satisfying experiences that would dramatically change my subconscious blueprints and my life. Through these two powerful tools, I was fully embracing my subconscious.

LUCID FANTASY TO HEAL THE INNER CHILD

All of your symbols—including your inner feminine and masculine, inner critic and nurturer, and inner child—can be regarded as windows to your subconscious, openings through which you can get to know yourself with more clarity and understanding.

Your inner child is an especially important symbol on which to do Lucid Fantasy. Although your Lucid Fantasy will not alter what happened to you when you were a child, it will create a different and more empowering blueprint for you to draw from. This positive experience is stored in your subconscious the same way a real memory is stored. And, when given a choice between an alternate memory that makes you more resourceful and a real memory that limits you, your subconscious will usually choose the one that helps you.

You will remember Dave, who used Inner Dialogue to discover his inner child and become friends with him. *(Chapter 2)* Not surprisingly, as a result of his Inner Dialogues, Dave immediately began to have some memorable dreams. Many of these dreams recalled unpleasant feelings he had when he was a child—feelings which he continued to experience subconsciously as an adult. Dave now had a wonderful opportunity to use Inner Dialogue and Lucid Fantasy to heal his inner relationship.

In several sessions, Dave explored symbols that revealed his childhood feelings of loneliness, isolation and distrust. These early feelings had become a blueprint for limitation—which held him back from the loving relationships he now craved. As Dave got to know Little Davey and healed his relationship with his inner child, his old fears gave way to a new experience of exuberance and joy in his life.

Dave described one of his dreams:

> I am beside a tall fence. I hear music, and through the slats in the fence I can see a lively party in progress on the other side. I want to join the party, but I can't find a way to get through the fence. I feel isolated now, with the party on the inside and me on the outside. I am frustrated that I can't join the fun.

Although this dream pointed out feelings of isolation and frustration in Dave, it also had some very positive aspects. The symbol of the party suggested a joyful energy in Dave that was ready to be tapped. In addition, although the fence held Dave back from joining the party, it was not a solid barrier; Dave could see through it. Dave's *strong desire* to get through the barrier and join the fun was a positive development; he was more conscious of the fun he was missing because of self-limiting beliefs and expectations. Now Dave was ready to dismantle the barrier that had made him feel separate for so many years.

> In his Inner Dialogue, Dave spoke as the fence, the party, and himself. He discovered that the fence was trying to *protect* him by keeping him out of the party—so that he would not get hurt or disappointed. Now, for the first time, Dave realized that the fence was also preventing him from being close to others.
>
> Dave negotiated an alliance with the fence in which he agreed that the fence could protect him some of the time. At other times, Dave realized that he needed to take some chances in order to make friends and have fun. As part of the negotiation, he told the fence he was willing to take this risk. Then he got the fence's agreement to let him through so he could join the party.

Dave's Inner Dialogue was a big step toward recognizing the reasons for the dullness and isolation he felt in his life. The fence symbolized a *subconscious barrier* whose purpose was to protect him from being hurt or disappointed by others. Until now, Dave had seen little reason to alter this protective barrier. But his dream seemed to invite him to change his mind, presenting him with a lively party on the other side of the fence— something good which he was sorry to miss.

Dave was ready to transform his dream. Through his Lucid Fantasy, he would fully experience what his original dream had only suggested as a new possibility—the excitement and joy awaiting him on the other side of the barrier.

I will never forget Dave's Lucid Fantasy. His eyes lit up with joy and excitement when he was able to transform his unhappy dream and *join the party*. His Lucid Fantasy was a major breakthrough in developing a satisfying, creative relationship with his inner child, and the benefits poured into his waking life.

In his Lucid Fantasy, Dave assumed an active role:

> I see the party on the other side of the fence, and I want to get in. Now I am more sure of myself. I walk along the fence. At first, it seems there is no door or opening. But I am determined to find a way in. I keep following the fence and in a few moments, I find a gate.
>
> Now I realize that I have an invitation in my hand—I've been invited to the party. I walk in through the gate, and everyone turns to greet me with smiling faces. They are congratulating me. *I am the guest of honor!*

At this point Dave paused, so I asked him, "Is there anyone here at this party who is special to you?" Right away, he said,

> "Little Davey is here. He wants to dance with me. Everyone is dancing in a big circle, with me and Little Davey in the center. We are all feeling very happy."

Dave became quiet while he enjoyed the experience he had created. After a few moments, he seemed ready to stop, so I suggested, "Does Little Davey want to give you a gift to celebrate this occasion?"

> "Little Davey is giving me the gift of a flower. It is a simple, fresh daisy. The daisy's special quality tells me that I am beautiful just the way I am."

This gift was so touching that Dave began to cry. He felt truly accepted.

After a few moments, I asked him if he wanted to give Little Davey a gift. He smiled and said, "Yes, a song. I want to sing to Little Davey and all my friends."

I knew that Dave was a musician, so I encouraged him to make up a little tune and sing the song directly to Little Davey and his friends. With great feeling, Dave sang his song of acceptance,

> "I'm a little flower
> And everybody loves me
> Just the way I am."

THE PURPLE ROBE AND THE WHALE

Lucid Fantasy enables you to change a pattern of limitation into a blueprint that promotes good feelings and success. No matter how unrealistic or magical your Lucid Fantasy may be, your subconscious will remember it in a way that will produce practical results in your everyday life.

When you do Inner Dialogue *before* doing your Lucid Fantasy, you will be surprised at the ease and creativity with which your Lucid Fantasy will unfold. In the following example, you will notice how well Kathy's Inner Dialogue prepares her for a Lucid Fantasy which provides a satisfying completion of the story suggested by her original dream.

> I am swimming naked in the ocean. Near me floats a purple robe. It is wadded up. I am reaching for it, trying to get it so I can

cover myself up. I am struggling, treading water, and the robe keeps eluding my grasp. This is very frustrating. I am also embarrassed about being naked.

I notice that a large, powerful whale is submerged near me in the murky water. I am afraid of it. I see a man in the distance to my left, who is also in the water.

Kathy's Inner Dialogue will give her new awareness of parts of her that have been "submerged." After creating an alliance with the whale and any other symbols, she will be ready to use her Lucid Fantasy to make her experience even more enjoyable and real. She speaks first as the whale.

WHALE: I am large and powerful and can do anything I want. I feel rejected by you, Kathy. You think I'm dangerous, but I'm not. I'm here because I want to have more contact with you, but your fear is keeping me away.

KATHY: I don't trust you, Whale. Maybe if I could see you clearly, you wouldn't be so frightening. But right now you are hidden under the murky water and you seem threatening. I don't like being in this water with you. I feel exposed and vulnerable.

As she went through the complete Inner Dialogue, Kathy discovered that the whale symbolized a valuable, instinctive and powerful part of her which she had rejected and submerged. As a result, she felt afraid and unable to express the self-confidence and power she needed in order to make her life more satisfying.

Before negotiating an alliance with the whale, Kathy decided to dialogue with a third symbol from her dream. The robe seemed unusual and significant to her. She was very curious about what its message would be.

ROBE: I am beautiful. My velvet is soft and sensual. My color, purple, suggests both spiritual clarity and royal status. Yet I am not being used properly. I am floating in the water, out of Kathy's reach.

Through her Inner Dialogue with the robe, Kathy identified an important contrast in her dream: sensuality-power. (The soft sensuality and spirituality of the robe is contrasted with the implied royal power also associated with it. In the same way, the robe's softness is contrasted with the hard, powerful form of the whale.)

Kathy's contrasts seemed to pit her feminine energies against her masculine energies, rather than using them together. She told me that she was afraid to use her masculine energy or power in her life. She wondered, "If I am powerful, will that make me less feminine or attractive?" Ironically, Kathy's dream seemed to indicate that rejecting her masculine qualities also distanced her from her feminine qualities (sensuality and spiritual clarity, symbolized by the robe). In her dream, both the whale and the robe are near her, but not in meaningful or cooperative contact with her.

In the negotiation stage of her Inner Dialogue, Kathy was able to resolve the conflict between herself and the whale, transforming the symbol she feared into a powerful ally.

> KATHY: It would be easier to trust you and let you get closer, Whale, if you would approach me slowly and give me time to learn to trust you.
>
> I will accept you and use your power more if you will not expect me to be powerful all the time.
>
> I need you in order to be able to move through this water and through my life.
>
> By joining forces with you and using your power and strength in my life, I will feel supported and unafraid. I will be able to choose the moments when I want to be powerful and protective, as well as the moments when I want to be sensual and open, making that choice out of strength and not out of weakness or fear.

Once Kathy discovered the hidden meanings of her symbols with Inner Dialogue, she was ready for Lucid Fantasy. "The Purple Robe and the Whale" provided her with several opportunities to change her subconscious blueprint—by transforming the limitations she experienced in her dream into empowerment and success. These changes, listed below, are useful goals for all Lucid Fantasies.

> • *Create more meaningful and satisfying interactions among the dreamer and the other main symbols:* in this case, between the dreamer and the whale, the dreamer and the robe, and the dreamer and the man.
>
> • *Have the dreamer reach the goal or complete the adventure:* in this case, have meaningful and friendly contact with the whale, the robe, and the man.
>
> • *Replace the dreamer's feelings of struggle, embarrassment, and fear with feelings of ability, confidence, and enjoyment.*

• *Do something that shows that the dreamer trusts and enjoys her power:* in this case, be allies with the whale and the man, and somehow utilize the robe.

• *Do something that demonstrates that the dreamer enjoys revealing who she really is:* in this case, get out of the water without using the robe to cover herself.

• *Resolve or clear up any problems or uncertainties that remain:* in this case, clear up the murky water.

Making a list of the actions or feelings which you want to transform, as shown above, is very helpful. Without needing to plan what will happen in your Lucid Fantasy, this list will remind you where you or a symbol were limited (by fear, isolation, being out of control, etc.). You will then find it easier to transform your experience to one that empowers you.

What would you want to change about the "Purple Robe and Whale" if it were your dream? Imagine yourself as the dreamer and close your eyes for a moment. Allow your subconscious to spontaneously show you some ways in which this dream could be transformed into an enjoyable and empowering adventure.

In the next section, you will see how Kathy used Lucid Fantasy to liberate herself from the fear and limitations of her original dream. Like Kathy, you, too, can create satisfying adventures, thereby conditioning your subconscious to expect success. (*See Exercise 1 in this chapter for the Guidelines for Lucid Fantasy.*)

FEAR INTO CONFIDENCE: RIDING THE WHALE

The whale comes to the surface where I am. I can see it now, and I am not afraid. I climb on the Whale's back. I am naked above the water, and the wind feels good on my skin. I'm not embarrassed that I can be seen this way.

I reach for my robe in the water and unfurl it above my head. I wave it gaily as the whale and I fly through the waves together.

Both the whale and I are singing joyfully. We splash toward the man, and when we reach him I pull him toward me onto the whale. Now the three of us are flying through the waves together.

Later, the whale leaves the man and me in a beautiful secluded cove. We make love and feel very close to each other. The whale dives down to the bottom of the ocean and brings me back a gift:

a large shell, a conch. This conch imparts the whale's power, helping me to move forward in my life. I can also communicate with the whale through the conch, and call him whenever I need him.

In her Lucid Fantasy, Kathy transformed her fear into confidence. She assumed an active role as the heroine of her story, so that she interacted with the whale, the robe, and the man (symbols for parts of herself) in meaningful and empowering ways. She took the opportunity to change her blueprint whenever her symbols expressed limitation, fear, or lack of completion. These changes allowed her to construct a blueprint for success, which her subconscious would remember and apply to other situations, whether awake or dreaming.

Significantly, Kathy made use of her five senses as much as possible (sight, touch, hearing, taste, and smell), so that she saw the whale clearly, felt the wind on her skin, grasped the robe in her hand, heard herself singing gaily, and perhaps even tasted and smelled the salty sea air—sensations which greatly enhanced the vividness and pleasure of her experience.

Have fun giving a title or name to your Lucid Fantasies, as well as to your dreams and waking dreams. Each of your dreams and Lucid Fantasies is a special creative expression, full of your own wisdom. Choose a title that captures the action of your dream or the special insight it gives you. What would you name Kathy's Lucid Fantasy? "Riding the Whale" or "A Whale of A Good Time" are two possibilities.

Lucid Fantasy can transform a nightmare into a pleasurable adventure. For instance, Louise, whose "Gold Elevator" shot out of the top of a building into space (*Chapter 3*), used Lucid Fantasy to redesign her dream:

> The elevator is shooting out of the building and going into outer space. But now, rather than being frightened, I am in charge of the flight! Now I can go further than I ever went before. I am excited about my new freedom. Instead of feeling angry with the elevator, I am grateful for its powers and happy to have it as a vehicle for my ride.
>
> I tell the elevator, "Now I see how valuable you are to me. I realize how beautiful and capable you are. Now your golden color is even more noticeable. Every part of you is glowing. I know I can trust you. I feel comfortable and I am so happy to take this ride in you."

Louise named her Lucid Fantasy "Enjoy the Ride." This title captured the wisdom of her dream, helping her value the part of her that wanted new risks and challenges.

HEALING A TRAUMA

Lucid Fantasy can serve as *mental first-aid* to help you heal a traumatic experience. Although your Lucid Fantasy cannot change a real event that has happened to you, it does help you to change the way you perceive the event and reduce your stress about it. Lucid Fantasy will empower you to resolve and heal an inner conflict that may be delaying your recovery or draining your emotional and physical energy. Because your Lucid Fantasy is an experience that is real to all your senses and to your subconscious, it will give you a boost of energy and well-being.

Although so far the examples of Lucid Fantasy have been on dreams, Lucid Fantasy is just as effective on waking dreams—real-life experiences that cause a strong emotional response.

Carly was a young woman who had been through a traumatic experience. Out late one night, she had been attacked and repeatedly bitten by a large dog. A year had passed, and although her physical wounds had healed, the wounds to Carly's psyche had not. She told me she was still afraid to go out at night for any reason. In addition, she felt terrified whenever she saw a large dog, even if it was on a leash.

Carly's trauma was real. We could not change the facts or circumstances that she had experienced, but we could help her to change her reaction to the event.

Before getting into the emotionally-charged memories surrounding her trauma, I explained to Carly that it was very important to set the stage by letting her experience Inner Dialogue and Lucid Fantasy with symbols that were pleasant, safe and nonthreatening. Carly would benefit greatly from spending one or two sessions exploring symbols from visualizations and dreams *before* working on the trauma. Carly agreed to use these first sessions to get comfortable with the process and to discover and enjoy some of her subconscious resources.

In her third session, Carly said she felt ready to tackle her waking dream nightmare of the dog attack. Our preparation this time was somewhat different, because when I work with an adult on a traumatic event, or with children on a scary dream, it is very important to ensure a feeling of safety. For this reason, I suggested to Carly that she imagine being surrounded by an impenetrable shield or bubble before beginning her Inner Dialogue; this would keep her safe so that nothing could harm her. Carly told me in detail what her "bubble" was like: clear, flexible, stronger than steel, and pleasantly warm and comfortable on the inside.

Now Carly began her Inner Dialogue. Although her trauma was terribly real, Carly agreed that something inside her needed to shift in order to let it go and complete her healing. For the purposes of her session, I asked her to treat the dog in the attack as a *symbol*. In her Inner Dialogue and Lucid Fantasy, she could talk to the dog, and she could also *change the outcome* of that meeting with the dog.

By changing her reaction and the outcome of the event in Lucid Fantasy, Carly would be changing a subconscious blueprint that had kept her terrified for a year; in its place, she would create a new blueprint that would help her move on:

> In her Inner Dialogue, Carly first imagined herself in her comfortable, protective bubble. From there, she felt safe to imagine seeing the dog again and talking to him.
>
> She was angry and told the dog, "I wasn't doing anything wrong. Why did you attack me?" She cried. "You hurt me very badly. Now I can't stand to be around dogs, and I always liked dogs until you hurt me."
>
> When it was time for Carly to shift her perspective and speak as the dog, I reminded her again that she was in her protective bubble and nothing could hurt her. The dog told Carly, "I was just doing my job, trying to guard my part of the street. I'm supposed to be tough. But now that you've talked to me, I am a little bit sorry that I hurt you."

Now, following the Lucid Fantasy guidelines, I encouraged Carly to imagine a much better outcome to her encounter with the dog. She could fight the dog and be victorious; she could make friends with the dog; the dog could become her ally. Whatever solution her subconscious spontaneously created, that was the best solution for now.

> In her Lucid Fantasy, Carly walks down the street again and the dog runs out to her. This time, though, she is not afraid, and the dog is friendly. She strokes the dog's head affectionately. They look into each other's eyes and feel a bond of trust. She appreciates his strength and his loyalty. Together, they go on an adventure into a wild, untamed land. She feels comfortable and able to deal effectively with the unexpected. She is tough and also loving, like her new ally, the dog.

In the week following her Inner Dialogue and Lucid Fantasy, Carly noticed a significant improvement. She told me that she did not think much about the dog attack any more; it seemed to have receded into the past. In the weeks that followed, she gradually became more comfortable going out at night. And when she saw a dog, she no longer was afraid.

The subconscious can be very adaptive and open to change. Although Carly's results may seem incredible, they were produced by the subconscious mind's ability to utilize fantasy events to create a new blueprint. Through her Inner Dialogue and Lucid Fantasy with the dog, Carly created a blueprint that provided her with the comfort and safety she had been lacking. Her Inner Dialogue and Lucid Fantasy completed her traumatic experience in a more satisfying way, enabling her to resume her normal life.

CREATING AN ALTERNATE MEMORY

Carly used Lucid Fantasy to create an *alternate memory* of a traumatic event, so that she could experience a safe, satisfying completion. It is also possible to create an alternate memory of a childhood experience. In the next example, a powerful healing fantasy will free Jane from the pain and limitation associated with the past.

Jane almost always got sad on her birthday. Now she was turning thirty-five and told me that rather than feeling more adult, she felt like a lonely child. At that moment, Jane's expression looked very childlike, so I asked, *What does that lonely child want to say?*

Jane looked surprised at my question. But there was a part of her that already knew the answer. I suggested that her sadness might be because she needed to pay attention to the lonely child inside of her—a part which still reacted with sadness to her birthday. I asked Jane,

> THERAPIST (T): Would you like to help that lonely child who gets sad on her birthday?
>
> JANE: Yes!
>
> T: Then close your eyes and imagine that child is in front of you now. Notice what she looks like and how old she is. What does she seem to be feeling?
>
> JANE: I see a child, about five years old. She's wearing a simple brown dress. She looks sad. More than sad. She looks defeated.
>
> T: Because you want to help that child, Jane, you can step into the picture now and make contact with the child. Let her know that you are her friend. Look into her eyes. Hold her hands in yours or hug her. In your own way, tell her that you are here to help.

JANE: I'm holding her in my lap. Her eyes are so innocent. I tell her, "I really care about you and I want to be your friend."

T: What would Little Janey like to say right now? What does she need in order to feel better?

JANE: Little Janey says, "I'm sad. It's my birthday, but no one cares. I don't get to be with my friends and do something that would be really fun."

T: What would be really fun to do on your birthday, Little Janey? What are some of the things you would like to do?

JANE (as Little Janey): First, I want all of my friends to come to my birthday party. We'll have lots of cake and ice cream. Then we'll play games—pin the tail on the donkey, the limbo, hide and seek.

Jane paused and looked thoughtful. She said, "I always wanted my mother to give me the kind of party the other kids had—so I could really be a kid for the entire day."

T: You can still give that experience to Little Janey. You can step in and be the loving mother Janey never had. You can give Janey the perfect birthday party. Help her to really enjoy being a kid, so she can be silly with her friends and do all kinds of wonderful things that kids like to do on birthdays. Are you willing to help Janey have a perfect birthday?

JANE: Yes!

T: Good. So close your eyes, Jane, and imagine being five years old. You have a chance now to experience something you have never experienced before, a perfect birthday. And now you have a loving mom—Adult Jane—to help you, too.

So, Little Janey, this is going to be a wonderful birthday for you. Your birthday party is starting now, and all of your friends are here. You can eat ice cream and cake, play games, and be silly. You can do anything you want to do today and go anywhere. What would you like to do first? Take your time and enjoy the whole day. Tell me all about your perfect birthday party as it happens.

JANE (as Little Janey): I'm waking up in my old bedroom. The sunlight is coming in through the windows, and I have a loving mom now who is smiling and kissing me. She has everything ready for my party. I'm really excited.

T: Good, Janey. And what happens next?

JANE: All of my friends are arriving now. There are lots of balloons everywhere, all different colors. We are laughing and playing games. Then my mom brings in a huge cake and ice cream.

T: Yes, and breathe into that. As Janey, take a breath now and feel how wonderful it is to be with all your friends...with your loving mom...eating cake and ice cream...having a perfect birthday.

Now, because this is your day, Janey, you can have anything and go anywhere. You and all your friends and your mom can continue the party outside the house, if you want to. There are lots of things you have always wanted to do, Janey, and you can do them all today. You and all your friends can be carefree and do whatever kids like to do. So imagine and feel what it's like now, going with your friends outside of the house and doing some things you enjoy.

JANE (*smiling with childlike happiness*): Me and my friends are going ice-skating. Then we go and play miniature golf.

T: Anything else?

JANE: Yes, now we're eating pizza and playing video games. We are having so much fun! We play and play, until it's time to go to sleep.

T: Good, Janey. And you can take all the time you need to have lots of fun with all of your friends, eating pizza and playing video games, and doing anything else you want to do. (*Pause*)

And now, it's the end of the day. Little Janey has experienced a wonderful day of having fun with her friends.

As Jane, imagine yourself now as Little Janey's mother. You are back at home. Janey is tired but happy—she has had a perfect birthday. You might want to hold Little Janey in your arms and say something to her.

JANE: "I love you, Little Janey. And I want to help you, so every day can be as happy as this one."

T: And would you like to give Little Janey a special birthday gift? Maybe something a loving mother would give her child.

JANE: Yes, it's a large pillow that is shaped like a heart. It's as large as Janey and very soft and cuddly. The heart-pillow will remind Janey of her perfect birthday, and the love, laughter and play she can enjoy every day.

COMPLETION

Jane felt a pleasant lightness in her heart after her Lucid Fantasy. Her "perfect birthday," experienced as both five-year-old Janey and as a loving mother to the child, gave her a sense of release from the past. Jane's Lucid Fantasy would be stored in her subconscious in much the same way a real memory is stored. Through her Lucid Fantasy, Jane had created an alternate memory of her childhood, one that empowered her and allowed her to *complete* a troublesome memory from the past.

Psychologists suggest that some memories persistently bother us, long after the event is over, because the experience is not complete. Like Carly's traumatic dog attack or Jane's birthday blues, the memory of an event continues to pain us because there remains something we still need to say or do. For many people, these incomplete experiences and memories work subconsciously to perpetuate self-limiting patterns and behavior; often, the incomplete experience is repeated as a waking dream with other people and in other situations.

Incomplete experiences do not recede with time, the way completed experiences do. These incomplete experiences hold powerful emotions and can sometimes cause significant physical tension. For Jane, it was as if her five-year-old self was frozen in time, unable to get beyond the hurdle of that unsatisfying birthday.

Lucid Fantasy gave both Jane and Carly a comfortable completion. Although their original experiences were quite real, so was the power of their subconscious to either perpetuate the unhappy feeling or help them create a comfortable ending and move on.

Lucid Fantasy works on a subconscious level to liberate you from self-limiting patterns. It really doesn't matter whether you use it on real events, memories, or dreams. You will feel more energized, capable and creative after your Lucid Fantasies.

RESOLVING RELATIONSHIPS, PAST AND PRESENT

Relationships we have with parents, lovers and friends often assume the form of a waking dream. For instance, after a relationship has ended or a parent has passed away, people may continue to have unresolved feelings of anger, sadness, or loss for many years. We may wish that we had just one more chance to try to communicate with that person, to clear the air, or simply to say "I love you."

Lucid Fantasy can serve as a wonderful opportunity to make peace with someone. You can complete communication with parents, as well as friends and lovers—even when the person you wish to talk to has passed away or is no longer in your life.

Whether the person you want to make peace with is living or not, you can meet that person in your Lucid Fantasy and talk to him or her. You can also "listen" to the other person responding to you. After saying what you need to say to each other, you can then imagine and experience a cooperative and enjoyable adventure with that person.

You can use Inner Dialogue and Lucid Fantasy to make peace with a parent—or rather, with the "parent" that you carry inside you. For instance, you may have noticed a critical internal voice undercutting your achievements and pleasures. This internal voice is usually linked to subconscious memories of a critical parent.

Inner Dialogue provides an opportunity to say what you need to say, and maybe never before had the chance to say to your parent. You may need to first express complaints and anger, then sadness, and then work out a negotiation with your parent that will increase cooperation. Whether or not this negotiation is possible with your real parent, it is always of value to create more cooperation with subconscious parts of yourself.

THE COSMIC PHONE CALL

A new year had just begun when Tom came in for a session. He was thinking a lot about his mother, who had passed away the year before. Because they lived on opposite coasts, Tom had always telephoned his mother on New Year's Eve, birthdays and holidays. For the first time, Tom told me, he had not been able to make his traditional New Year's Eve phone call to his mother. Because of this, he felt especially sad.

I suggested to Tom that he could place a "cosmic phone call" to his mother; with Lucid Fantasy, he could carry on the tradition, if he wanted to. Tom's face brightened at this idea. He asked, "What will I say?" I explained that he could say anything he wanted to say to his mother. He would also be able to "listen" and hear from her, too.

Tom began his cosmic phone call with, "Hello, Ma—happy New Year." He described to her the important changes that had taken place in his life since their last conversation. He said he was sad that she was no longer alive. He added that he was also sad that they had not been closer; there were problems they had not resolved while she was alive.

When he was ready, Tom imagined listening to his mother. She said that she, also, was sorry they had not been closer in life. At this point, Tom became very sad. As when she was alive, he felt as though his mother was blaming him for not being a better son. He said he had kept his distance from her because she didn't understand him and didn't like his choices of jobs, friends, or even his wife.

Tom needed to use Lucid Fantasy to resolve his relationship with his mother. I stepped in to suggest that although in life his mother had difficulty understanding him and appreciating his choices, it was possible that now his mother might have a larger perspective. She need no longer be held back by her human fears and limitations; she could love him more freely. Maybe from her new soul-perspective she could have a fuller understanding of their relationship, both past and present.

> I asked Tom to imagine his mother saying something to him from her new soul-perspective. Was there some way in which she wanted to give him more acceptance, or was there something special that she wished for him in his life?
>
> From a position of more acceptance, Tom's mother said that she now released him from any blame or obligation she had placed on him in the past. For the first time, she took part of the responsibility for their troubled relationship. She wished Tom a happy and productive life and a loving marriage.
>
> I suggested to Tom that just as his mother could give her love more freely now, so he could receive her love more freely, also. Tom said he could feel the love from her soul. He felt a deep acceptance from her. And he took comfort in knowing that he could make another cosmic phone call whenever he wanted to or needed to. His new relationship with his mother could continue to develop in ways that brought him more peace, as well as greater freedom to enjoy the present.

Like many others who have used Lucid Fantasy to make peace with their inner parents, ex-spouses or friends, Tom felt a noticeable sense of relief after his cosmic phone call—because his unresolved feelings were no longer draining him. Making peace with his mother enabled him to be more accepting of what had happened in the past, so he could move on. Lucid Fantasy helped him to free the emotional energy caught in that previously incomplete communication. As a result, his subconscious blueprint changed from one that limited him, making him feel sad and unresolved with his mother, to one that supported him in enjoying his life and accepting himself and others more fully.

Like Tom, you will find that when you make peace with someone in your Lucid Fantasy, you are also making peace with yourself.

(Exercise 3 in this chapter gives specific directions for doing Lucid Fantasy to complete communication and make peace with parents, lovers, and friends.)

VISITATION DREAMS

Sometimes we have special dreams that seem to reach beyond the boundary of time and space, reuniting us for a brief time with someone who is no longer alive. For thousands of years, people in other cultures have believed that the spirits of their loved ones appear in dreams and visions to guide and advise them.

Many of the special characteristics of visitation dreams also apply to lucid dreams—the vividness and intensity levels have been turned way up. The emotional level is high. The special person we meet looks younger and more robust than he or she did at the end of life. There is often a luminous light shining from that person's face or eyes. While dreaming, you may remember that this person has died and ask yourself, "Am I dreaming?"

People often ask me if these are real visitations. I don't know. No one can say for certain. But I do know that on a symbolic level, in these dreams we are making contact with a part of ourselves—in which we also carry the memory of that person. Our rational, left-brain consciousness tends to think of visitation dreams in either/or terms: either it is real or it is symbolic. But since dreaming is a right-brain, multi-leveled experience, anything is possible—it could be both.

Your dreams and waking dreams give you an invaluable opportunity to complete communication. If you have had unsatisfying dreams of a certain person *before* your Inner Dialogue and Lucid Fantasy, you will notice a more satisfying sense of cooperation and connection *after* you have completed communication.

(See Exercise 3 , Making Peace with Parents, Lovers and Friends.)

Exercises for
Your Subconscious

EXERCISE 1
Guidelines for Lucid Fantasy

Lucid Fantasy works equally well on dreams and waking dreams, transforming any experience into an enjoyable and life-affirming adventure.

GUIDELINES FOR LUCID FANTASY

1. You are the creator of your Lucid Fantasy. You have the power to change your symbols and your subconscious blueprint—so you look, feel, and sound more comfortable, empowered, and effective.

Just before you do your Lucid Fantasy, look again at your dream or waking dream and notice where you may have missed an opportunity to be confident, assertive, and creative. Note where the action or feeling was incomplete or unsatisfying. You may want to write a list, but you do not need to plan what the specific changes will be. Trust what comes to you spontaneously in your Lucid Fantasy, to make your experience satisfying and complete. (When working with a partner, remember that different people will create different solutions, in keeping with the issues each individual is working out presently.)

2. Now, close your eyes. Take an easy breath. You can start at the beginning, middle or end of your original dream or waking dream. See, hear and feel yourself there again. Only now, you can take advantage of the opportunities you missed before. Your purpose is to make the experience as satisfying as you can. There are no limits or rules. In your Lucid Fantasy, you have the power to do whatever you want. You can even have magical powers.

As the hero of your Lucid Fantasy, you can now make choices that resolve dissatisfaction or conflict and transform the experience into a confident, creative, satisfying, and joyful adventure.

If you were on the sidelines observing in the original experience, you can use your Fantasy to transform yourself into an active participant. You can also *consolidate* the good qualities of one or more other symbols into yourself, so that you are now the main symbol or hero of your adventure. Your purpose is to make your Lucid Fantasy as wonderful and satisfying as you can. You are now the star and you have the power to do whatever you want. You can even have magical powers. Remember to trust the images and feelings that come to you; let them develop into a story.

Describe your Lucid Fantasy as it happens, in the present tense. Saying your Lucid Fantasy aloud *(into a tape recorder or to a partner)*, helps you to experience it more vividly and to get more benefit.

3. If you had a problem or conflict in the original experience, imagine actively resolving that situation now—be assertive, confident, creative, and compassionate in your solution. You may have physical powers or clarity of understanding in your Lucid Fantasy that you did not have before. Look into the other person's (or symbol's) eyes and see that person more clearly and lovingly than you ever did before. Some specific suggestions:

FEAR. If you were frightened or overpowered by someone or something in your dream, turn and confront your dream enemy or adversary, rather than run away frightened. Resist the temptation to make the "bad symbol" disappear completely. Remember that the flip side of every nightmare symbol is a symbol that encourages your personal power or growth. Make the energy of this symbol work for you as an ally.

ANGER. If someone or something antagonized you or caused you to be angry, hurt or embarrassed, confront your antagonist. Demand that this symbol be your friend and ally. You have the power to transform the enemy (a subconscious part of you) into a useful, friendly symbol. In doing this, you are creating an *internal ally*—forming a beneficial relationship with a part of yourself with which you have lost conscious contact.

ATTACK. If you were attacked in any way, defend yourself now. Be aggressive and attack your enemy; or create an impenetrable bubble that keeps you safe. Call on allies to help you, if needed, but you must continue to defend yourself before they arrive. The defeat or death of an enemy-symbol is sometimes appropriate; imagine the defeated symbol releasing its energy to be used in a new and positive way, or perhaps transforming into a new symbol that will now be your ally.

See, hear and feel yourself as an active participant in your Lucid Fantasy. Take a position of strength and express yourself with confidence—you're the hero!

4. Now move toward the most pleasurable experience possible. Create a joyful, creative adventure, experiencing pleasant sensations of flying, dancing, singing, embracing, making love, etc. Use your senses as fully as possible: sight, sound, touch, smell, taste.

- Ask for a gift from your new friend, ally or other symbol. (Or, extract a gift or creative product from a beautiful place you've discovered.) What gift do you receive? What special qualities or magical powers does this gift give you? What do you want to do with the gift? Where do you want to wear it or place it?

- Now imagine that you can experience the power or quality of your gift *inside your body.* Feel its special energy inside you, filling you. Wait a moment, then ask: is there any special place in your body that you feel this energy? Breathe into this spot and enjoy the way it feels.

- Do you wish to give a gift? What special qualities or magical powers does the gift give to your ally? The gifts received and given strengthen the bond between you and your ally, helping you to integrate the valuable qualities of your ally, which is a subconscious part of you.

5. Bring back your gift or creative product and recreate it so you can share it with others in art, song, poetry, pictures, etc. Recreating your gift and sharing it also strengthens the bridge between conscious and subconscious, waking and dreaming, which are aspects of the same creative process. *(Chapter 7 will suggest many ways to share gifts from the artist within.)*

WHAT TO DO: Use these guidelines to help you create a Lucid Fantasy. Begin simply, with one or two guidelines at a time.

It doesn't matter where your Lucid Fantasy begins. You can start anywhere—at the beginning, middle or end of your original experience. What is important is that you include the symbols (the main characters, location and situation) from your original experience—because it was a powerful and spontaneous communication from your subconscious.

You can ask yourself, "What would make this experience more satisfying and joyful?" Notice what opportunities you may have missed to express yourself clearly and actively. Is there something you left unsaid or undone? Once you have done Inner Dialogue on your dream, you will have a better idea how to use your Lucid Fantasy to change a situation of limitation into one of success.

Feel free to do Lucid Fantasy on the same dream or waking dream. Experiment with different kinds of solutions for the same dream to become more familiar with how Lucid Fantasy works—and how enjoyable it feels. With practice, the creativity of Lucid Fantasy will become second-nature to you in a short time. You will gradually incorporate more and more of the suggestions outlined here, adding power and dimension to your experience. Take your time and enjoy!

Be patient with yourself. Through familiarity and practice, your Lucid Fantasies will gradually become more vivid, story-like, and richly symbolic. Regardless of length, the most important thing is to *do* Lucid Fantasy. Trust the healing images and ideas that your subconscious gives you.

After your Lucid Fantasy, be on the lookout for changes in your reactions, whether in real life or in dreams. *Even a small shift in your attitude and behavior is worth noting and celebrating,* because it means you have successfully reached the subconscious level, where all change begins. Keep track of changes, noting them in your journal. When you do Inner Dialogue and Lucid Fantasy regularly, you will accelerate your self-discovery and healing. Inner Dialogue and Lucid Fantasy will help your subconscious to work as your ally, so you can more easily achieve your goals.

(You may want to tape-record the Guidelines in your own voice, speaking slowly, with pauses between each step. Pause the tape whenever you need more time.)

EXERCISE 2
Healing Your Inner Child

Lucid Fantasy can help you to contact and heal your inner child. It can be used in many ways to help you enjoy an exciting, ongoing relationship with your inner child. You can also use Lucid Fantasy to create an alternate memory for a troubling or incomplete childhood experience.

If at first you don't get clear, spontaneous images or feelings from your subconscious that transform your dream or waking dream into an enjoyable experience, remember to *trust the first image or feeling that pops into your mind* when you begin your Lucid Fantasy. Many times, by ignoring this first clue, or deciding it is not good enough, you lose contact with the healing potential of your subconscious and return instead to a conscious, left-brain perspective.

Some people are concerned that trying to "program" your subconscious might be interfering with Nature. Don't worry. Your subconscious is open to useful suggestions and a productive partnership with your conscious self, but it cannot be controlled or overridden. For instance, if you try to "program" a dream about someone, or a solution to a problem, your subconscious will follow your suggestion if it is consistent with what it needs to do. If your "program" does not fit with what is needed at this moment, though, your subconscious will bypass your request and your symbols and dreams will reflect concerns that are more important or pressing. With this built-in safeguard, there is little worry about interfering with Nature. Lucid Fantasy and Lucid Dreaming are respectful processes that promote the insight and healing energy your subconscious naturally offers.

WHAT TO DO: Close your eyes and allow yourself to get a spontaneous image of yourself as a child. (Or, if you prefer, select a photograph of yourself as a child and use this image to dialogue with.) Now do the Inner Dialogue with this symbol. If possible, imagine holding the child in your arms. Look into the child's eyes. Talk gently to your inner child. For example:

> "Little Davey/Donna, I really care about you and want to be your friend. You may not be sure of that right now, and that's okay. I'll keep coming back to be with you and we'll get to know each other a little at a time. Your thoughts and feelings are important to me. I want to help you to feel safe and loved."

Listen to what your inner child wants to say to you. Listen to his/her needs in the caring way of a loving parent, without criticism. Speak gently to your inner child. Give reassurance when needed, and be available to play. You can also use Inner Dialogue to identify what valuable qualities your inner child has to offer you, as well as what it is that your inner child needs from you in order to thrive.

Next, do a Lucid Fantasy in which you put your new understanding of your inner child into action. Experience a magical, healing adventure with your inner child. Experiment with magical powers; you can both fly and do things you would not normally be able to do. Let your subconscious provide you with some spontaneous ideas and images. Take this opportunity to give to each other the special kind of loving attention that both of you need. Make sure to give your inner child a gift, and see if your inner child has one to give you as well.

EXERCISE 3
Making Peace with Parents, Lovers, and Friends

When you experience unresolved feelings of loss, anger or regret after a relationship has ended, Lucid Fantasy gives you a wonderful opportunity to complete communication and to make peace with that person where it counts most—inside yourself.

Whether the person you are thinking about is living or not, and whether you will be having further contact with the actual person or not, your Lucid Fantasy has great value—because the person-symbol you are making peace with is also a subconscious part of yourself. You will notice a significant improvement in your subconscious blueprints, dreams, waking behavior and outlook as a result of your Lucid Fantasy.

Your Lucid Fantasy is most effective when you imagine that you can *see, hear, and feel* the person with whom you need to make peace. However, if you prefer, you can make a cosmic phone call, a method that is especially useful when the telephone was a frequent means of contact with that person in reality.

WHAT TO DO:

• *Making Peace with a Parent.* There may be things you never had a chance to say to this parent, which you can say now. Express yourself fully and freely, and then give your parent a chance to respond to you. Follow the Inner Dialogue steps and continue to dialogue for as long as you need. This is also a good opportunity to express any anger or resentment you still have toward this parent. Inner Dialogue is a safe place to do this, so that you can complete communication and free yourself of old, unresolved feelings.

Next, do a Lucid Fantasy in which you imagine and experience your parent giving you the understanding, love, and attention that you especially need. If you need to, you can create a new or different parent—the parent you have always wished for. Remember, you are the hero of this story and you can create whatever you want!

Imagine your parent in detail, the way you have always wanted that parent to be. See a kind face, loving smile, and gentle eyes. Feel your parent's arms around you. Notice what your parent does to show caring and support. Hear the caring tone in his or her voice as your parent talks to you.

If it is difficult to imagine your parent as a loving presence, or if your parent seems unable to change, you can bring in an ally to help you. Your ally might be a wizard who waves a transforming wand, a respected expert who explains certain things to your parent and persuades him or her to behave differently.

• *Making Peace with Lovers and Friends.* Follow the same guidelines as above. There may be something you wish you could say now to this person, or something you wish this person would say to you. There may be a specific event that you want to redo with more satisfying results. These are all things you can experience in your Lucid Fantasy.

You will be amazed at how much satisfaction your Lucid Fantasy can give you. Through completing communication with a parent, lover, or friend, you are making peace in two ways. You gain a clearer and more loving acceptance of yourself as you are now, and also a clearer and more loving understanding of the other person.

• *The Cosmic Phone Call.* If it is difficult for you to imagine seeing the other person, or if you often talked to your parent, lover or friend on the phone, a cosmic phone call can be very effective. Imagine picking up the telephone and putting through a phone call to wherever that person is now—whether s/he is alive or not. Hear the telephone ring and the person's voice on the other end saying "Hello." Now, follow the suggestions described above.

Although it is not necessary to see the other person or make physical contact with him or her during a cosmic phone call, you may find that all of your senses spontaneously become involved, making the experience more vivid and memorable.

EXERCISE 4
Noticing Moods

You may experience a variety of moods in a given day or week, both while awake and dreaming. The moods which you experience regularly, as well as those which are rare for you, indicate much about your subconscious blueprints. For example, today have you been...

Happy	Loving
Excited	Frustrated
Angry	Afraid
Sad	Other

Put a check by each word that describes a mood you've had today. Next, review your recent dreams and waking dreams and put a check by each word above for each time you experienced that mood. When you are done, notice which moods occur most often.

Notice also which moods you seldom experience or do not seem to experience at all. If, for example, you seldom experience happy, loving feelings, awake or in dreams, this exercise is for you. Similarly, if your feelings are predominantly unhappy—sad, angry or frustrated—this is also an important exercise to do.

WHAT TO DO: In your journal, review some of your recent dreams and waking dreams. Notice what mood or feelings you had in each experience. Perhaps the feeling shifted from one mood to another in the same experience; perhaps the feeling remained constant throughout; or perhaps the feeling increased in intensity. You might want to underline the words or phrases that describe your feelings in each experience.

Now, notice if any particular mood or feeling is more frequent than the others. Notice also if any particular mood or feeling is conspicuously absent from your dreams and waking dreams.

Next, do Lucid Fantasy on a dream or waking dream where you would have liked to experience a pleasant mood but didn't. Imagine what it would be like to experience that pleasant mood now. How would you look, feel, and sound? How can you change your actions in this dream or waking dream to be more exhilarating and enjoyable? Experience a story-like adventure that improves on the original experience—and which doesn't have to make sense or be realistic.

Your time will be well-spent. You will notice a change in both your dreams and your life.

For example, for many years I had a recurring dream in which I was expected to perform on stage, in front of a large audience. Typically, I did not know the words to the song I was supposed to sing or the steps to the dance I was supposed to do. I had terrible performance anxiety and a feeling of inadequacy.

I did Inner Dialogue on a few of these dreams—and followed with a Lucid Fantasy in which I took an active role and performed with skill and enjoyment. Right away, my dreams changed dramatically. My mood changed from one of fear and inadequacy to one of confidence and ease. In many of the dreams that followed, I was singing and dancing with great pleasure and freedom. In some dreams, I discovered that even if I did not know the words or the dance steps, I could enjoy performing anyway! My performance dreams changed into playful, self-accepting adventures. In real life, I experienced a direct benefit from these Lucid Fantasies and dreams: I became much more comfortable and confident speaking and performing in front of groups.

EXERCISE 5
Power and Resource Symbols

Take some time to appreciate the power and resource symbols that appear in your dreams and Lucid Fantasies. These symbols may be powerful human or animal friends. They may energize or inspire you—like a healing stone, a special place, or something unusual or awesomely beautiful.

WHAT TO DO: Speak as your power or resource symbol, following the steps of the Inner Dialogue. Next, close your eyes and feel your power or resource symbol inside of you. Notice where you feel your symbol the most (chest, arms, throat, stomach, etc.).

Review the Lucid Fantasy guidelines and do a Lucid Fantasy in which you have an enjoyable adventure with your symbol. Be sure to utilize your power or resource symbol in a new way.

Remember, anything is possible in your Lucid Fantasy. Take your Fantasy to its most pleasurable limit! Be active both physically and vocally in your Lucid Fantasy—you are now the hero or heroine!

Afterwards, notice how you feel. Also, note where in your body you feel more relaxed or energized.

Lastly, to stretch your creative muscles, think up two more possible endings for your Lucid Fantasy. Give your Lucid Fantasy a title, and be sure to write it down in your journal.

5

Recreating Reality:
Planting a New Belief

"I'm Here to be Your Friend and Defend You"

Hypnotic states happen so naturally that, like most people, you may not even notice them:

- You are driving a car and become so engrossed in your thoughts that you are no longer conscious of changing lanes or traveling toward your destination; distance and time seem shortened. Before you know it, you have arrived.

- You watch a movie and become so involved in the story and the characters that you temporarily forget they are not real. You respond with excitement, fear, anger, happiness and tears, as if it were happening to you.

- You go home to visit your parents and you feel like a child again. Perhaps the childlike feelings are pleasant and nostalgic, or maybe your adult confidence seems to evaporate—you get "small."

- You reminisce about a relationship—either one you had in the past, or one you are having in the present—and you can "see" the person with great clarity and feel again the emotions and sensations you associate with him or her. Suddenly vivid details and feelings come rushing in—either pleasant or not—that allow you to reexperience being with the person, even though he or she is not physically present.

Unlike what you might see in a stage hypnosis show or the dramatic way trance is often depicted in a movie, hypnotic states in everyday life happen so naturally that most people don't think of them as trance or hypnosis. The characteristics of a hypnotic state are common, everyday experiences. Your attention becomes focused on one particular area, and the rest of the world seems to go away. Your perception of time and space may become shortened or lengthened. Your emotions and physical sensations become intensified, or dulled, to an unusual degree. Your ability to recall past events may suddenly improve; or you may forget recent events or recall them only vaguely.

This chapter will show you how to use hypnotic states of consciousness to your own advantage. You will learn how to distinguish between *positive and negative trance states* and turn a hypnotic state that occurs randomly into one you can control and use for your own benefit. You will increase your ability to choose subconscious blueprints that produce comfort and well-being. You will learn several powerful self-hypnosis techniques you can do on your own. In addition, this chapter will demonstrate how Inner Dialogue, Lucid Fantasy and self-hypnosis can be combined in a hypnotherapy format that creates deep and lasting change in your subconscious.

IT'S HOW YOU USE TRANCE THAT COUNTS

Like most people, you can probably remember a pleasant and empowering experience. If you remember it in enough detail, very pleasant feelings and thoughts often follow:

> Remember a time when you experienced a deep feeling of happiness...of oneness with someone or something...A time when your mental or physical powers seemed unstoppable...Your senses so acutely alive that everything looked brighter, sounded clearer, and felt more pleasurable.

Unfortunately, usually these *positive trances* occur at random. We're happy when they happen, but most of us do not know how to consciously reach this positive, empowered state of mind. Particularly when you are nervous about doing well in a challenging situation, or when you are in a bad mood, wouldn't it be nice to be able to switch tracks and choose a more resourceful, comfortable state of mind?

In this chapter, you will go deeper to learn how to turn an experience of limitation or negativity—what I call a *negative trance*—into an experience of comfort and positive expectation.

In the following pages, you will learn how you can direct your conscious awareness in a way that empowers you and increases your comfort and confidence.

NEGATIVE TRANCE

Most people do not realize that when you feel "stuck"—when you can't stop feeling upset, when you think you are powerless, or when you are ill or in pain—you are experiencing a negative trance. Have you ever noticed that when you think about a pain, you feel it more? The mind is powerful, and it will take you where your attention leads you.

Most of us have, at one time or another, been in a state of mind where everything seems to go wrong. As though we are looking through a dark filter at ourselves and the world, all that we experience seems tinged with negativity. Even a small annoyance can get blown up to catastrophic proportions. In earlier chapters, I referred to this experience as a waking dream—a situation in which subconscious feelings may surprise you by causing you to react more strongly than you expected.

Some people are masters at putting themselves, or others, into negative trances. As in a waking dream, we find ourselves very upset about something and caught in what seems like an endless feedback loop of negative emotion. We might be experiencing a challenging situation, and suddenly we feel "small"—everyone else seems powerful or important, and we are tiny and powerless. We've lost our confidence to deal with the situation.

On a subconscious level, your negative trance could be described as a *Blueprint for Limitation*:

> **Visual:** You look small, powerless, maybe like a child.
>
> **Auditory:** You might be saying to yourself: "They won't listen to me. What I have to say isn't important. I'm not safe."
>
> **Kinesthetic:** You feel weak, tense, nervous.

When a negative trance happens—when you feel powerless or experience pain—it seems like it will last forever. Perhaps that is because the subconscious is not limited by rational ideas of time and space. Yet you can *interrupt a negative trance* which is making you feel weak and use the same mental principle to *put yourself into a positive trance or resourceful state:*

> Think about a pleasant, relaxing experience, like feeling the warm sunshine on a beach in Hawaii. You can hear the surf and see the deep aquamarine blue ocean. The air smells fresh and salty. There's nothing you have to do. You can just soak in the comfort and enjoyment of this place.

As you read this description, you may notice something interesting. Your breathing may deepen and you may feel more relaxed. Just as your thoughts can make you feel bad, so they can also make you feel good.

On a subconscious level, your positive trance could be described as a *Blueprint for Success*:

> **Visual:** You look relaxed and calm.
> **Auditory:** You might be saying to yourself: "Life is good. I can be safe and happy at the same time."
> **Kinesthetic:** You feel the warm sunshine flowing over you. Inside, you feel warm, soft and relaxed.

Your blueprint serves as a direct command to your nervous system, producing either tension or relaxation. This is true because *your body responds instantaneously to your thoughts*—whether they are conscious or not—in this case, with lowered blood pressure and relaxation.

Mind and body are no longer regarded as separate. They are so interconnected that what affects one immediately affects the other: they are a unified field. Deepak Chopra, M.D., states in his book *Quantum Healing* that brain receptors (neuropeptide receptors) have been found outside the brain, circulating in the blood stream as neurons and immune system cells. Since 1985, mind-body research has been revolutionized by neuroscientist Dr. Candace Pert and others who have found that neuropeptides are the means of intercellular communication throughout the brain and body. According to Dr. Pert, these neuropeptides and their receptors allow us for the first time to identify "the biochemical correlates of emotions."

(Exercises 7, 8 and 9 in this chapter offer guidelines for breaking out of negative trance.)

HEALTHY TRANCE STATES

You can learn how to use hypnotic states to your own advantage. You can break out of a negative trance in which both mind and body are stressed—and imagine yourself into a resourceful, positive trance in which you feel relaxed and energized.

In this section, you will learn a simple self-hypnosis technique that will enable you to tap into the energy and vitality of your subconscious any time, anywhere. The mini-vacation technique only takes a few minutes. You can do it to recharge yourself during a busy day, and you can do it before bed to relax yourself for a sound night's sleep.

Mini-Vacation Meditation

Take in a full breath, and let it out slowly. Relax and focus on one spot in front of you. Take in another full breath, all the way into your chest and abdomen, and release it slowly. On your next breath, imagine breathing in through the top of your head, and releasing the breath through the bottoms of your feet. And you can close your eyes if you want to.

Now let your subconscious bring into your awareness *a natural place* where you can feel very comfortable today.

A place that is peaceful and safe. Maybe a place with trees or water. And it might be a place where you've felt very good in the past, or maybe it's a place in your imagination—a place where you can feel very good.

Trust the first place that comes to mind, a place that is comfortable and safe for you. And you can notice what this place is like—*feel* what it's like to be here. Notice the warmth of the sun, the softness of the ground under your feet. *Look* around and notice the colors, the shapes, the landscape. *Listen* to the natural sounds, maybe of birds, or a gentle breeze stirring in the trees. *Smell* a special freshness in the air.

And with your next breath, you can *breathe in* the comfort and peace of this special place. Imagine and feel that comfortable warmth spreading through you now—into every part of you— so every part feels comfortable, peaceful, relaxed and energized.

If you want to, you can *anchor* this good feeling of comfort and special energy in your body. You can touch your hand to your heart and anchor this comfort deep in your body, and you can do that now.

It's good to know that any time you need to or want to, you can touch your hand to your heart and feel very good. You can automatically recall the peace, comfort and special energy of your natural place.

This self-hypnosis technique is surprisingly simple and very effective. When you take even one or two minutes of mini-vacation during the day, your breathing will deepen and you will feel more comfortable and energized.

Research has shown that we all need to experience regular shifts away from our normal consciousness, into a relaxed state of hypnotic awareness, in order to maintain mental and physical health. Many creative, successful people regularly use daydreams, dreams and playful fantasies as indispensable tools to keep their creative juices flowing.

Rather than use something external and potentially harmful to relax—such as watching television, drinking alcohol, or many other potential addictions—self-hypnosis gives you a healthier alternative. While television or alcohol may temporarily alter your awareness to help you forget about worries, they leave you drained and without resources. On the other hand, healthy trance, produced by taking a mini-vacation or doing Inner Dialogue and Lucid Fantasy, gives you the relaxing hypnotic state you need. It also gives you increased access to subconscious resources that empower you to be more confident and effective.

(See Exercises 1-5 at the end of this chapter for more ideas for using self-hypnosis to promote health and relaxation.)

IS YOUR BLUEPRINT HEALTHY?

Your thoughts, both conscious and subconscious, have immediate impact on your physical and mental health. Someone once half-joked, "I'm this way because of all the bad things that happened in my life—most of which I imagined!" This jest captures a truth. Sometimes we make our lives more difficult by worrying about *anticipated* problems which do not really exist. The trouble occurs when we use our imagination to create anxiety and discomfort, rather than to enhance our best resources.

A blueprint can limit your mental and physical well-being:

> **Visual:** You look weak, pained, sick, unhappy.
>
> **Auditory:** You might be saying, "I'll never feel better. It's taking too long. No one really cares about me."
>
> **Kinesthetic:** You feel drained, tense, afraid, depressed.

You can change a self-limiting blueprint to one that empowers you and promotes healing:

> **Visual:** See yourself vibrant, happy and healthy.
>
> **Auditory:** You might say to yourself, "I am getting stronger and healthier every day. My mind and body know how to heal."
>
> **Kinesthetic:** Feel inside the warmth and comfort that let you know you are energized and strong.

Whether problems are real or not, the obstacles you perceive have their own kind of reality in your subconscious. Unpleasant waking dreams, upsetting thoughts, frightening daydreams, and threatening dream situations are indicators that your physical and emotional health are out of balance. Symbols such as explosions, storms, dangerous whirlwinds or whirlpools should alert you to pay attention to your physical health.

Like a detective, you can use your thoughts and symbols as clues that can lead you to discover beliefs and attitudes that are limiting you or hurting your health. You can do Inner Dialogue on any symbol that suggests limitation or illness. You can explore something that has happened while awake: an event, image, feeling, or thought.

When you are experiencing illness, pain or depression, you can increase your insight and comfort by exploring it as a waking dream. Do Inner Dialogue on your illness and pain—treating it as a symbol that has something to say to you. Find out how that symbol can be of value to you. For instance, your pain may be telling you that you are working too hard and need to provide more relaxation time for yourself. Negotiate some kind of agreement, so that you and the symbol can become allies. Then create a Lucid Fantasy in which you and the symbol work together cooperatively to create health and well-being. *(See Exercise 7 in this chapter.)*

Whether you are presently happy and healthy, or want to be, you now have the tools to transform your symbols into life-supporting resources that promote your health and happiness.

(To dialogue with your body or a part of your body, refer to Chapter 2, Exercise 3. After your Inner Dialogue, remember to do a Lucid Fantasy in which you enjoy a magical adventure while feeling powerful, energetic and healthy.)

ILLNESS AS A NEGATIVE TRANCE

Negative trances occur when we can't stop thinking about an annoyance, injustice, or problem—when it seems to take over. For instance, it might seem that you can't stop seeing your own or other people's shortcomings; or maybe you become preoccupied with a physical or emotional pain; or maybe there's a critical inner voice that keeps sabotaging your efforts to feel good or reach a goal. Even when you want to stop dwelling on a problem, breaking out of a negative trance can be very difficult.

An extreme form of negative trance may occur with serious or chronic illness. The physical dimension of illness, which often involves painful symptoms and chemical or cellular changes in the body, also influences the mental dimension. Healing is usually addressed on a physical level—and yet many times physical healing is not enough to produce full recovery.

The powerful mental dimension of illness is often overlooked. The more you worry and imagine the worst, the more your weakness or pain seems to intensify, perpetuating illness.

> **Visual:** You see yourself sick in bed, powerless against the illness. No improvement or change can be seen, now or in the future.
>
> **Auditory:** You might say: "I'm not getting better. Maybe this is going to last forever."
>
> **Kinesthetic:** You feel weak, constrained, uncomfortable or in pain. The more you notice the pain or weakness, the worse it seems to get.

Many people who have experienced physical or emotional pain for a long time have difficulty remembering what it felt like to be healthy. Their illness seems to have blocked out the possibility of anything else. *This is what makes it a negative trance.*

With self-hypnosis, you can *interrupt a negative trance* and increase comfort, relaxation and health. By remembering a specific experience where you were healthy and energized, you can turn that memory into a powerful resource.

Resource Memory Meditation

Recall a time when you felt very good—maybe a time in the recent past, or long ago. You can allow your subconscious to bring into your awareness the memory of a time when you felt very healthy and energetic. And trust what comes, a memory that is safe for you; and it might be something quite small and simple.

And notice where you are in this memory, and how old you are. Notice what you're doing that is enjoyable and feels good. And now, step into that memory and feel yourself and see yourself in that experience.

Notice what you look like—healthy and happy. And now look out through the eyes of the healthy person.

Sense what you feel like—strong and energized. Breathe and move with the ease of a person who is completely well.

Hear yourself speak, sing, and laugh with the voice of a person who is filled with comfort and energy. And listen to what you might be saying to yourself as you enjoy this healthy way of being.

At first, the experience of being healthy may be difficult to remember and feel again, even in fantasy. It is not unusual to see and sense only glimpses of this resource memory in the beginning—a moment of lightness, a quick vision of yourself and what you were doing that felt good. But with practice, these moments will lengthen until all of your senses are involved in experiencing again what it is like to feel good and be healthy. Through self-hypnosis meditations, you can break out of a negative trance and use any memory of being healthy and energized to encourage a positive attitude that will contribute to your comfort and recovery. *(See Exercises 1 and 2 in this chapter.)*

MIND-BODY HEALING

The revolutionary new information linking body and mind as a unified field has yet to have its full impact on modern medicine. A profound reworking of old premises and methods will have to occur in the decades to come. Although the scientific evidence of the unified mind-body field is very new, the concept is thousands of years old. *"There is no illness of the body apart from the mind"* could be the observation of a 21st century neuroscientist; yet it is a statement made by Socrates in 600 B.C.

In his book, *Getting Well Again,* Dr. Carl Simonton recognized the connection of subconscious symbols to physical health. Dr. Simonton found that when he asked his cancer patients to draw a picture of their disease process, their drawings revealed important information about their subconscious beliefs, as well as their attitudes toward their illness.

Dr. Simonton views disease as the "physical manifestation of the battle being waged between two parts of the self: the toxic or self-destructive parts and the nurturing or life-sustaining parts." Just as you have discovered various parts of yourself through your symbols, Dr. Simonton's patients use symbols to discover how their self-limiting patterns relate to their illness.

The drawings made by Simonton's patients represent their "battles" on both a physical and emotional level. For many of them, their first drawings depict the cancer cells as very powerful and the patient's immune system as very weak. At the beginning of treatment, many patients feel that they cannot fight their disease.

Dr. Simonton has contributed greatly to understanding the powerful link between subconscious beliefs and health. Dr. Simonton works with his patients to help them become aware of their self-limiting beliefs about their disease, their treatment, and their life situation. Then he teaches his patients how to *create new images* of powerful symbolic allies that can battle the cancer cells and emerge victorious—a process that resembles Lucid Fantasy.

For example, a patient will visualize the cancer cells as "slow-moving sloths"—stupid and vulnerable to attack. Next, the patient will see the white blood cells as an army of "white knights on horseback" which destroy the sloths with their lances and swords. The white blood cells, envisioned now as powerful and determined, defeat and destroy the vulnerable cancer cells.

This kind of visualization helps to restore the patients' feelings of hope and power. In addition, the visualizations appear to stimulate the *physical response* of the patients' immune systems, increasing their body's ability to combat the disease. Many of Dr. Simonton's patients believe that this image therapy has prolonged their life and improved the quality of their living.

If you experience a symbol which suggests illness or a health problem in some form, by all means go to your doctor for a checkup. But don't forget that you have the power to influence your own health. You can use self-hypnosis, as well as Inner Dialogue and Lucid Fantasy, to support your emotional and physical well-being.

TOXIC THOUGHTS: FANTASY OR REALITY?

If you ever wonder, "What do these techniques have to do with the real world?"—remember that *what you think* can produce negative consequences that are only too real. You are probably aware of the way in which "toxic" or self-critical thoughts can disrupt your life and cause unnecessary misery. This is because what you think can create either tension or relaxation, self-limitation or enhanced confidence. And when you worry about what "might have been" or "could be," you make yourself tense and unhappy fantasizing about something that is not real!

It's interesting to notice that the same mental process that in the past has made you feel terrible can be used to help you feel terrific. The mental tools you are learning through this book are the antidote for toxic thoughts: they enable you to take charge of your thoughts and blueprints—so you can experience more relaxation and resourcefulness, both mentally and physically. Your ability to understand your symbols and messages, and change limiting blueprints, *empowers you* to be more effective in the real world.

In the next several sections, you will learn specific ways to change a blueprint for limitation into one that harnesses your resources and promotes physical and mental health.

BUBBLES AND ADRENALS

Like many others suffering from Chronic Fatigue Syndrome, Susan was physically exhausted almost all the time. Unable to work full time or enjoy sports the way she used to, Susan's life had changed radically. After three years, she realized her condition was not improving, and she was very discouraged about her health.

Susan's exhaustion was a physical reality, but it was also a symbol for something important—a signal or encoded message from her subconscious. I suggested to Susan that we work on her exhaustion as a waking dream. To begin, I asked,

> THERAPIST (T): Susan, I'd like you to think about what your exhaustion *looks like.* Even though this is not a logical question, your subconscious can help provide you with an answer. Trust what comes.
>
> SUSAN: I see my adrenals. They look withered.

Having read about her illness, Susan was aware that her adrenal glands were not giving her the energy she needed in order to feel well. The withered appearance of her adrenals, as a symbol, reflected her lack of vital energy.

Now that Susan had a symbol to dialogue with, she was ready to do an Inner Dialogue.

> SUSAN: I am Susan's adrenals. I am withered. I am green and yellow. My job is to provide Susan with energy. But I am weak and withered. I don't seem to have anything to give.
>
> What I want to say to Susan is: I need nourishment.
>
> T: Now I would like to ask Susan's adrenals, what would that nourishment look like?
>
> SUSAN (As the adrenals): Bubbles. Crystalline blue bubbles.
>
> T: Good, Susan. Now imagine yourself as the bubbles. Speak as the bubbles and describe yourself.
>
> SUSAN: I am the bubbles. I am a beautiful shade of crystalline blue, like a gemstone. Only I am alive with energy and light. There is lots of me—plenty to nourish Susan's whole body.
>
> T: Bubbles, would you like to nourish Susan's adrenals?
>
> SUSAN (As the bubbles): Yes, but I can't find them. They seem far away. I don't know where I am, either.
>
> T: Adrenals, how can the bubbles find you?
>
> SUSAN (As the adrenals, in a low voice): Listen to my pain— and follow it.
>
> T: That's good, Susan. Take an easy breath and let that go. *(After a few moments)* Now imagine yourself as the bubbles again. You have lots of nourishing energy to give, but first you have to find the adrenals. So listen very closely now; listen for the sound

of pain from the adrenals that need you so badly. *(After a pause)*
And what is it you hear?

SUSAN (As the bubbles): I hear a low moaning, like an animal
that is trapped and scared. It's a very faint sound.

T: Adrenals, would you be willing to make that sound a little
louder, so that the bubbles can hear your pain more clearly and
find you?

SUSAN (As the adrenals): I don't like to make any sound at
all. I'm not supposed to call attention to myself. This is the best I
can do.

T: Bubbles, can you hear that sound well enough to follow
it—so you can find and help the adrenals?

SUSAN: Yes, I think so.

T: Let the bubbles follow that sound now. The bubbles are
flowing through your body now, Susan, and they have plenty of
nourishment to give. They can give nourishment to all the parts
they pass through, and still have enough for your adrenals. And
when the bubbles find your adrenals, let me know.

SUSAN: *(After a moment)* The bubbles are here now, at the
adrenals.

T: Good, Susan. And what's happening now?

SUSAN: There's no opening for them to go in. That's why the
adrenals are so withered.

Susan needed to find a way to comfortably open her adrenals so they could
let in the healing energy of the bubbles. But first she needed to find out why
her adrenals had no opening.

T: Susan, I'd like you to imagine yourself now as the adrenals.
Become aware of what it's like to be the adrenals now, and notice
what is happening around you. Can you sense the bubbles out
there?

SUSAN: *(Looking agitated)* Yes.

T: Adrenals, those bubbles are offering you nourishment and
energy, but they can't find a way to get in. Would you be willing
to give them a way to get in?

SUSAN (As the adrenals): No, *I'm afraid to be open.* I'm afraid
of being overwhelmed by the bubbles.

In Susan's subconscious, there were reasons for not having an opening, even a symbolic one. Like her adrenals-symbol, Susan had difficulty opening up to others, even when it meant getting the help she needed.

One of the strongest impulses of the subconscious is to protect. Although Susan's blueprint might be outdated and unnecessary in the present, her subconscious was still afraid to let in what it needed for emotional and physical health.

I thought that perhaps the adrenals could negotiate with the bubbles—to find a way to help the adrenals without overwhelming them. In this process, Susan could enlist the help of her subconscious to keep her safe, while also creating an opening through which she could receive the nourishing energy she needed.

> T: Susan, I'd like to speak to your adrenals again. Adrenals, would it be okay to let the bubbles float on your surface, so you could get some of their energy that way?
>
> SUSAN: Yes, I think so.
>
> T: Good. So imagine and see the crystalline blue bubbles now. Feel what it's like to let them float on your surface, as the adrenals. The bubbles are outside, giving you support and energy, and you don't have to let them in if you don't want to. Just feel what it's like to let those bubbles gently be there. *(Pause)* And what are you noticing as you do that?
>
> SUSAN: They feel light and feathery.
>
> T: Good. Breathe into that pleasant, light and feathery feeling. You can breathe into it and enjoy the comforting energy of those crystalline blue bubbles floating outside, on your surface, as the adrenals. *(After a minute or so)* And Susan, how do your adrenals feel now?
>
> SUSAN: *(Surprised)* A bit better. Maybe I will let a few bubbles in now to try it out. *(After a moment to try it)* It feels okay.

From watching Susan's expression and body language, I knew that letting the bubbles in was difficult for her. Though I did not know the exact reasons, her difficulty had all the signs of a hurt or trauma that might have been experienced early in life. Susan's adrenals, representing a subconscious part of her, found it very difficult to make any sound—even when in pain and needing help. If her adrenals felt they had to suffer in silence and were afraid to be open, even to nourishing and revitalizing energy, then on a deep subconscious level these were Susan's feelings also—feelings that perpetuated a pattern that began when she was a child.

If she was willing to explore that, we could; otherwise, it was very important to respect her limits and go no farther than she was ready to go. Her subconscious might have a faulty blueprint that was robbing her of energy and health, but like most subconscious blueprints, it was probably designed long ago to protect her in some way. Rather than try to interfere with or directly challenge a protective pattern, it was better to negotiate *a more adaptive form of protection.*

> T: What would you like to do now, Susan? Would you like to go back to having the bubbles outside of your adrenals? Or maybe have a few bubbles inside for now? Or would you like to let more bubbles in?
>
> SUSAN *(Her courage winning out over her fears):* I'm letting more bubbles in.
>
> T: How does that feel, letting more nourishing bubbles inside the adrenals now?
>
> SUSAN: It's upsetting. *If I feel good, I will be punished.*

Susan looked surprised at her own words and paused. A new awareness was coming through the "opening" she had created. She was beginning to remember why her subconscious had chosen this blueprint in order to protect her as a child.

> SUSAN: When I got sick three years ago, my career was just about to take off. I was enjoying myself more than I ever had. I was finally going to be happy—then bam! I got sick.
>
> When I was a child, my happiness was always ruined for me. If I felt good, I was punished. It wasn't safe to be happy, to enjoy life, or to succeed in my family.
>
> T: What would that little girl like to say, Susan? That little girl's experience in her family convinced her that it wasn't safe for her to be happy, or enjoy her life, or succeed. Imagine that you can speak now as that little girl who was punished if she felt good. What would that little girl like to say?
>
> SUSAN (As Little Susan, in a soft, childlike voice): I'm used to being mistreated. I'm so used to it that now I punish myself— I don't let happiness in anymore.

Susan's last statements identified the subconscious belief that blocked her recovery: that if she felt good, she would be punished. As a child, she had learned that it wasn't safe to let happiness in.

T: What do you need, Little Susan, so you can feel better?

SUSAN (As Little Susan): I need to be safe and loved, so I can change, a little at a time.

T: And how will you know, Little Susan, that you are safe and loved? What do you need so that you can feel safe and loved?

SUSAN (As Little Susan): I need to be held. I need someone to help me be happy, and to defend me. Then I'll know I'm loved.

T: Now I want to talk to Adult Susan. Adult Susan, are you willing to be there for Little Susan, to hold her and help her be happy?

SUSAN: Yes. *(Susan's eyes became moist with tears.)*

T: And would you, the adult, be willing to defend that child's right to be happy and keep her safe, so she can feel loved?

SUSAN: Yes, I will!

Susan's dialogue with her "Bubbles and Adrenals" had led her to another dialogue with her inner child. Like Susan, many people who experience chronic physical symptoms can benefit from discovering the subconscious belief or blueprint that may be perpetuating the problem.

SELF-HYPNOSIS TO HEAL THE INNER CHILD

Change doesn't happen all at once. Susan was now willing to give her inner child the love and protection she did not get before, as well as the reassurance that she would no longer be punished for being happy. But to fully change an old belief that had operated for years, Susan would need to give love, protection and reassurance to her inner child many more times.

In her next session, Susan learned how to do the Inner Child Meditation. This self-hypnosis technique provides the opportunity to gradually increase contact, trust and communication with your inner child.

Like Susan, you can use the Inner Child Meditation for a variety of goals, including changing subconscious beliefs, increasing confidence, improving health and building self-esteem. The Inner Child Meditation has three parts:

1. Visualize a comfortable, safe and natural place.

2. Experience a nurturing visit with your inner child *in the present*, with your adult self giving love and reassurance.

3. *Anchor* the good feeling of connection with your inner child—that is, touch your hand to your heart to create a body/mind association that will help you experience this good feeling again.

Inner Child Meditation

1. Take in a full breath, and let it out slowly. Relax and focus on one spot in front of you. Take in another full breath, all the way into your chest and abdomen, and release it slowly. On your next breath, imagine breathing in through the top of your head, and releasing the breath through the bottoms of your feet.

Now let your subconscious bring into your awareness *a natural place* where you can feel very comfortable today. A place that is peaceful and safe. Maybe a place with trees or water. It might be a place where you've felt very good in the past, or maybe it's a place in your imagination—a place where you can feel very good.

Trust the first place that comes to mind, a place that is comfortable and safe. Notice what this place is like for you—*feel* what it's like to be here. Maybe you can sense the warmth of the sun and the softness of the ground under your feet. *Look* around and see the landscape, notice the colors. *Listen* to the natural sounds, maybe of birds, or a gentle breeze stirring in the trees. *Smell* a special freshness in the air.

And with your next breath, you can *breathe in* the comfort and peace of this special place. Imagine and feel a comfortable warmth spreading through you now—into every part of you—so every part feels comfortable, peaceful, and relaxed (or energized).

If you want to, you can *anchor* this good feeling of comfort and special energy in your body. You can touch your hand to your heart and anchor this comfort deep in your body, and you can do that now.

It's good to know that any time you need to or want to, you can touch your hand to your heart and feel very good. You can automatically recall the peace, comfort and special energy of your natural place.

2. Now, as you continue to enjoy your natural place, you may notice that *a small person is here with you.*

You can pay close attention now to that small person, and as you do, you may be surprised to discover that this child is somehow familiar; in some strange way this small person is the child you once were, long ago.

Notice now what that child is doing...what that child's expression is like...how you feel as you watch that child.

And now, if you want to, you can make contact with that child in your own way. You can say hello to the child now, and look into her eyes.

Maybe you want to explain to the child that you've come here today to meet her, and to be her friend.

And, *(your name)*, if you are ready to help that child feel safe and loved, you can look lovingly into her eyes. And you might want to tell her: "Little *(your name)*, I want to be your friend. And I'll be here for you, to help you be happy. Because every child deserves to be happy. And I want to listen to you, and play with you, and protect you, so you can feel safe and loved."

Notice now how it feels to talk to the child, and to look into her eyes. Here in this comfortable place, you can take the time now to listen to that child and let her tell you how she is feeling today.

And because you are that child's grown-up self, you have the special ability to understand that child and to love her. And it's interesting to notice that the child may tell you how she is feeling with words, or maybe with her body language, or maybe by showing you something like a drawing or a picture. And you can listen to that child, now. *(Pause)*

It's good to know that as you take the time to listen to that child, understanding her thoughts and feelings, a bond of trust can begin to grow—maybe not all at once, but a little bit at a time.

And that child may be ready to trust you right now, or not. That child might need more time to learn to feel comfortable with you as a new friend, and you can give her all the time she needs. You might want to reassure her in your own way now—maybe by telling her, "Little *(your name)*, you can take all the time you need to feel comfortable, and I'll keep coming back to be with you and listen to you. Your thoughts and feelings are important to me. I love you."

And as you let that child know you care, you might notice that something changes—that child feels more relaxed and happy.

3. When you feel a comfortable sense of connection with your child, you can anchor that good feeling in your body. You can touch your hand to your heart and anchor that comfortable connection deep inside.

And it's good to know that you can return to this comfortable connection with your inner child, any time you need to or want to, whether you're in a trance or asleep, dreaming or fully awake.

You can benefit the most from this self-hypnosis meditation by recording it in your own voice, speaking slowly and gently. Listen to it once a day, allowing twenty minutes or so of uninterrupted private time. *See Exercise 4 for guidelines on creating a Lucid Fantasy with your inner child.*

(This or any meditation will induce a hypnotic state that will absorb your attention fully. For this reason, you should not combine self-hypnosis with driving a car or operating machinery, as this would be hazardous.)

CHANGING YOUR BLUEPRINT WITH HYPNOTHERAPY

As children, we cope as best we can with difficult situations—but our age and inexperience limits our awareness and ability to protect ourselves.

When we have to cope with a crisis at an early age, we come to conclusions about ourselves and the world that are based on a child's attempts to understand. Unfortunately, these early conclusions can follow us into adulthood, preventing us from feeling good about ourselves, and sabotaging our achievements. A Blueprint for Limitation created in childhood might, for example, cause someone to believe (consciously or subconsciously) that he or she is not lovable or capable; or cause difficulty trusting; or inhibit spontaneity and self-expression. A decision made in childhood may also result in a blueprint that perpetuates difficulty in forming lasting relationships (i.e., "They never stay; I'm always left alone and abandoned").

An early blueprint may also cause a belief that contributes to poor health. Susan's belief, "If I'm happy, I'll be punished," led to a conclusion that it was not safe for her to be happy. To Susan, being happy meant having the freedom to express herself, both physically and mentally. When she perceived that this freedom was not all right in her family, Susan's early solution for protecting herself was to shut down her self-expression and energy. Without energy, the freedom to be happy and spontaneous is no longer much of a threat.

In her next session, I assisted Susan in changing her subconscious blueprint with powerful hypnotherapy techniques. During her session, she would recall an early memory when the blueprint for limitation was put into place; she could then come to a new, adult understanding of that event and imagine responding in a more empowering way. By creating an alternate memory to replace the original experience, *even in fantasy,* Susan would be able to change a self-limiting blueprint into one that promoted both mental and physical health.

RESCUING YOUR INNER CHILD

Since our last session, Susan had been practicing her Inner Child Meditation every day. She told me that using self-hypnosis every day relaxed her and gave her more energy. And she also noticed that with time and attention, Little Susan was opening up and becoming more trusting and playful with adult Susan.

Another sign of Susan's progress was that now Susan could catch herself thinking, *"If I'm happy, I'll be punished."* Susan's increased conscious awareness of her self-limiting inner voice was an important step toward changing her faulty blueprint. Even though that old belief no longer made sense, Susan realized that it was continuing to inhibit her recovery.

To help Susan change the blueprint that was holding her back from enjoying her life, we would need to go further in our next session and use another hypnotherapy technique, Rescuing Your Inner Child.

> In a therapeutic session, you can imagine going back in time. As an adult, you can help the child you once were.
>
> Many times, this method involves asking the subconscious to bring into your awareness *a memory, maybe of the first time a particular problem or self-limiting belief occurred.* Then the hypnotherapist helps you to comfortably review what happened at that early age, understand what you were experiencing as a child, and discover what happened as a result.
>
> Then, as your adult self, you can step into the early situation where the problem or faulty blueprint began and, in imagination, help and protect your inner child. You can now *change the outcome* of the situation, following the Lucid Fantasy guidelines. And because your subconscious doesn't know the difference between a fantasy that is experienced with all your senses and a real event, this alternate memory is stored the same way as a real event—giving you an experience that empowers you.

Susan's hypnotherapy session will incorporate seven important steps:

1. Experience *a comfortable, safe and natural place* (and *anchor*).

2. Ask the subconscious to provide a *symbol or clue* to help achieve the goal. Develop the symbol into a *metaphor.*

3. Ask the subconscious to provide a *memory* of an early experience when the limiting pattern first began. View that memory *over there* on a "television screen," while remaining comfortable *over here*—producing

a therapeutic dissociation to ensure a safe, comfortable, and resourceful experience.

4. *Review* the Blueprint for Limitation and its effect up to the present.

5. *Rescue the Inner Child.* The adult self steps into the past to intervene on behalf of the child.

6. *Create a New Blueprint for the Inner Child*, one that supports an empowering new *belief* and behavior, i.e., "I can be safe and happy at the same time."

7. *Create an Alternate Memory of Growing Up.* Experience the inner child growing up safe and happy into an empowered adult.

When there is a need for the inner child to be safe, as well as valued, a hypnotherapist can help. A safe and healthy trance can be experienced, with a hypnotherapist's guidance, and an empowering blueprint set into place. For Susan, as well as others needing to change a self-limiting blueprint from childhood, reexperiencing early memories can be painful or difficult. For this reason, it is very important to explore or reexperience early memories (or any painful memory) only with the assistance of a qualified hypnotherapist or psychotherapist.

PLANTING A NEW BELIEF

We began our session with Susan taking several relaxing breaths. After some imagery to further relax her, she imagined and felt herself in her *Comfortable and Safe Place.* When Susan was able to experience and enjoy her natural place with all of her senses, I suggested that she anchor the feeling of comfort and safety in her body, by touching her hand to her heart.

Now that she was in a resourceful state, she was ready to work on her subconscious blueprint.

Providing a Symbol or Clue

Therapist (T): So now I'd like to ask your subconscious, Susan, to provide you with a *symbol or clue* that can help you to experience more happiness in your life; a symbol or clue that can help you to feel safe and protected while you enjoy the happy feeling of being fully yourself. And this symbol or clue might be an energy you *feel* in your body; it might be something you *see*, like a color or image; or it might be a *word* or phrase or sound that you *hear*.

Just let your subconscious bring into your awareness now a *symbol or clue* that can help you to experience being happy in a safe and comfortable way. And you can do that now. And trust what comes, whatever it is. It might surprise you.

And what are you aware of?

SUSAN: I see a beautiful rose. It's red and has a long stem. It also has a lot of big thorns.

T: And can you smell the fragrance of that beautiful red rose?

SUSAN: *(Taking in a deep breath)* Yes, it smells very sweet.

T: And can you touch the petals of that rose and feel their softness?

SUSAN: *(Smiling)* Yes, it feels soft and velvety.

T: And is there anything else you're aware of?

SUSAN: There's a honey bee near the rose. It's busy gathering nectar. *(Laughing)* It has a big stinger.

T: And can you hear that honey bee as it gathers nectar from the rose?

SUSAN: Yes, I hear its hum and the fluttering of its wings. Now it's flying away.

T: And so just breathe into that beautiful red rose, Susan. Smell the sweetness of that rose, and feel it's velvety softness. And with every breath, you can take that sweet softness inside of you, that pleasant feeling of being happy in a safe and comfortable way. Letting that good feeling spread through every part of you, so that every part feels safe, comfortable and happy.

And a red rose knows how to open and show its soft flower to the world, and share its sweet fragrance, even while it uses its big thorns to stay safe and protected.

And like that rose, Susan, you can let yourself be happy in a soft and sweet way, while knowing that you also have the ability to keep yourself safe and protected.

And as you breathe into that beautiful rose, you can feel yourself beautiful and strong, *soft and at the same time protected.* And if you want to, Susan, you can *anchor* that good feeling in your body. You can touch your hand to your heart to anchor that comfortable happy feeling, safe and protected, deep in your body. And that's good.

And it's good to know, Susan, that those big thorns keep the rose's softness and sweetness safe and protected. And in the same way that the honey bee knows how to gather nectar to make something sweet, it also knows how to use its stinger to defend itself.

Viewing the Memory

Now, Susan, as you continue to feel the comfort and safety of your natural place, I'd like you to imagine that in front of you is a blank television screen. In a few moments, I'm going to count from one to ten, and on the count of ten your subconscious is going to show you on that screen *a memory* that is safe for you. A memory, maybe early in your life, of the first time you felt that "if you're happy, you'll be punished." A memory of a time when you felt it was not okay for you to enjoy your life or be happy.

As I count from one to ten, your subconscious can select a memory that is safe for you—and you can see that memory separate from you, on the TV screen. You can stay comfortable and safe, *over here;* while you view that memory separate from you, on the screen *over there.* Beginning to count now, Susan—

1 - going back in time,
2 - to a time, maybe early in your life, when you felt it was not safe to be happy;
3 - a memory over there, separate from you,
4 - while you remain safe and comfortable over here;
5 - going back in time,
6 - to a memory that is safe for you;
7 - feeling safe and comfortable *over here,*
8 - as your subconscious brings that memory onto the screen *over there;*
9 - breathing comfortably and
10 - letting that memory come into your awareness now.

And just notice what you're aware of now, Susan—a memory, maybe of a time early in your life. And you can see that memory *over there* on the TV screen, separate from you. You can feel safe and comfortable *over here,* while you view that memory on the screen, *over there.* And your subconscious can show you in some way how old you were when this limiting belief began, the belief that "if you're happy, you'll be punished."

And are you aware of what age you were?

SUSAN: Yes. I was about 5 years old.

T: And are you aware of a memory, something that's happening on that screen over there?

SUSAN: Yes. I'm having fun. It's summer and I'm running through the grass and the sprinklers. I'm wearing my bathing suit bottom, but not the top.

T: And so watch that memory, over there, Susan. That little girl of five or so who is having fun running through the grass and the sprinklers. And what do you think that little girl feels about herself as she has fun in that natural, innocent way?

SUSAN: She feels very good about herself. She's full of energy and joy. She feels safe in the world. (*Now Susan's expression changes to a look of annoyance.*)

T: And what happens next, Susan? What are you seeing over there on that TV screen?

SUSAN: My dad comes out of the house. He looks at me having fun. He's frowning. Then he tells me to put my top on.

T: And pay close attention now, Susan, to what happens next on that TV screen. Dad comes out of the house, looks at the little girl having fun, and then tells her to put her top on. What does five year old Susan say to her Dad, if anything?

SUSAN: I say, "Why? I'm having fun."

T: And as you watch that screen, over there, Susan, notice what your dad says back, if anything.

SUSAN: He says, "You're too old to be running around without a bathing suit."

T: And what does that little girl feel when her dad tells her she's too old to run around without a bathing suit?

SUSAN: She feels ashamed. She feels criticized.

T: Take a nice easy breath now, Susan, and slowly release it. And as you look at that little girl on the screen *over there*, you can continue to feel comfortable *over here*.

And what happens next, Susan?

SUSAN: I put on my top. But I don't feel happy any more.

T: When your dad told you to put on your top, did you feel that you were being punished in some way?

SUSAN: Yes. I was having fun and being natural and free. I was not self-conscious. And then I had to cover up.

T: Did you think you were being blamed in some way?

SUSAN: Yes. It was like there must be something wrong with me if I have to cover myself up. There must be something wrong with being so natural and happy, if my dad didn't like it.

T: And did your dad seem concerned about your welfare when he told you to put your top on?

SUSAN: I'm not sure. It was like there was something dangerous that he wouldn't talk about. I don't know what. Maybe he was afraid someone would abuse me.

T: So before this happened, Susan, back when you were five years old, you knew how to have fun and be fully yourself. You had lots of energy, didn't you, and lots of joy, before this happened.

SUSAN: Yes.

T: And, in fact, most five-year-olds enjoy running through the sprinklers and grass, just like you did back then. And children that age are very natural and free of self-consciousness; they don't worry about what they are wearing or not wearing. Children that age have a natural ability to just have fun, don't they?

SUSAN: Yes.

T: But what happens, Susan, when that innocent, fun-loving child is stopped in some way? When your father told that five year old girl to put her top on, what do you think that young girl thought or decided from that experience?

SUSAN: She thought, "When I'm having fun, feeling natural and free, I'm doing something wrong, something dangerous. I should cover up and keep myself under wraps."

T: Yes, that little girl felt there was something wrong and maybe risky about having fun and being fully herself.

So now, as you remain comfortable over here, Susan, you can put that TV screen on "Pause" over there. And the screen goes black and white and the images freeze.

And I'd like you to think about what happened to the little girl who loved to run through the grass and the sprinklers. Did she have fun and feel natural like that again?

SUSAN: I don't think so. I thought, "Something must be wrong with me, something must be dirty and dangerous about my body. Something must be wrong with having fun and feeling natural."

T: So is it possible that when five-year-old Susan thought there must be something wrong with her, she was beginning to believe *"if I'm happy, I'll be punished"*?

SUSAN: Yes.

T: And do you think that a belief was getting set in place at that time, long ago, *that feeling natural, energetic, and being fully who you are* was something that brought disapproval and criticism?

SUSAN: *(Crying)* Yes, that's what I thought.

T: What did that little girl do after that to avoid being punished? What did Little Susan do to cope with that belief that "if she's happy, she'll be punished"?

SUSAN: I kept myself covered up. I stopped feeling natural. I worried about what would happen if I showed too much of myself to others.

T: And what happened to the abundance of energy and joy which that little girl once enjoyed?

SUSAN: They went away. The energy and joy withered and dried up. *(Susan looked surprised, and added:)* Yeah, I guess they withered and dried up like my adrenals.

T: And did it seem like you were protecting yourself at a big cost to yourself? What was it like for you to keep yourself covered up and lose your joy and energy?

SUSAN: Yes, it cost me. I felt like I was in a little box. There wasn't any joy, just fear of punishment and shame. After that, I always felt self-conscious in a bathing suit, like something was wrong with me, I wasn't good enough. It was hard to feel relaxed enough to be myself and have fun.

T: And were you giving up an important part of you in order to be safe?

SUSAN: Yes.

T: And was being in that little box, afraid to be yourself, like a punishment? A punishment that continued for a long time after that?

SUSAN: Yes.

Reviewing the Blueprint for Limitation

T: In a moment, Susan, I'd like you to turn that TV back on and review what happened to that little girl's life after that. I'd like you to notice how this early belief, this early blueprint or belief that "If I'm happy, I'll be punished" affected and shaped her life after that. Because from this point on she's decided to cover up and try to keep herself safe, even if it costs her to do that.

So I'd like you to watch that screen, over there, and see again that five year old girl, having just experienced this really unfortunate situation where her dad made her feel ashamed of having fun and being a natural child. From this moment in time, that belief, "If I'm happy, I'll be punished," that blueprint, is going to affect her decisions, her relationships, her life, and even her health for the next several years, right up to the present.

And Susan, you can watch that screen, *over there*—while you remain safe and comfortable *over here*. And with your adult, reasoning mind, you can watch that little girl grow up, the same way you would watch a movie. And you can begin that movie, now.

You can comfortably watch that movie, over there, and notice what happens to that little girl while she grows up; notice how that belief, that blueprint, affects her life.

And follow her all the way up to the present. And a short time can seem like a long time, a comfortable time for you to review key moments in your life when that belief really cost the little girl you were, and the woman you became.

And when you're done, you can let me know. *(After a minute, she nodded)* And that's good.

And just turn off the screen now, Susan. Take a nice easy breath, coming back to your safe, natural place. And you can call to mind again that beautiful rose with its protective thorns. You can breathe in again the sweet fragrance of that rose, and remember that like that rose, you can learn how to feel soft and sweet and happy, even while you use your thorns to keep yourself safe. You can breathe in, and allow the soft, comfortable feeling of that rose to spread through your body.

And what did you notice, Susan, from that review?

SUSAN: There were lots more times when I felt something was wrong with me, like I wasn't good enough. And I thought I was ugly. I was very self-conscious in bathing suits. If I started having fun, I got very nervous—like something bad was going to happen.

T: Okay, good. So here is what we've learned so far, Susan: Five-year-old Susan experienced an unfortunate situation and formed an early belief that it was unsafe for her to have fun and be herself. And she basically said, "If I'm happy and energetic and having fun, I'm going to get punished. So I'm going to keep myself safe by keeping my natural self covered up. And that may mean giving up a part of myself; it may cost me emotionally to do it. It may even cost me my physical energy and health to do it." Is that right?

SUSAN: Yes.

T: And at different points in your life since then, this belief or blueprint has led you to feel nervous about having fun and made you want to cover up and protect yourself, hasn't it?

SUSAN: Yes.

T: Now, five-year-old Susan did the best she could with a difficult situation; but we know that a child of five doesn't have a lot of choices about how to best protect herself in a situation like that. Unlike that child, Adult Susan of the present knows and understands a whole lot more than that little girl did—*so you have a lot more choices.*

And it's really up to you, Susan—Do you want to continue with that old belief, that blueprint for limitation, which costs you your natural, joyful self? Do you want to continue with a belief that costs you your happiness?

That little girl had good reason to think that if she was happy, she'd be punished. But as an adult, you have a lot more power and choice than you did back then, and now you can defend your right to be happy and feel good about yourself.

So here is your choice, Susan. Do you want to continue to expect to be punished whenever you're happy? Or do you want to replace that old belief with a new blueprint that helps you to feel good?

SUSAN: I want a new blueprint!

Rescuing the Inner Child

T: Now, Susan, that little girl needed help when her dad told her to put on her top. She needed someone to hold her and love her and defend her. Someone to let her know she is beautiful and deserves to be a natural, happy child. Would you be willing to go back in time to help that little girl?

SUSAN: Yes.

T: Good. So I'd like you to imagine now that as an adult you can go back in time...all the way back to when Little Susan was five years old. And when you can see Little Susan there, running through the sprinklers and the grass, let me know.

SUSAN: I see her.

T: Okay. So now I'd like you to step into the scene. I'd like you, as an adult, to stand behind Little Susan. And now Little Susan's dad comes out of the house and frowns, and tells her to put on her top, because *he thinks* she's too old to run around without a bathing suit.

And now, *as the adult standing behind the child*, you can look at that man with your adult, reasoning mind. You might be older and more mature than he is at this moment in time. You have many years of experience now, so as an adult you can probably sense what is going on with him that would lead him to say something like that to this little girl.

And what are you aware of?

SUSAN: I *am* older than he is—he looks so young. He's very tense. He's not really thinking about Little Susan. There's a lot of things bothering him, and he's taking it out on her.

T: What do you want to say to him, to defend Little Susan's right to be happy?

SUSAN: I'll tell him: "No! I'm not going to let you hurt this child. You're teaching her to cover up and feel ashamed and afraid, when you should be showing her that you love her the way she is. You should be protecting her naturalness and joy, not shutting it down!"

T: Good. And what would you like to say to Little Susan, to give her the love and acceptance she needs?

SUSAN: "Little Susan, you deserve to feel good about being free and natural and happy. You don't have to cover up if you don't want to. I'm here to be your friend and defend you."

T: That's good. Breathe into that, Susan. Look into that child's eyes now. And, if you want to, you can say to little Susan what she needed to hear from a loving parent, both then and now: You can tell Little Susan that you will protect her and keep her safe so she can have fun and be a natural child.

SUSAN: "You are beautiful, Little Susan, and I like it when you have fun and play. I won't let anyone shame you or make you hide yourself again. You deserve to believe the world is a safe place, and I'll look out for you and make sure you're safe. I'll let you enjoy yourself and the world your way, because you're unique. I like it when you're energetic and active and show all of who you are."

T: And it's good to know that you can give Little Susan what she needs so she can feel happy and safe. And you can hold that child in your arms now, and feel that child's softness and innocence. Breathe into that softness. Maybe you can feel some of that softness inside of you now, as you hold that beautiful child.

Creating A New Blueprint for the Inner Child

T: As you continue to look into that child's eyes and hold her, you can imagine and feel that you are together now in your safe and natural place.

And here in this comfortable, natural place, you and that little girl can *plant a new belief*, a new blueprint, that can help her to feel safe and happy. Like planting a seed that will grow up strong and beautiful, you and that little girl can plant a new blueprint now that can help her to feel good about having fun, being energetic and active, and expressing who she is.

Because that little girl deserves to *see* herself as beautiful and natural, like a red rose. And she deserves to defend herself, when she needs to, to keep her softness and sweetness safe.

And that little girl deserves to *say to herself*, "I *can* have fun and be happy. The more I express myself, the more energy and well-being I feel."

And that little girl deserves to *feel inside* that joyful, good feeling. Active, warm, and trusting.

Every time you imagine that joyful, energetic little girl, a *new blueprint* is being planted in your subconscious, Susan. A little at a time, in a way that is comfortable for you.

And you can imagine and see that little girl now, Susan: She looks strong, healthy and beautiful. She knows that she deserves to be happy, and that she can defend herself. She feels energized and active, loving and loved.

And with this *new belief*, Little Susan will grow up in a very different way than she did with that old, limiting belief. Knowing that you, her future self, are there to help her and love her, that little girl can grow up strong and happy.

Creating An Alternate Memory of Growing Up

T: You might be curious to know what that little girl's life will be like with that new blueprint in place, a *belief* that she deserves to be happy.

So you can take the time now to imagine Little Susan growing up *strong and happy*. Like watching a movie, you can scan forward in time and experience her growing up, a little at a time—safe, energetic, healthy, and happy. And you can begin that movie, now.

And notice how comfortably that little girl is growing up—through her grade school years, where she can have fun with many friends. Through her junior high and high school years, where she may discover that she likes to sing and dance; where she enjoys learning and is busy with creative projects; and where she is respected and valued by many friends and teachers. Into her adult years...feeling beautiful and strong, doing productive work, keeping her sense of humor, still having fun, knowing the world is a safe place for her to be herself...all the way up to the present.

And being happy is a very attractive quality, Susan. And people you like to be with, people who treat you well and respect you, are people who like you to be happy.

And you can feel happy and protected at the same time. The rose's thorns allow the soft petals and sweet fragrance to be there; the bee collects the sweetness and can use its stinger if necessary.

It's good to know that you can take all the time you need, take all the space you need, to keep yourself safe, strong, and happy. So your inside feels warm, safe, respected, and happy.

And if you can feel that happy, safe feeling inside now, Susan, you can *anchor* it in your body. You can touch your hand to your heart and anchor that good feeling deep inside.

And that's good.

Any time you want to, any time you need to, you can return to your safe and natural place and be with your inner child. You can hold Little Susan in your arms and reassure her. You can let her know that you will keep her safe so that she feels loved and happy.

And any time you hear an inner voice say, "If I'm happy, I'll be punished," you're going to stop and think. You're going to recognize that voice is part of an old belief that has made you miserable. And you're going to challenge that destructive voice and say, "I deserve to be happy. I deserve to be healthy and energetic. I have the power now to be safe and happy at the same time."

You can talk to your inner child, have fun with her, and give her the time and space she needs to feel safe and happy. And every time you give your inner child that safe and happy experience, you are creating a *new blueprint*, one that makes you happy. Every time you talk to your inner child and encourage her to have fun and be natural, you are making that new blueprint stronger. And the more you help Little Susan to feel safe and happy, the easier it will be for *you* to feel energized and healthy, to enjoy being fully yourself, safe and happy at the same time.

In a few moments, I'm going to count back from 5 to 1. And on the count of 1 you will awaken, feeling refreshed and energized. And you will awaken with a sense of having done something very well; bringing that comfortable, safe and happy feeling back with you.

And it's good to know that you can return to this loving connection with your joyful, natural inner child any time you want to or need to, whether you're in a trance or asleep, dreaming or fully awake. And you can remember everything you need to remember from this experience. And this healing and strengthening process can continue, naturally and easily, over the next 24 hours and during the next several weeks.

So, beginning to count now,

5 - taking in a deep, satisfying breath;

4 - beginning to bring your awareness back into your body, feeling your body resting here;

3 - and you can move your fingers and toes as you wake up, feeling refreshed and energized;

2 - returning to normal, bringing that comfortable, happy feeling back with you as you get ready to open your eyes, and,

1 - opening your eyes, wide awake.

SAFE AND HAPPY

Susan's old belief had blocked her energy and freedom to be happy for a long time. That belief was part of a Blueprint for Limitation:

> **Visual:** Somber, alone. Passive, inactive. Covered up.
> **Auditory:** "If you're happy, you'll be punished."
>   "You must suffer in silence."
> **Kinesthetic:** Low energy, health problems. Sad, nervous,
>   afraid.
> **Taste:** Bad taste, bitter.
> **Smell:** Stale, closed in *(like in a box)*.

Susan's new blueprint was designed to free her energy and promote the new belief that she could be *safe and happy at the same time.*

> **Visual:** Smiling, active, expressive *(both child and adult).*
> Red rose with big thorns; busy bee with stinger.
> **Auditory:** "You deserve to be safe and happy.
> "You deserve to be natural and have fun."
> "It's okay to express your needs and feelings."
> "It's safe to let your pain be heard and let in the nurturing you need."
> Sound of buzzing bee.
> **Kinesthetic:** Zestful, happy, natural. Enjoys expression and movement.
> **Taste:** Sweet *(honey).*
> **Smell:** Fresh, fragrant *(rose).*

Susan felt more relaxed and comfortable than she had in a long time. Her stress decreased, her energy increased. Her attitude toward her illness changed: she was determined to interrupt the inner voice that told her that if she was happy, she would be punished.

Over the next few months, hypnotherapy sessions allowed her to create many more alternate memories that supported a dramatic improvement in her health and happiness. She now had the tools to replace negative thoughts with positive, empowering experiences.

Susan reinforced her new blueprint every day. She regularly visited her inner child and listened to her. They would go on adventures together, using Lucid Fantasy. Susan also enjoyed creating playful adventures with other allies—including superheroes, animals and famous people—who served as special resources for both her inner child and her adult self.

Through embracing her inner child and creating loving alternate memories, Susan learned how to have more fun—and to express herself with greater confidence and ease. As she paid more attention to her good feelings, Susan broke out of her illness-induced trance and reclaimed her life. She was able to return to her career with new creativity and excitement.

(Refer to all the exercises in this chapter for more self-hypnosis techniques. See Exercises 5 and 6 for guidelines on using Lucid Fantasy and Super Allies as part of your inner child meditations.)

Exercises for Your Subconscious

To practice self-hypnosis, one to three minutes is all you need. You can take a "mini-vacation" to a comfortable, energizing place any time, anywhere. At the same time, you will be giving your subconscious a Blueprint for Success that can help you experience more comfort and confidence.

Your subconscious will understand and remember the positive experiences you suggest to it. This is because your self-hypnosis meditation is personalized to your needs and uses your unique symbols and resources.

To achieve a specific goal, do self-hypnosis three times a day (*for one to three minutes at a time*). Create a personalized meditation by selecting one or more subconscious resources from the following:

- A comfortable, safe place (mini-vacation)
- An ally, guide, or symbol
- A meeting with your inner child
- A resource memory (remembering something you did very well or a time you felt very good)
- A mental rehearsal (preparing for a real situation).

Separately or combined, the subconscious resources listed above will give you added energy and motivation to help you feel capable and comfortable in achieving your goal. The more you practice personalized self-hypnosis meditation, the more automatic these positive trances and resourceful experiences will become. Make them an integral part of your day:

- Imagine your subconscious resources accompanying you in the most ordinary of circumstances, while you are wide awake.
- Take a "mini-vacation" for a minute or two during the day— Practice seeing, feeling and hearing your comfortable place while brushing your teeth, during your lunch break, or when you walk the dog.

- In the morning and before bed, take a minute or two to say hello to an inner ally or your inner child. Give yourself an extra boost of energy by reexperiencing a resource memory and practicing mental rehearsal before going into a challenging situation.

(See Exercises 1-6 for self-hypnosis meditations.)

EXERCISE 1
How To Take A Mini-Vacation

You can do this self-hypnosis technique to relax and energize yourself in the morning, when you take a short break during a busy day, and in the evening. It only takes two minutes!

WHAT TO DO: Before you begin, select a specific goal or intention for this exercise. You may want your mini-vacation to relax you; or maybe you want to experience *a safe and comfortable place* that will energize you or give you healing. The more specific you are, the more your subconscious can provide you with resources and allies that fit a particular need, so you'll maximize your results.

Mini-Vacation Meditation

Take 3 slow breaths; exhale slowly.

And now let your subconscious bring into your awareness a place where you can feel very good. It might be a place that relaxes you, and maybe it's a place that energizes you. You can imagine and feel yourself now in a safe and comfortable place.

And trust the first place that comes into your awareness—a place that feels comfortable and safe, a natural place where you can feel very comfortable today.

And you can *look* around you and notice what this place is like. *See* it: notice colors, plants, special details. *Feel* what it's like to be here. Notice how the ground feels under your feet, the temperature of the air, and the sensations you are experiencing in your body. *Listen* and notice the pleasant natural sounds in this place. Maybe you can hear the water flowing in a nearby stream, or the birds, or the wind in the trees. Perhaps you can *smell* a special freshness in the air—as you breathe in the comfortable energy of this place. Let that comfort spread throughout your body, warm and soft.

And when you feel the comfort and relaxation of your special place, you might want to touch your hand to your heart—to *anchor* that good feeling deep inside.

EXERCISE 2
Resource Memory

A resource memory is a real event in which you felt energized, healthy, and empowered. You can recall that past event in conscious awareness or, more effectively, during self-hypnosis—by allowing your subconscious to select the right one for you to help with a specific goal. You can then use that memory as a *resource* to help you turn a Blueprint for Limitation into a Blueprint for Success.

Recalling only one resource memory helps you to recall many others. Once you tap into a positive trance, other enjoyable and empowering experiences will be easier to recall by association. During self-hypnosis and afterwards, your resource memory will work on a subconscious level to increase well-being both physically and mentally.

WHAT TO DO: Before you begin, select a specific goal or situation on which to concentrate during this self-hypnosis exercise. During the meditation, your subconscious will provide you with a resource memory that can help you to feel more confident and motivated in achieving your goal.

Allow thirty to sixty minutes in a quiet, uninterrupted place to do this exercise. First do the Mini-Vacation Meditation *(Exercise 1)* to relax and experience a comfortable hypnotic state. Once you are relaxed, do the Resource Memory Meditation. (You can read both scripts onto a tape and play it back, or have a friend read them to you in a slow, soothing voice.)

Resource Memory Meditation

There have been many times in the past when you have been full of energy, when you felt very good about yourself, strong and comfortable. And in a moment your subconscious can bring into your awareness a resource memory that is safe and comfortable; a memory that can help you to achieve your goal. And it's nice to know you can *remember a time* when you felt very good about yourself, strong and comfortable. Maybe a time when you achieved a goal and felt very satisfied; or a time when you were motivated to learn or do something important; or a time when you felt very healthy and energetic. And maybe you remember a time from the recent past, or maybe a time from long ago. And trust what comes, a memory that is safe for you; and it might be something quite small and simple.

And notice where you are in this memory, and how old you are. Notice what you're doing that feels good. And now, step into that memory and feel yourself and see yourself in that experience.

Notice what you look like—strong and comfortable.

And now look out through the eyes of that person.

Sense how you feel—strong and energized. Breathe and move with the ease of a person who is healthy and energized. You are alert, smiling and confident.

Hear yourself speak, sing, and laugh with the voice of a person who is filled with comfort and energy. And listen to what you might be saying to yourself as you enjoy this healthy way of being.

And when you feel the strong, comfortable energy of this experience inside of you, you can touch your hand to your heart and *anchor* that strength and comfort deep in your body.

And it's good to know that you can bring that comfortable experience with you into any situation. You can remember that feeling of comfort and ease, and experience it again, any time you need to, any time you want to.

EXERCISE 3
Mental Rehearsal

When you are preparing to go into a challenging situation, take an exam or perform in front of a group, mental rehearsal can help you clear away self-doubt and maximize your physical and mental ability.

Mental rehearsal lets you experience *in advance* the comfort, energy and resourcefulness you need in order to do your personal best. Athletes and performers of all kinds have found that mental rehearsal helps them to excel both mentally and physically.

You can mentally rehearse each part of your task—the beginning, the middle and the end: *see* yourself doing it confidently, *feel* comfort and energy to spare, and *hear* an encouraging inner voice tell you that you are doing well.

Recent brain research revealed a surprising benefit: even when mental rehearsal is done *in imagination only*, it fires the same neurons that would fire in the real situation. In other words, your mind and body experience your *fantasy* as though it were absolutely real!

Mental rehearsal primes you both emotionally and physically to do your best: You can *see, feel and hear your audience:* see their interest; feel their excitement in what you are doing; hear their applause. At the end of your task, you can *feel a sense of satisfaction at a job well done.* You know that you have been noticed and appreciated, and that you did very well.

If feeling empowered and expecting to succeed are not common experiences for you, that is all the more reason to *get those neurons firing now.* Experience it on the inner level first, so that when the real opportunity arises, your mind and body will be ready. You can build a blueprint for success that helps you to say, "Oh, I know how to respond to this. I know how to embrace this situation and make the most of it."

WHAT TO DO: Allow thirty to sixty minutes in a quiet, uninterrupted place to do this exercise. First do the Mini-Vacation Meditation. Once you are relaxed, do the Mental Rehearsal Meditation. (You may read both scripts onto a tape and play it back, or have a friend read them to you in a slow, soothing voice.)

Mental Rehearsal Meditation

It's easy for you now to imagine yourself in a situation *in your present life* in which you *would like to feel* capable and confident, comfortable and energized. Whether it is at work, or in a relationship, or when you do some of the things you want to do or need to do to *feel good*. Imagine yourself now in a situation in which you want to feel comfortable and capable today.

And you can feel yourself and see yourself in that situation now, knowing that *you are strong and comfortable*. You look calm and comfortable, your eyes are sparkling, and you're smiling. Your voice is clear and calm, and you can stand and move in this situation with perfect comfort and ease. And the comfort and good feeling of this experience can spread into every part of you, so that every part feels calm, energized, and confident.

And you can comfortably imagine yourself doing everything you need to do to *maintain that comfort and ease* throughout the first part of this situation; maintaining that comfort and ease throughout the middle part of this situation; continuing to feel strong and comfortable as you complete what you need to do. And long after you have finished that comfort will continue, and you will enjoy a sense of having done something very well.

And if you want to, you can touch your hand to your heart, anchoring that comfort and strength deep in your body.

When you are familiar with Exercises 1-3, you can do a meditation that includes the Mini-Vacation, Resource Memory, and Mental Rehearsal. Together, these three scripts make a very powerful combination.

EXERCISE 4
Inner Child Dialogue and Meditation

In relationships, many times the child and adult parts of you and the other person seesaw: You may try to solve a problem or disagreement by talking to the other person's adult self, when it is their inner child that needs a special kind of reassurance.

Many attractions, as well as disagreements and hurt feelings, arise when one person's adult is talking to the other's child, and vice versa. To get past the emotional confusion and explore your part in a difficult communication, do an Inner Child Dialogue on one of the three choices listed below.

An Inner Child Dialogue might reveal, for instance, that the child part of you needs to say "I'm afraid," "I'm hurt," "I'm angry," or something else. Giving your inner child an opportunity to express her feelings, either positive or negative, will also help you to understand and balance your inner child's feelings in the relationship.

WHAT TO DO: Do all of the Inner Dialogue steps for:

- Your adult self and your inner child (in a specific relationship or present situation)
- Your inner child and the other person's adult self
- Your adult self and the other person's child self

Inner Child Meditation

First, go to your safe and comfortable place *(Exercise 1)*. There might be a special place you like to go in order to be with your inner child. Notice where your subconscious takes you. Once you're in your safe place, do one of the following:

- Walk with your inner child in your safe place. Take the time to notice how s/he is feeling today. Ask your inner child if there is something she needs in order to feel happier or more comfortable. Listen to what your inner child has to say and then gently acknowledge her thoughts and feelings. You can also ask your inner child what she would like to do to have fun with you today.
- Imagine that you are with your inner child in a natural place *in the present*; talk about a present-day concern, both from the child's point of view and your adult point of view. For example, your

inner child may not like all the demands being put on you at work. While it's true you have to keep your job, you can still comfort your inner child and tell her you will spend some time with her every day, or once a week, to play together and have fun. If your inner child is hurting, the best thing you can do is just be there and listen. Then you can tell that child, "I really care about you, and I'm sorry you feel bad. Your thoughts and feelings are important to me. I'm going to do whatever I can to help you feel better."

• Again, visit with your inner child *in the present*. This time, you may want to listen to what your inner child has to say about *a relationship you are presently having*. (Remember, it is possible that if your inner child is unhappy, it might have to do with the present as well as with the past.)

• This time, imagine that you are visiting your inner child *in the past*. Imagine stepping into a situation in the past *as a friendly ally*, perhaps at a time when the child you once were needed someone to talk to, someone who could help and reassure him or her, or someone to have fun with.

(See Chapter 3 for an example of relationships as waking dreams, and in particular the child-adult dynamics in two married people, Sarah and her husband.)

EXERCISE 5
Lucid Fantasy with Your Inner Child

As your friendship with your inner child grows, you will be ready to make your visits more playful. Taking your inner child on a Lucid Fantasy adventure is a very effective way to change a limiting blueprint into one that empowers you to have fun, be playful and active, and to express your unique abilities and talents.

WHAT TO DO: In your Lucid Fantasy, you can begin anywhere. Perhaps you would like to start in your safe and natural place *(Exercise 1)*. Once you are relaxed and comfortable, follow the Lucid Fantasy Meditation below. Allow thirty to sixty minutes of uninterrupted time.

Lucid Fantasy Meditation

Look into the eyes of your inner child, and sense the love and innocence there. And on your next breath, your subconscious can bring into your awareness a *pleasant adventure* that you and your child can go on together.

Just trust what comes—an adventure that is safe and comfortable for you and that child to share. And it's easy for you now to imagine a very pleasant and safe adventure—going someplace very special, doing something together that feels good. And notice what this adventure is like for you—*look* around and notice where you are; *feel* what it's like to be here with your inner child.

Imagine for a moment that you can step into your inner child. Look out through the eyes of your inner child. Look at the loving adult who is here with you now. Feel what it's like to be safe and loved. Experience a child's curiosity and zestfulness inside of you.

You can be playful now and notice what happens next. It doesn't have to make sense. This adventure can be magical. You can have special powers—fly, go to magical places, be playful and lighthearted in new and unexpected ways. You can enjoy your adventure, in your own way, now. *(Pause for one minute.)*

And that's good. As you comfortably enjoy your adventure, you can notice how you and your inner child *look* as you enjoy yourselves together;

Notice how you *feel* inside, sharing this childlike playfulness and trust;

And notice now if there is anything you want to *say to your inner child*, and if there is something that your inner child wants to *say to you*.

And if you want to, you can *give your inner child a gift*, a gift that lets her know that she is safe, loved, and free to be a happy, playful child. And you can give that gift, now.

And notice if your inner child wants to give you a gift. Maybe it's a gift that can help you to remember this good feeling of playfulness, trust, and love. And you can receive that gift, now.

And when you feel that special energy of your child's gift deep inside, you can touch your hand to your heart, and *anchor* that energy deep in your body. You can touch your hand to your heart and anchor that child's playful, loving energy deep inside. And breathe into that good feeling.

And it's good to know that you can return to this comfortable connection with that zestful, loving child within, any time you want to or need to, whether you're in a trance or asleep, dreaming or fully awake. Any time you want to or need to, you can touch your hand to your heart, and remember this loving, playful adventure.

EXERCISE 6
Super Allies for Your Inner Child

Another exciting possibility for a Lucid Fantasy adventure features a Super Ally who helps, encourages, and has fun with your inner child.

WHAT TO DO: Let your imagination and your subconscious guide you in creating a Super Ally adventure with your inner child. Follow the Lucid Fantasy guidelines, allowing your subconscious to suggest a Super Ally from cartoons, movies, or even history. Or, there may be a Super Ally you particularly liked *when you were a child*—such as Superman, Batman or Wonder Woman.

Super Allies can have magical powers to fly, make things materialize and dematerialize, and do other things that can be playful and fun for a child. Remember to *anchor* the experience when you are done.

EXERCISE 7
Hypnotic First-Aid for Illness or Pain

When you are ill, afraid or in pain, many times you pay so much attention to the problem that it seems to take over. Here is a more constructive way to pay attention to your problem—while also creating part of the solution.

WHAT TO DO:

1. For the purposes of this exercise, treat your pain, illness or symptom as a *symbol*. After visiting your safe and comfortable place, let your subconscious bring into your awareness what the problem *looks like* (a shape or image), *feels like* (its weight and texture) and *sounds like* (its sound or what it wants to say).

2. Do an Inner Dialogue with the symbol (representing your illness, pain or symptom). As an additional step, ask it: What do you need in order to feel better?

3. Create a Lucid Fantasy and give the symbol what it needs to feel better. Now experience the desired change on every level—see it, feel it, hear it. Make other adjustments, if needed.

4. Again, see, feel and hear what you are like, now that you are completely healthy and comfortable.

5. Anchor the good feelings this change gives you.

EXERCISE 8
Identifying and Disarming Your Inner Saboteur

A faulty belief or self-limiting blueprint has *a voice of its own* that you can learn to recognize and resist. This voice is very good at rationalizing a destructive belief or excusing a behavior that may feel good in the short-term but is damaging to you in the long term.

This "saboteur voice" may say,

> "You'll never be happy."
> "To hell with it."
> "It doesn't matter."
> "One more chocolate (or cigarette) won't hurt me."

Your inner saboteur may criticize, demean, or sabotage your efforts and achievements:

> "Whatever you do, it's just not good enough."
> "If it's not perfect, it's not worth doing."
> "You'll never make it."
> "You've got to do it perfectly or else you've failed."
> "You don't deserve to succeed."

Sometimes you may not even be aware of what the "voice" is saying—it happens subconsciously. But by thinking about what happens between the moment when you feel good and the moment when you begin to feel discouraged or defeated, you can often figure out what your inner saboteur has been saying to you.

WHAT TO DO:

1. List some of the negative beliefs or arguments your inner saboteur, or inner critic, has used on you in the past and is likely to try again in the future. Write whatever phrases or thoughts come to mind in your journal. (If you experience your inner saboteur on a more physical level—with anxiety, knots in the stomach, or panic attacks, note this as well.)

2. Now plan a strategy to deal with your inner saboteur. For example, "Whenever I hear myself say "to hell with it," I will remember and know it is my inner saboteur talking—and I will do (my strategy) instead."

Strategies to Counteract Your Inner Saboteur

- "Any time I am aware of being in a negative trance (self-limiting blueprint), I will interrupt it by imagining my comfortable place and visiting with my inner child."

- "The next time I feel nervous or insecure about an upcoming situation, I will mentally rehearse a positive outcome: I will see, hear and feel myself being comfortable and strong in that situation, doing my personal best and getting the results I want." *(See Exercise 2 for details on mental rehearsal.)*

- "I will counteract my self-critical thoughts by keeping a gratitude journal—where I list the good things that happen every day, no matter how small."

- "Any time I am aware of a self-critical thought, I will read my gratitude journal or add one more good thing."

- "The next time I want to eat/smoke/watch TV, I will call a friend or exercise instead."

- "The next time I am tense and want to eat/smoke, I will go outside and breathe deeply instead."

- "This week, I will do one of the exercises in *Embracing Your Subconscious* for half an hour." *(Do only one exercise per sitting. If you have not finished a section after a half hour, return to it next week. By keeping your sub-goals small, you will increase your motivation .)*

- "This week, I will create an Inner Dialogue with my inner saboteur or inner critic." *(Follow guidelines given in Chapter 2, Exercise 3, Inner Dialogue on Contrasting Parts.)*

EXERCISE 9
Breaking Out of A Negative Trance

The more *strategies* you have available to break out of a negative trance and create a resourceful state of mind, the more *choices* you will have to help you deal effectively with stressful situations.

WHAT TO DO:

1. To break out of a negative trance—when you are depressed, obsessed, in pain or upset:

- Change your physical position. Get up, walk around, stretch, breathe, exercise. Splash water on your face, drink a glass of clear, fresh water.

- Change your physical environment. If you're with others, excuse yourself and take a short break. Walk away for a minute; go to the restroom or make a phone call.

- Distract yourself. Change your focus to something else. If you're with someone, change the subject, tell a joke, sing a song. If you're alone, exercise, dance, read the paper, look out the window, play some music, sing to yourself. Seek an enjoyable activity that can absorb your interest, where you feel the reward of time well-spent: such as sports, gardening, art-making, carpentry, or even cleaning house.

- Ask others to support and encourage you to meet your goals.

- Do self-hypnosis and call on special allies and resources (like peaceful, calm scenes, inner guides or people who are models of success) that increase your comfort and support you in remaining free of a self-limiting blueprint.

2. Use Hypnotic First-Aid:

- Sing a favorite song (or a power song) to your inner child. Try "Forever Young" or "Born Free."

- Draw the way you feel with paper and crayons.

- Imagine the situation on a television screen: make it black and white; make it smaller; turn the sound all the way down. Then turn the set off.

- Imagine the situation on a television screen: change it to look like a comedy act, sit-com or carnival; give the people involved comical voices, masks and costumes.

- Imagine and feel yourself in your safe and comfortable place.

- See and feel a protective shield or bubble around you. Repeat key words from self-hypnosis, such as "comfortable and strong."

- Use "power words" or key words that help you feel relaxed, capable and strongly committed to your goal.

EXERCISE 10
Achieving Goals—Realistically

The reason we are often unable to change or get rid of unwanted patterns and habits is that *we try to do too much too soon* and then get discouraged or overwhelmed. We invite failure by expecting ourselves to accomplish our goal perfectly at the moment we begin. In order to succeed, we need to break the goal into several steps, or *sub-goals*—each of which can be comfortably achieved.

With a gradual accomplishment of your sub-goals, you will be able to stay within your comfort zone while you complete each step toward the lasting change you want. A secret to success is making your first sub-goals *so easy and ridiculously small* that they require little or no effort at all.

When you complete your first sub-goals with ease, you will have a feeling of accomplishment and increased motivation. This confidence enables you to *gradually* increase your sub-goals from week to week. As a result, you will notice some real changes in your behavior and attitude. And your satisfaction will motivate you to continue adding sub-goals from week to week.

For example, to set a realistic sub-goal, you might say:

- "In the next week, I will do **one thing** that takes me closer to my goal. I will—*(something specific)*.

- "This week, I will practice self-hypnosis **one time,** for one minute or more."

- "This week, I will catch myself **one time** when I'm being self-critical, and I will do an inner child meditation instead."

WHAT TO DO:

1. Set your sub-goal: *For This Week's Sub-Goal, I'm Certain I Can..."*

Write your sub-goal for this week in your calendar or journal. Make sure your sub-goal is small enough that you are *certain* you can do it once in a week's time. Remember, the smaller and simpler the sub-goal, the easier it is to accomplish. Making your sub-goal painless builds your confidence and motivates you to want to do more. If you accomplish your sub-goal *just once* during the week, you have achieved your sub-goal for the week. This simple formula *guarantees success!*

2. Reward yourself as soon as possible after completing your sub-goal or responding with the desired behavior (i.e., after you interrupt a self-critical thought and do a self-hypnosis meditation instead.) No matter how small the gain may seem, rewarding yourself *reinforces and encourages the new behavior.* Think about an appropriate reward now—something that is meaningful to you (which preferably does not cost money or involve eating). You can be creative and playful in designing your rewards. You may be surprised how good it feels to reward yourself, for example, when you:

- Keep a gratitude journal and list positive changes there.
- Place a gold star on your calendar, marking the day and the sub-goal (behavior or activity) you accomplished.
- Put on a record of your favorite music and sing or dance.
- Compliment yourself—and your inner child—for the change in behavior.

6

Lucid Dreaming:
Manifesting Your Heart's Desire

"The More I Enjoy Myself, the Faster I Fly"

> *"I am flying. I have beautiful white butterfly wings. I am so surprised by my wings that I realize I must be dreaming. Many butterflies are with me. All of us have white wings, except for one, whose wings are amber. Experimenting, I move my wings subtly and skillfully. Riding the air currents, I swoop upward and glide down, letting the air carry me. I'm not afraid of falling. The more I enjoy myself, the faster I fly."*

Lucid dreaming involves a change in consciousness that is unmistakable and often dramatic. You enjoy a sense of boundless energy and power. Confidence and mastery are the norm, as in the "Butterfly Dream" above.

In a lucid dream, you are *aware that you are dreaming*. At the same time, you are fully participating in your dream—seeing, hearing, and feeling it. You experience a heightened state of awareness in which you can make decisions and choices that change and improve any part of your dream.

Lucid dreams often involve brilliant colors, pleasurable sensations and a significant communication—using words, touch or music. When you feel a strong connection with a symbol in a lucid dream, that symbol serves as a mirror: you also feel a deep and loving connection with yourself.

You are drawn irresistibly toward a symbol. You look deeply into his or her eyes and move closer. This irresistible attraction is the force of your own subconscious, pulling you into an embrace with a forgotten part of you—so that you can experience greater wholeness.

When you know you are dreaming, you can look at a symbol and know that it is also a part of you. You can ask questions, demand cooperation, experiment with your responses, make *lucid choices*, and change the outcome of your dream to manifest your heart's desire.

And you feel very loving and full of compassion for the subconscious parts of you. There ceases to be a sense of separation. In this lucid state, you are likely to say, "I realize that you are me. In opposing you, I am really opposing myself. I know that I have much to gain from being your ally. In loving you, I am loving a valuable part of me."

Lucid dreaming helps you to use more of your mind's potential. Yet it is a paradox: how can you be *conscious* while dreaming? This amazing phenomenon has been studied scientifically in sleep lab experiments conducted by researcher Stephen LaBerge. LaBerge's experiments with lucid dreaming give scientific validity to a phenomenon which has been recorded and practiced by many cultures—American Indian, Tibetan, East Indian, Malaysian, and others—for thousands of years. Like these ancient lucid dreamers, you, too, have the ability to explore the rich dimensions of your own consciousness.

The miracle of the human brain is more baffling than the most complex computer—and our brain is said to be more efficient. Even today in our increasingly technological society, scientists admit that they do not know what 90% of our brain is there to do. It follows, then, that there is still much to learn about the experience we call consciousness.

What is consciousness? Sociologists tell us that consciousness is awareness of our existence, of our thoughts, our emotions, and also our mortality—and that it is this consciousness of ourselves that separates us from other animals. Further, psychologists tell us that being conscious is being mentally alert, known to oneself, and able to act with intention.

We have only a few terms to describe consciousness, hypnotic states and lucid dreaming—while the Eskimos are said to have over one hundred words in their language to describe snow. Even researchers at the leading edge of scientific inquiry, who are dedicated to mapping the potential of the human brain, grope to find words to adequately describe the unique consciousness available in *lucid dreaming*. Our vocabulary is, as yet, too small to communicate the variety of outcomes and different levels of intensity that are possible.

Einstein once said, "Problems are never solved on the level on which they were created." If Einstein was right, then working with your subconscious is one of the best methods to reach beyond your conscious mind and gain the resources to solve real-life problems. Lucid dreaming, Inner Dialogue, Lucid Fantasy, and self-hypnosis engage the creative part of your mind, which your normal consciousness cannot.

LUCID CUES

Over the ages, dreamers and explorers of consciousness in many cultures have noticed some special phenomena or *lucid cues* that provide a *doorway* through which you can enter into lucid dreaming. Once you are able to recognize these cues, either while dreaming or afterwards, the heightened state of consciousness known as lucid dreaming will open to you.

Many of the lucid cues seem almost playful, as though your subconscious is saying, "How big a sign do I have to give you in order to get your attention?" But when you *read the signs* that help you to recognize a lucid cue and become aware that you are dreaming, you often experience an immediate surge in vitality and enjoyment, as though your subconscious is saying, "Now that we've connected, let's have some fun!"

Once you step through the lucid doorway and are aware that you are dreaming, there is a dramatic increase in freedom. Your choices and actions become more creative and empowering. The more you participate in your dream with lucid awareness, the freer you are to experiment and stretch yourself with new interactions and responses.

> As the degree of your lucidity increases, you will be able to make choices while dreaming: to ask questions of your symbols; do what you want or need; transform conflicts into alliances; change self-limiting patterns into empowering experiences; explore places of transcendent beauty; and gain an inspiring new vision of yourself and the world.

I first learned about lucid cues from Patricia Garfield, author of *Creative Dreaming*. In *Pathway to Ecstasy*, another marvelous book, she shares in detail her lucid dreaming experiences and the lucid cues that they contain. The following is a summary of lucid cues:

Lucid Cues

1. *An intense body movement,* often in air or water, followed by a different state of consciousness or awareness.

- Flying or rising in the air.
- Like Alice stepping through the looking glass, you may *break through a barrier* of some kind, crossing over into another dimension—a highly energized, creative state of consciousness.

2. *Sensations of light-headedness, coolness, or other bodily changes.*

- Dizziness, being swept in a current, diving into deep pools, cool night, light rain, downpour, snow.

- Extreme fatigue or falling asleep (within the dream). Awakening again within the dream, which is also called false awakening— thinking you have awakened when you are still dreaming.

- Making love and/or experiencing an orgasm within the dream.

3. *Experiencing intense visual focusing;* staring at something with total absorption.

- Looking deeply into someone's eyes (a person or an animal).

- Becoming absorbed in studying, handling, or looking at something.

4. *Seeing or experiencing something that fills you with wonder, awe, or inspiration.*

- Seeing or feeling the essence of something or someone—reaching a state of heightened awareness or understanding.

- Seeing or sensing *energy:* pulses, auras, luminosity *(light emanating),* brilliant colors, etc.

5. *Incongruity or Improbability:* Experiencing or observing something unusual or unlikely.

- A change in anatomy or appearance, i.e., something is growing out of your head or you have new body parts.

- A change in natural laws, i.e., defying gravity by flying; or you may have magical powers or experience something that you know couldn't "really" happen, like walking through walls or x-ray vision.

- An unlikely act of nature, such as a tidal wave or tornado; or meeting someone you are unlikely to meet, such as a celebrity or someone who is no longer alive.

6. *Experiencing doubleness.*

- Doubleness of people—seeing twins, seeing your own or someone else's double.

- Seeing yourself in a mirror—gazing at yourself with wonder and new vision. Tibetan Buddhists call this "the wisdom of the mirror."

- Dreaming *the same sequence* a second or third time.

- Remembering a sequence from another dream while still dreaming. Or, remembering this dream as part of a recurring theme (something you keep dreaming about).

- *Deja vu*—a feeling that a dream scene, activity or symbol has occurred before; a feeling that "I have seen, felt, or experienced something like this before."

- Double awareness—you are both the doer and the observer. You can participate in the action of the dream and also be aware that you are dreaming and interacting with symbols that are parts of you.

These lucid cues provide *a specific vocabulary for lucid consciousness.* As you will see throughout this chapter, these cues can serve as indispensable *guideposts* to help you cross the threshold to lucidity. Becoming familiar with these cues will increase your mastery of lucid dreaming.

MY FIRST LUCID DREAM

When I first decided that I wanted to experience a lucid dream, I was not sure what to do to make it happen. How do you make a leap in consciousness occur?

For several weeks, just before going to sleep I would say to myself, "Tonight I will have a lucid dream." But when I tried to imagine *how my dream would feel, look, and sound when I was lucid,* I had trouble being specific. After all, it was an experience I had not yet had. When my consistent efforts produced no lucid results, I realized that I would have to do something different.

I looked at the list of lucid cues for ideas. I noticed that one of the most striking things about my dream states was that I had *recurring dreams:* I would dream about a person or situation one week, then dream about the same person or situation a week or a month later. This experience always gave me déjà vu. Sometimes I would even remember, while in the dream, "This has happened to me before."

Previously, I had thought of my recurring dreams as something unpleasant that I'd rather avoid. Now, because they were a phenomenon that appeared on the list of lucid cues, my recurring dreams became an experience I chose to seek out and use.

Although I had more than one recurring dream to choose from, I picked my "Tidal Wave Dream." This dream appeared so regularly that I could almost predict its return within a month.

In the dream, I am standing on the shore watching the ocean.
It is a warm and sunny day. Everything is fine, until I look up
and see a huge tidal wave advancing toward me. The wave is

coming too quickly for me to get away from it. I become more and more afraid as the huge wall of water gets closer and closer, towering over me. I feel powerless as it crashes over me. I am so afraid that I wake up.

When I thought about this dream, it became obvious to me that in normal reality, it was very unlikely that I would ever encounter a tidal wave. *Incongruity* is one of the lucid cues: something seems out of place or doesn't make sense. (The same idea applies to flying in dreams or having unusual body parts; in normal reality you know this is not possible or likely.)

While awake, I practiced *seeing, hearing and feeling* the tidal wave. I practiced saying, "There's a tidal wave—therefore I must be dreaming!"

Within a month, there I was again in my recurring dream, confronted by a huge tidal wave.

This time, I am being lifted very high on top of the wave. I am afraid the wave will crush me under its weight when it breaks. **At this moment, I become lucid.** I say to myself, "I am having another tidal wave dream!" Even as the wave lifts me higher, I say, "Since I am dreaming, I know this can't hurt me!" For the first time, I feel liberated from dream terrors. I am certain the wave can't hurt me—and no longer feel that I have to get away.

Experiencing a lucid dream for the very first time, I feel an amazing surge of excitement—a new world of possibilities is opening to me. At this point, I know that I can do anything I want to—fly, ride the wave, discover something magical.

Then, I start to worry. "What should I do now? I should think of something really good." I get anxious about making the right choice and draw a blank about what to do next. My worry disrupts the delicate balance of lucid awareness, and I wake up.

My first lucid dream showed me that when I thought about my dream too much, my rational mind interfered with the dream state and I woke up.

Many dreamers, when they first become lucid, have difficulty in continuing to be lucid. This is because when you start to think and plan, you *change your brain waves.* Your efforts to problem-solve engage your rational left-brain hemisphere, so your brain waves speed up, causing you to either lose the lucid state (and return to normal dreaming) or wake up.

On awakening, my consolation was that I was on the right track. I had succeeded in having my first lucid dream! I had the right formula for *becoming lucid*—what I needed now was a way to *stay lucid* and enjoy the dream.

In my Lucid Fantasies after that, I repeated what had worked to make me lucid, and then carried it further: I imagined doing something pleasurable with my new-found awareness. Within a few weeks, I had another opportunity to be lucid.

> I am swimming in the ocean. Suddenly a tidal wave builds up near me, lifting me higher and higher. I look down from what seems a great height, and just before I panic, *I realize that I'm dreaming!* I say to myself, "This can't hurt me, because it's a dream!" Then I add the thought or intention, "Now I can have some fun with this dream."
>
> This time I feel comfortable and playful. The next thing I know, I am *riding the wave!* Like a surfer, I am being propelled in front of the wave's curl, the wind and foam flying by me, going very fast. I seem to ride the wave for miles. I feel a tremendous exhilaration and freedom.

This lucid dream was truly liberating. My lucid state was already teaching me to be more playful, while helping me to master my fear. Lucid dreams came regularly after this, each one unique, playful, exhilarating, touching, and inspiring in its own way.

When you do Inner Dialogue and Lucid Fantasy once a week, your first lucid dream will come with much less effort than mine. The guideposts are in place, and the doorway is very near.

BRIDGING STATES OF CONSCIOUSNESS

Lucid dreaming gives you the opportunity to bridge conscious and subconscious states. In lucid dreams, you have *double awareness* as both the observer and the doer, the conscious and subconscious parts of you:

You are aware that you are dreaming
(you are the observer)

And at the same time,
You are involved and participating in the
action of the dream
(you are the doer)

The challenge of lucid dreaming is to learn to balance your *observer* with your *doer.*

Your chances of having a lucid dream are greatly enhanced when you incorporate lucid cues into your Lucid Fantasies. By *rehearsing* your recognition of the cues and imagining an adventure that utilizes lucid awareness, you are very likely to have a lucid dream soon. *(See Exercise 2 for guidelines on incubating a Lucid Dream.)*

As your lucid dreams become more frequent, you may notice that *lucid consciousness* also happens while awake: you may recognize a repeating pattern in your life and use it as a cue to change that experience and make it more satisfying.

Paradoxically, you do not have to be aware that you are dreaming in order to benefit from being lucid. As a culture, we tend to simplify the mysterious and complex phenomenon of lucid dreaming—seeing it in black and white, "either you are lucid or you are not."

Lucidity has no simple on-off switch. Rather, there is a continuum of lucid awareness. On this lucid continuum, you can experience *semi-lucid* dreams in which you don't realize you are dreaming, but:

- You notice and enjoy something unusual or wonderful happening, like flying or experiencing magical powers.
- You notice your own double, or that you've had this dream before.

To move from a semi-lucid dream into a fully lucid dream, you need to recognize a lucid cue, as I did in my tidal wave dream. For example, you might say, "This experience is so strange and unlikely, I must be dreaming!"

My firsthand experiences with lucid dreams have shown me that many levels of consciousness are possible. I have had lucid dreams in which I was able to fully participate in my dream—and at the same time know that I was dreaming. I have also had semi-lucid dreams in which many of the characteristics of lucid dreams were present—such as flying, a feeling of high-energy, vividness, and a clear understanding of the significance of the actions in my dream—but at the same time, I did not have full awareness that it was a dream; I didn't say to myself, "I must be dreaming!"

Even if lucidity occurs for only a moment at a time, it is important, even vital, to be proud of it. Semi-lucid dreams and lucid cues, no matter how small or inconsequential they may seem, are openings through which you can begin to experience your consciousness in a new and exciting way.

In the subconscious, everything is permitted. You may look deeply into a symbol's eyes and be irresistibly drawn into an embrace. Every time you embrace a symbol, you are really embracing yourself—loving and accepting yourself more fully.

Invariably, I have found that when people *encourage and appreciate* their small gains, their lucidity while dreaming steadily increases, bringing more and more clarity and enjoyment to their dreams.

When you appreciate your progress in gaining lucidity, you also encourage more lucid dreams, as well as lucid awareness while awake. You will become more "clear" or lucid about ways in which you can influence your subconscious perceptions and responses, and in turn you will also become more aware of the ways in which your subconscious colors and shapes your waking life experience.

LUCID CHOICES

In a lucid dream or Lucid Fantasy, ask yourself, *"What is my heart's desire in this situation? What needs to happen here?"* You can say, *"I want to..."*

Rather than trying to plan your dream with your *head*, or rational mind, approach the dream with your *heart* and intuitive feelings. Simply feel and say your intention. Then leave it up to your subconscious to do the rest.

You can make *lucid choices* whether your dream is fully lucid or not. Your lucid choice will *create a different outcome* than your usual non-lucid response—either dreaming or awake. You will gain some important insights, as well as new awareness of how changing your behavior can affect the outcome of any situation. The advantage of experimenting with lucid choices while dreaming is that you can try out many different responses without risk to yourself or others.

Once you know you are dreaming, you can *choose to respond to the dream situation in a playful or healing way.* For instance, my tidal wave dream was a great opportunity to playfully ride the wave for miles! You can also lucidly choose to leave the current dream situation and create another. For example, you can jump into the air and fly on to another adventure.

Follow your heart and your intuition. You don't always have to do something (like fly or complete a task) in order to experience the magic of lucid awareness. Another lucid choice is to continue participating in the dream without trying to change it.

RESOLVING CONFLICTS LUCIDLY

Recurring dreams or patterns are a sure sign that your subconscious is searching for a solution to some problem or seeking to complete some past experience.

For many years after high school and college, I experienced a recurring theme (in both dreams and conscious thoughts) involving a school friend named Simon.

Simon was a boy I knew in grammar school. I remember him fondly as the first boy who told me he loved me, at age 8. I never really knew him well, although we attended the same schools for the next ten years. Perhaps because I did not get to know him, my subconscious chose Simon to represent a part of me that I needed to know better.

In a typical Simon dream,

> I am at a party where I see Simon. Usually he is in the distance, across a crowded room. I try to cross the room to talk to him, but there are too many people and it takes too long. By the time I get there, he's gone. (Or else I forget about him until it's too late and he is gone.) I feel frustrated.

I did Inner Dialogue on many of these dreams—speaking as Simon and becoming more familiar with the part of me that he represented. After many Inner Dialogues with Simon, I finally succeed in reaching him and talking to him in the dream. As a result, I began a *new trend* in my dreams of him. Once a mystifying and frustrating symbol, Simon began to symbolize my quest for lucidity. *Now the frustration I associated with him became my lucid cue.* I practiced recognizing Simon as a lucid cue in many Lucid Fantasies, and played with different choices I could make in my lucid state to talk to him, fly with him, and have an adventure with him.

Because of my lucid rehearsals, in later Simon dreams I was able to immediately recognize Simon as a lucid cue.

> At first, I would say to myself, "There's Simon. He's a cue to remind me of something important." And then I would remember, "He's a cue to remind me that I'm dreaming!"

In my semi-lucid Simon dreams, I did not realize that I was dreaming, but I still was able to make lucid choices.

> I see Simon and know that it is very important to talk to him. (Sometimes I remember previous experiences in which I tried to reach him and failed.) While I do not realize I am dreaming, *I remember my intention or lucid choice*: talking to Simon is important for some reason. When I see him, I say to myself: "I know it's important to connect with him; I know I must reach him." That is usually all I need to say.
>
> Without having to plan what happens next (which would probably disrupt my dream), my intention sets my energy into

motion, and the dream shapes itself accordingly. The next thing I know, I am saying hello to Simon, getting to know him, or even embracing him.

Another important theme involved a school friend named Eliot. Eliot was known as the class "brain" throughout my school years. My first few Inner Dialogues with Eliot revealed something surprising: my relationship with the Eliot symbol reflected my relationship with my own "brainy" qualities.

My relationship with the Eliot symbol has been more complex and challenging than with the Simon symbol. This is because I was friends with Eliot in school, but our friendship ended abruptly. After doing Inner Dialogue on many of my Eliot dreams, I began to suspect that my subconscious had not chosen Eliot simply as a symbol for my braininess, after all.

Typically, in an Eliot dream:

> Eliot is acting distant or even unfriendly to me. He won't talk to me. He won't even acknowledge me. I feel very hurt and disappointed.

My subconscious had cleverly chosen a past failure to help me discover that I was not communicating effectively with my own outgoing, masculine, brainy energy. My Eliot dreams helped me realize that I needed to make good friends with my brainy side. I also needed to have a dream of *reconciliation and renewed friendship* with the Eliot part of me.

Over a short period of time, I saw Eliot in a few more dreams, but did not have a chance to talk to him. I continued to do Inner Dialogue on those dreams, and noticed where I could have been more active—where I could have approached him and shared my feelings clearly. I did Lucid Fantasy on these dreams and practiced taking an active role. My intention was to talk with Eliot and become friends again.

Then, within a month, another dream—this time, a dream of reconciliation:

> I see Eliot again. We're our present ages. He is cold and dismissing toward me, but I am very certain that I want to be his friend. This time, I realize that his coldness is because of a misunderstanding. In this moment, I have *a lucid awareness* that he must have felt rejected by me, and has been angry ever since.
>
> I walk over to him and say, "Eliot, I'd like to be friends with you again. I can understand that you're upset with me because of something I did. But that was many years ago and I wish you'd

forgive me. I was a lot younger then and I was confused. I'm sorry I hurt you."

At this point, I see his face very clearly and he is really listening to me. He softens and holds out his arms a little, like he's willing to embrace me but is still uncertain. I step into his arms and we embrace each other. I feel very good now. I am marvelling at the special way in which I understand everything so clearly, and at how effectively I am communicating with Eliot.

Now he is gentle and says to me, "I really did care for you and I was very hurt when you seemed to reject me. But I think of you whenever I see something beautiful."

I'm very touched by this and start to cry. I say, "Back then I really had a lot of trouble believing that you cared for me. I didn't think you did, and that's why I got scared and avoided you." He reassures me, "I did care for you." Hearing him now, I'm able to believe it.

I'm looking closely at his face. We gaze into each other's eyes, and now it is as if I am seeing *into* him. I can feel, very vividly, his caring, his soulfulness, and his considerable mental power.

We're still embracing, and then we start to dance together. I am surprised at how light he is on his feet and how well he dances. We move together in harmony now, dancing in step. I feel very close to him.

My reconciliation dream with Eliot was not fully lucid, and yet I made many lucid choices in it. While dreaming, I seemed to reach a new understanding of both myself and Eliot, which greatly aided our ability to say what we needed to say and heal our friendship. I did not realize that I was dreaming, and yet I acted on my intention to reconcile. Without planning it, my semi-lucid dream unfolded in a way that was more beautiful and touching than would have been possible if I had tried to lucidly direct it.

Shortly after our reconciliation, I had several more friendly dream encounters with Eliot. After real-life occasions where I communicated well, or when I did well in an interview or presentation to a group, I often embraced Eliot in my dreams and celebrated with him.

MASTERY OVER FEAR

Some people wonder if lucidly directing your dreams could be misused as a way to avoid working out inner conflicts. It is true that if you become lucid in a dream where you are in an unpleasant situation or in danger, you can often use your lucidity to change to another scene or escape. Many times, though, if you choose the escape route, you spend the rest of the night having to extricate yourself from other difficult or unpleasant situations. Being able to lucidly direct your dream is not going to just make the bad situations go away.

When I first began to dream lucidly, I often used my lucidity to enable me to rise in the air and fly away from dangerous or threatening situations. But I found that when I avoided facing my fear, what I flew on to was not a wonderful adventure. Each dream scene that followed would present me with a similar difficulty.

In many cases, the longer I avoided facing my fear, the more my fear increased. I finally realized that the only way to master fear was to remain in the difficult or scary situation, using lucidity to change the experience into a more positive one.

We dream what we need to dream. Your symbols are there for a reason—to teach you something about yourself. In lucid dreams, as in life, you can choose whether to remain in or leave a particular situation. But wherever you are, your subconscious will present you with situations from which you need to learn. How you respond emotionally to a situation, with fear or with lucid awareness, determines much of the outcome.

Your symbols and dreams are, essentially, energy states which change and reconfigure each step of the way, reflecting your intention to approach or avoid something. Every dream presents you with many possible choices and many possible responses, each of which will lead to different outcomes. Because this is true of real life as well, your dreams are excellent opportunities in which to try out new attitudes and responses.

For instance, if you react with fear—feeling frightened or paralyzed, or trying to escape—this response usually leads to more fear in the dream (and the dreams that follow). On the other hand, you can create a very different outcome by choosing to face your fear and master it: confront your antagonist and try to resolve the conflict. This response usually leads to a satisfying sense of completion, as it did in my reconciliation dream with Eliot.

Your choice at any given moment will shape the outcome of your experience. *Mastering your fear* will shape your dream in surprising ways. At one moment you may be arguing with a difficult person. Then, as your *intention to resolve the conflict* shapes the dream, you may be able to look into that person's eyes and express yourself more clearly than ever before. When you embrace that person-symbol, you may suddenly find that the symbol has changed and you are now embracing someone else—a lover, mate, friend, or child. By resolving conflicts with your symbols, you will free yourself to be more *lucid* in real life, as well as more loving in your relationships.

Tibetan Buddhists, Hindus, and American Indians, as well as the Senoi of Malaysia, believe it is essential to gain mastery over fear in dreams. Tibetan Buddhists regard lucid dreaming as a preparation to free themselves from the cycle of birth and rebirth. The Tibetan Book of the Dead warns departing souls,

"O nobly-born, whatever fearful and terrifying visions
thou mayst see, recognize them to be thine own thought forms."

By mastering fear during their lifetime, Tibetan Buddhists hope to free themselves from the illusions or thought-forms (subconscious patterns) that keep them from achieving oneness with the Divine.

In my own dreams, mastering fear has been a very exciting challenge. I mentioned earlier that as a child, I used to have very frightening dreams. Inner Dialogue and Lucid Fantasy gave me the tools I needed so that, when faced with what *used to be* a frightening dream situation, I could remain and feel little or no fear. As a result, my trust and confidence in myself increased, and my response to difficult dreams and waking dreams became more creative. You, too, can learn how to use lucid awareness to master fearful situations and transform them.

LUCID NIGHTMARES

We tend to think of lucid dreaming as a wonderful adventure. But it is possible to have lucid nightmares. This may seem a contradiction in terms—how can a lucid dream be a nightmare? Yet sometimes when you are learning to master fear in dreams, your subconscious may choose just this kind of experience—in order to drive home the lesson you need to learn.

My own lucid nightmares have been dramatic, incredibly vivid and, in the long run, very educational. Like other lucid dreams, lucid nightmares have the special capacity to help you understand any conflict more clearly: to experience a problem from a perspective quite different from your conscious mind, to recognize your part in creating it, and to gain wisdom as to how it may be solved.

My concept of consciousness was stretched by my pleasant lucid dreams. But my lucid nightmares ripped through the boundaries of what I thought possible in a dream and redefined consciousness in an unforgettably dramatic way. For instance, some people say that you cannot die in a dream without really dying. This is untrue. In one of my early lucid nightmares:

> I plunge off a cliff in a car. Luckily, I realize that I am dreaming and I am not afraid. Then I lucidly choose to continue the dream—to see what it is like to float around as a spirit. It really isn't so bad. But I do miss being alive.

When I awoke from this dream, I thought about the gift of being alive with renewed appreciation.

In another lucid nightmare:

> I encounter a woman on a horse who looks, oddly enough, like me. *(The lucid cue of doubleness.)* When I get closer, she reaches out and stabs me in the heart with a small knife. I vividly feel pain as the blade pierces my breast. The pain is so surprising and intense that *I realize I am dreaming.* I know her attack is not going to kill me, which quiets my fear, but I still feel the pain. I am aware that I can change the dream, but the pain is too distracting. I decide to wake up instead.

This rather brutal dream sent me a wake-up call I could not ignore. My Inner Dialogue with "the Woman on the Horse" made me realize that I needed to integrate the primal strength she represented. The woman used the knife to cut through my resistance, fear, and self-limiting patterns. Resisting her primal energy is what caused me intense pain.

> Through her dramatic action, she is saying to me, "You've got to let your heart energy out, let your vitality out into the world. We need to be connected. We need to be allies."

My most recent dream about mastering fear required me to *step into the unknown*, a situation that would have frightened me in the past. This time, I did not need to have a lucid nightmare. I was ready for a different kind of lesson:

> I am being tested by an old man. I am told to follow a guide through something like a dimensional door. I understand that this is a test of my ability to master fear. I am going through the door and stepping into the unknown. I am not afraid and sense that if I just follow my guide, I'll be all right. The test is a series of trips into the unknown, stepping through the door and coming back.
> The first time I step through the door after my guide, I find that I am floating in a black void. I relax and wait, unafraid. Then I am back with the old man.

Before I step through another time, the old man says to me, *"Let your shoulders be light."* I concentrate on his direction and find that I am flying with great joy in a yellow-gold sky. Somehow I realize that this incredible, luminous sky also represents the color of my life.

I feel that my performance on the test does not have to be perfect—just so long as I try. I sense that I will pass this test of mastery.

DREAMS OF WONDER

Flying in dreams is a very popular goal of lucid dreamers. Research has shown that flying dreams provide a psychological boost to self-esteem, helping you to feel more powerful and capable in directing not only your flight, but also your life. Flying dreams also provide a boost of well-being to the body.

You can enjoy breathtaking flying adventures to beautiful places and thrill to the freedom and movement of your flight, as I did in my "Butterfly Dream." You can also use flying as a lucid cue to realize that you are dreaming, because you know that for most humans, flying without help is unlikely.

Dreams of wonder are among the greatest rewards of lucid dreaming. These are dreams in which your personal freedom, pleasure, sense of humor, and lucid awareness are enhanced and particularly vivid. Often, dreams of wonder involve flying. Most of all, these are dreams in which you may be filled with astonishment upon seeing something incredibly beautiful. You may be struck with wonder upon encountering something magical or inspiring:

> I am flying through the universe. I vividly see the stars all around me, shining brightly in the blackness of space. I see a group of beings flying near me. They are holding globes of light which glow brightly in their hands. They fly by me. I am in a spell of wonder. I feel high energy inside me.

In this dream, which I call "Flying through the Universe," I am flying with the same kind of wonder that I experienced in my "Butterfly Dream." And yet there are differences. As a butterfly, I was enjoying the pleasure of soaring on air currents, in what might be called earth-zone flight. In "Flying through the Universe," flight has taken on much larger possibilities. The symbols of the Universe and the Light Beings give this dream a mystical or cosmic feeling.

In your lucid dreams and dreams of wonder, you will enjoy a similar feeling of exhilaration and heightened awareness. And the more you pay attention to and encourage these experiences, the more you will be rewarded with inspiring dreams—and increased pleasure and creativity in your life.

FLYING HIGH

"Angels fly because they take themselves lightly," says philosopher Alan Watts. To enjoy a lucid flying dream, we must also take ourselves lightly and recapture some of the playful wonder of being a child.

> Leap into the air and fly. A pleasant surge of energy propels you lightly above the trees. You fly higher, then swoop down and up again. You playfully turn somersaults and dance in the air. Way up here, there is wonder, beauty and power. Feeling deeply contented, you awaken, inspired and energized.

As children, we often fly in our dreams. As we get older, though, many of us lose this special ability. Instead of the lightness and energy of flying, our dreams get heavy and anxious and may involve both struggling to fly and falling.

The good news is that you can learn how to change the anxiety of falling dreams into the pleasure of flying dreams.

> Surprisingly, falling and flying dreams are connected. The same anxiety that you feel in a falling dream or other unpleasant dream can be transformed into the energy and excitement that propels you into flight.

Because there are different degrees of pleasure, frustration, and fear in flying and falling dreams, it is important not to generalize. Take the time to notice the specific details and feelings in your flying dreams, and in any dream, because each one is a personal message from your subconscious. Flying dreams can be better understood as a metaphor for your ability to "take off" and be in charge of your life:

- **Falling dreams**—You experience your worst fear, that you will be hurt or even killed by falling from a high place. In these dreams, you feel panicked and out of control. *As a symbol or metaphor for your life,* falling dreams tell you that you feel very afraid or insecure about a certain situation or aspect of your life. Further, the dream may indicate that subconsciously you feel powerless to change a real-life situation into a safer experience.

"I fly high, hey, ho!"

- **Pleasurable falling dreams**—You may be a little afraid, but your fear is more than compensated by the excitement of flying while you glide downward. Like diving into a pool, you feel in control in these dreams and know you will not be hurt. *As a symbol or metaphor for your life*, pleasurable falling dreams tell you that although you may currently be facing a challenging situation, you are prepared to make the most of it.

- **Flapping dreams**—Like a bird that has wings but cannot fly, you have to work very hard to get off the ground. You may flap your arms vigorously and struggle against gravity to lift off. Unlike the burst of energy that comes with successful flying and soaring dreams, when you flap, the energy is uneven or seems insufficient to get you into the air. The experience is frustrating, and sometimes you are afraid you will fall. You may lift only a few inches or feet off the ground. *As a symbol or metaphor for your life*, flapping dreams show that you are feeling stymied in a particular area of your life. Perhaps you have focused on a goal, but are having trouble reaching it.

- **Flying and soaring dreams**—You feel like Superman or Wonder Woman. You are in control of your energy and feel confident, powerful and playful. You are able to direct your flying, so you can go anywhere you want. *As a symbol or metaphor for your life*, flying and soaring dreams let you know that you are taking off in your life and feeling in charge; in general, you are energized and confident about your goals and accomplishments.

Although we tend to feel excited in flying dreams and anxious in falling dreams, the *physical sensations* of flying and falling are actually quite similar. What changes the experience is the *feeling* that goes along with the *action*.

You can use Lucid Fantasy to change a falling dream into a flying dream. While awake, imagine making a *lucid choice* to master your fear of falling and to empower yourself with flight.

> Use all of your senses to imagine swooping out of a fall and soaring comfortably above the trees. Feel the pleasure of flying to a place of transcendent beauty and peace. Or, imagine gliding downward, unafraid, and landing softly on the ground.

When you experience the pleasure of flying in a Lucid Fantasy, you plant the experience in your subconscious so you can dream about it later. Your dream flights will become more frequent, playful and exciting— and your confidence both dreaming and awake will soar. Even more, while in dream flight you can become lucid—and fly to the wonder of another realm.

TURN ANXIETY INTO EXCITEMENT

Just as the sensations of falling and flying are similar, so are the sensations of anxiety and excitement. Clearly, one is very unpleasant and the other is wonderful. But if the sensations are similar, why are our reactions so different?

When we are afraid, we tend to take very shallow breaths and tense our bodies. While designed to protect us, this reaction does not put us into the most resourceful state to deal effectively with a situation. Fritz Perls, the founder of Gestalt therapy, has said, *Anxiety + Oxygen = Excitement:*

> When you breathe fully, you can experience the situation (awake or dreaming) with more comfort, and as a result, a pleasant sensation of excitement will develop.

Let's say you had a dream in which you were falling from a great height. In the dream you were afraid and anxious. While awake, you can use Lucid Fantasy to re-imagine your dream—transforming it so you feel in control and can land safely.

> While falling, imagine that you know you are dreaming, so you are certain there is no real danger. You can breathe easily and relax. Notice the sensations of falling—aren't they very similar to flying? Now you can lucidly choose a safe landing. See and feel yourself landing softly and safely on your feet, a soft cushion or a landing pad.
>
> Now try a different solution. Turn the sensations of falling into sensations of flying. Imagine falling again and then lucidly choose to swoop out of your fall and begin to fly. Notice that your anxiety has changed into a very pleasant feeling of excitement.

By using Lucid Fantasy to change anxiety and fear into pleasure, you are taking charge of the situation. Your Lucid Fantasy will communicate an empowering experience to your subconscious, and in your subsequent dreams you will be more likely to have both safe and pleasurable flying experiences.

In your dreams, you can also notice both flying and falling as *lucid cues.* When you become conscious that you are dreaming, you can lucidly change a falling dream into a flying dream, or you can land softly, as just described.

To become lucid in a falling dream is a good test of mastery over fear. If you are afraid, it is difficult to become lucid and stay lucid long enough to change a falling dream into a flying dream. This is why I recommend that you use Inner Dialogue and Lucid Fantasy on your dreams, to help you prepare for your next lucid opportunity.

Lucid dreams, like hypnotic experiences, are adventures in consciousness. And now—with Inner Dialogue, Lucid Fantasy, and Lucid Dreaming, you have entered into an exciting partnership with your subconscious. Use this partnership to search out the solutions to problems, transform fear into confidence, turn anxiety into excitement, increase your creativity, go on spiritual quests, and more.

SONGS OF JOY

Music often has special associations and meanings to us, evoking powerful feelings, both dreaming and awake. Musical expression, like dreams, comes primarily from the right brain hemisphere and is strongly linked to our emotions. Music that has a strong effect on you, either awake or dreaming, has much to say to you as a symbol.

Music often occurs spontaneously in dreams. Sometimes, the music is playing subtly in the background, but later when you think about what the song was or what the lyrics were saying, the meaning of your dream becomes crystal clear. Other times, the music might be playing loudly like a musical score, amplifying the feeling in your dream quite noticeably and reinforcing the message.

Enjoyable music often occurs in lucid and semi-lucid dreams:

> I am flying with great enjoyment to the song, "Born Free." The beautiful music of this song seems to lift me higher in my flight. I hear the lyrics very clearly. My heart feels warm and happy as I continue to fly with even more energy, knowing the meaning of my flight.

When you dream that you are hearing music, playing it or singing it:

- Notice the situation in which your dream music appears and how you are relating to it. Are you playing the music yourself? How near or far is it? How well can you hear it, and how much are you enjoying it?

• Use Inner Dialogue afterwards to explore your music as an important symbol. Speak as the music itself, and note your special qualities, your style (*classical, jazz, rock, etc.*), your rhythm, and your mood or feeling. (You can also speak as the instrument playing the music.) Then dialogue between the music and yourself.

• Using the symbol of music as a *metaphor for your life*, discover what specific areas in your life you need to *play, orchestrate or tune up* with more awareness and appreciation. Your Inner Dialogue will yield many rewarding insights as to how well you are expressing yourself emotionally and creatively in your life.

You can express feelings of power and healing by incorporating music or songs in a Lucid Fantasy. Whether or not the music was in your original dream, you can choose a song that conveys to you joy, healing, empowerment, playfulness, or gratitude. Sing, hum or play this music in your Lucid Fantasy as a way to anchor positive feelings and access a healthy trance state. You can put yourself into a resourceful, enjoyable state of mind, anytime, any where, by humming or singing the music.

You can also do an Inner Dialogue between the music and yourself, treating the music as a symbol for *the music of my life, my life-song, or my power song*. This Inner Dialogue usually creates a powerful metaphor which encourages you to express more of your unique "music" (feelings and abilities) in the world. You will also enjoy the beauty, harmony and joy that *your song* brings to yourself and others. *(See Exercise 4 for further instructions.)*

THE WONDERS OF THE UNIVERSE

You are ready now for your own personal adventure. There are many wonders awaiting you. Explore and experiment. Be playful and curious. Discover how far you can go.

Exercises For
Your Subconscious

EXERCISE 1
Appreciating Lucid Cues

Begin to notice lucid cues—either while dreaming, or later, when you recall the dream. Flying, intense visual focusing, changes in anatomy or appearance, unlikely occurrences, experiences of doubleness, and *déjà vu* (knowing that something in your dream has occurred before), are only a few of the lucid cues possible. *(The full list of lucid cues is contained early in this chapter.)*

WHAT TO DO:

- Underline your lucid cues in a bright color ink, when you record your dream in your journal. Whether you recognized a lucid cue while you were dreaming, or not, think of these cues as opportunities you can use to become fully lucid. Congratulate yourself for any lucid cues, no matter how small they may seem!

- Write "Lucid Cues" next to the date of the dream, or at the top of the page, to remind you that you reached a higher level of awareness in the dream. This notation will help you to find these cues again so you can track your progress with greater ease.

- When you have a dream in which you are nearly aware that you are dreaming, underline this part of the dream and write "Semi-Lucid" at the top of the page. Similarly, when you experience even a moment of lucid awareness, underline that part of the dream and note "Lucid Awareness" at the top of the page. Doing this will help reinforce your ability to dream lucidly and invite the experience again.

- When you have become fully lucid in a dream, write "Lucid Dream" at the top of the page when you record the dream.

By keeping a record of your dreams, Inner Dialogues and Lucid Fantasies, you will also be able to *track the evolution of your lucid dream experiences*. You will notice a natural progression from lucid cues which you did not utilize in one dream, to lucid cues which you were able to recognize and utilize in another. You will become so familiar with your semi-lucid dreams and lucid cues that when another opportunity arises in your dreams, you will recognize it as a doorway to lucid dreaming—and become fully lucid.

As you continue to pay attention to both your dreams and waking dreams, this process gains momentum. You will be amazed at the shifts in consciousness you can encourage and experience.

Take special pride in your experiences on the lucid continuum. Remember to appreciate the special insight or gifts you receive, as well as the wonder and exhilaration you feel.

EXERCISE 2
Incubating A Lucid Dream

If you did not recognize a lucid cue while dreaming, create a Lucid Fantasy now in which you are able to recognize one. For example, you were flying in your dream, but you did not realize that you were dreaming. Use Lucid Fantasy to feel and see yourself flying again—but this time recognize it as a lucid cue: "I'm flying, therefore I must be dreaming!"

WHAT TO DO: Create a Lucid Fantasy that incorporates one or more lucid cues. Imagine and experience a lucid adventure in which you use your lucid cues creatively and enjoyably. Trust your subconscious to spontaneously suggest the creative and healing solutions that are just right for you. Your Lucid Fantasy is an incubation for a fully lucid dream. *(For a guided meditation using many lucid cues, see Exercise 7.)*

Practice recognizing a particular lucid cue and saying to yourself, "There's my lucid cue—I must be dreaming!" Enjoy the surge of excitement and the feeling of liberation that this lucid awareness brings.

See, hear and feel your Lucid Fantasy as fully as possible, while awake. By planting lucid cues, you can reexperience any dream *as though it were a lucid dream*. Your subconscious will not know the difference between your *fantasy* of a lucid dream and a *real* lucid dream. The more you use Lucid Fantasy to rehearse becoming lucid, the more likely you are to have a lucid dream!

Remember to record your Lucid Fantasy in your journal, the same as you would a dream. Write down your Lucid Fantasies while they are fresh. These marvelous, healing adventures can provide insight, inspiration and enjoyment for a long time.

EXERCISE 3
Lucid Waking Dreams

As lucid dreaming becomes more frequent and familiar, you will also gain an ability to experience *waking situations* lucidly.

When you find yourself in a difficult situation, you may discover that you are responding in new ways and with increased awareness. As in a lucid dream, you may have a broader perspective of what it all means. You may interact with a difficult person and discover that you are communicating your feelings and views more effectively. You may even be able to see a particular person more lucidly, with more compassion and clarity, as though you can recognize a bit of yourself in him or her.

WHAT TO DO: Record a waking event as a lucid waking dream, writing it in the present tense in your journal. Choose a situation in which you responded to an event with greater awareness than before. You may have gained a new perspective and deeper understanding, or maybe you were able to act with more confidence and effectiveness than in the past.

Perhaps for the first time, your lucid waking dream has brought you the lucid awareness that you have *the freedom to choose* either your habitual response or a more conscious and effective response. Notice how your new response is different from the old one. You may want to ask yourself, "In what way was my intention different this time? How am I being more lucid in my life?"

EXERCISE 4
Songs of Joy

Dream music symbolizes the way you are currently expressing yourself in your life. Music as a symbol may also be there to remind you of needs and potentials of which you have lost track.

Enjoyable music often occurs in dreams when you are close to or in a state of lucid dreaming. Like a musical score which enriches a movie by expressing the mood of the scene, dream music may be in the background, subtly playing, or it may be quite obvious. It might be a song you are singing or creating in the dream; or it might be a piece of music you are playing or hearing.

WHAT TO DO:

- Do Inner Dialogue and speak as the music (or the instrument playing the music). As that symbol, note your special qualities, your style (classical, jazz, popular, blues, honky-tonk, rock, etc.), your rhythm, and your mood or feeling.

- Notice the situation in which your music appears and how you are relating to it. Are you playing the music yourself? How near or far is the music from you? How well can you hear it? How much are you enjoying it?

- If there are lyrics with your music, notice what the words are saying or implying. Notice in what way(s) the lyrics may connect with the action of your dream, pointing out or emphasizing the dream message. For example, remember the dream I recounted in which I was flying high to the song "Born Free." In this dream, the music and the words perfectly expressed my feelings of joy and freedom as I glided through the air.

- Do a Lucid Fantasy on the dream or waking dream involving the symbol of music. Express your *song of joy* (or your song of empowerment, healing, playfulness, gratitude, or something else) in an enjoyable and meaningful way. Bring the music as close to you as you can—and play it, dance to it, or sing it with pleasure and expression. If your music was sad or not satisfying in some way in your original dream, allow your subconscious to suggest a way to change it now into a more energizing and pleasurable form. If there are lyrics, hear them clearly now and let their meaning or message inspire and uplift you.

- Use your Lucid Fantasy to have a joyful adventure with allies and friends, using the music as inspiration. Remember, this is your adventure! Take an easy breath and let your subconscious suggest some possibilities. Use all of your senses to see, hear and feel the music welling up within you and around you.

- Lastly, explore your *song of joy* as a symbol. Do Inner Dialogue and speak as "the music of my life," "my life-song," "my power song," or "my song of healing." You can base your symbol on the music that appeared in your dream, or you can allow your subconscious to provide you with a fresh symbol. After your Inner Dialogue, create a Lucid Fantasy in which you experience the joy and fulfillment of expressing your music (or its quality) in a specific real-life situation.

- Look for helpful messages regarding specific areas of your life which you may need to *play, tune up or orchestrate* with more attention and appreciation. Inner Dialogue and Lucid Fantasy with your music-symbol will yield many insights and give you a joyful awareness of the creative, expressive part of you.

EXERCISE 5
Creating a Lucid Storybook

Collect your Lucid Fantasies and lucid dreams in a special Lucid Storybook. Every time you read your Lucid Storybook, you will feel inspired—because you will be reminded of your lucid awareness and the wonder of these experiences.

Your Lucid Storybook elevates your lucid experiences *into art.* In this form, you can continue to draw insight and enjoyment from them for a long time. And it is also very satisfying to share this gift with people who are close to you.

WHAT TO DO: First, select a blank book or notebook (separate from your journal) in which to write or assemble your dream stories, Lucid Fantasies and lucid dreams.

Next, select a special image or combination of images for the cover of your Lucid Storybook. For example, my Lucid Storybook is covered with a beautiful array of blooming flowers.

It is very important to make your Lucid Storybook look and feel special to you as a container for these wonderful stories and experiences. By preparing your Lucid Storybook in this way, you are acknowledging the creativity and wisdom of your own mind.

Next, select inspiring dreams, lucid dreams, Lucid Fantasies, and waking dreams and copy them into your Lucid Storybook.

- Illustrate your Lucid Storybook entries with colorful images, montages, or drawings.
- Write and include a dream haiku or poem with your dream or Lucid Fantasy *(see Chapter 7).*
- Give each entry a title that captures its special message.
- Date each entry, so that you can later cross-reference it with your journal.
- Include dreams and lucid dreams that were particularly inspiring, and follow each with your Lucid Fantasy on that dream. (This makes it possible to trace the evolution of your lucid dreams.)

Your Lucid Storybook will be inspiring to read, since the level of energy and awareness of your Lucid Fantasies is very high. I keep my own Lucid Storybook handy to read as an incubation before bed or when I need a "hit" of inspiration.

EXERCISE 6
Recognizing Dream Patterns

Patterns have a way of repeating in your dreams and waking dreams until you consciously recognize them and gain insight. According to learning experts, pattern recognition is an essential part of learning. So, in order to learn more about yourself, a Dream Overview will help you to *recognize repeating patterns of symbols, action and feelings.*

WHAT TO DO: Read through both recent and older dreams to observe some of your dream patterns. You will probably want to do this review over a period of time and on several occasions. Each time you look at your dreams, you will gain a slightly different impression that can lead to further insights. You will recognize new patterns each time and even discover levels of meaning you had not noticed before.

Now, write down as many similarities among your dreams as you can:

> Similar Symbols
>
> Similar Themes or Action
>
> Similar Messages

Similarities in each category may be either *in physical appearance or feeling.* (Remember to refer to each dream by a date, a description, or a title.) For example:

1. Similar Symbols

- Dream of 8/1, dark-eyed woman
- Dream of 9/22, pregnant woman

2. Similar Themes or Action

- Theme of attack. Dream of 5/10, an explosion (a feeling of attack). Dream of 5/29, a rhinoceros attacks me.

- Theme of women. Dream of 8/1, A dark-eyed woman helps me. Dream of 9/22, I am friends with a pregnant woman.

- Theme of school. Dream of 11/15, I am taking a test and I'm worried I don't know enough to pass. Dream of 12/21, I am back in school; I can't find my locker (or remember the combination) to get my books to study for a test.

3. Similar Messages

- Dreams of 8/1 & 9/22. "I am opening more to my feminine or feeling side (i.e., *the symbols of women*), allowing myself to be more vulnerable. As I value my feeling side more, I receive needed help and support from it."

- Dreams of 5/10 & 5/29. "There are powerful, aggressive and scary feelings in me *(i.e., the symbols of the explosion and the rhino)*, which I need to express more openly, rather than avoid or run away from them. If I do not express these feelings, I end up turning their energy against myself or running the risk of exploding."

- Dreams of 11/15 and 12/21. "I feel I am being tested by recent events in my life *(i.e., the symbols of taking a test or remembering my locker combination)*. I feel worried and unprepared for the challenges I'm facing; I'm not sure if I can deal with them successfully. There are resources I need to get to *(my locker and books)* which I have forgotten, cannot find, or cannot open.

EXERCISE 7
A Guided Meditation to Incubate a Lucid Dream

In this meditation, you will travel to a magical world and meet an animal ally. You will experience an exciting, heightened state of awareness, as well as many of the characteristics of lucid dreaming: brilliant colors, bright light, sensations of physical freedom, and lucid awareness.

WHAT TO DO: To prepare for this hypnotic meditation, read it slowly into a tape recorder, with plenty of pauses between sentences. Or, you may want to have a friend read it to you, also at a slow pace and in a soothing tone of voice.

Find a quiet place where you will not be disturbed for thirty minutes to an hour. Have your journal ready so that you can record the experience when you are done, while it is fresh.

You do not need to plan this journey. As I guide you through it, whatever happens is right for you. Trust the images that come. Every image has important meanings that you will discover later. Just let your subconscious supply you with the images and feelings. (Do not listen to your critical mind if it says they are not good enough.)

Lucid Dream Meditation

Relax and close your eyes. Take a deep breath and let it out slowly. During the next half-hour, you can take a journey that is safe and comfortable for you. Anything is possible. Anything can happen. You can start your journey now by imagining your favorite place, a place where you feel peaceful and safe. Or you can imagine a special place where you feel energized. Maybe it's a place where you've been before, or maybe it's a place in your imagination.

Trust whatever pops into your mind...Notice what this place looks like. *(Pause)* Now, step into the picture. See and feel yourself in your special place. Enjoy what is around you. See and feel the clothes you're wearing. *(Pause)* What is the landscape like? *(Pause)* Listen and notice what sounds you hear. And become aware of how you feel, here in this special place.

And now, nearby in your special place, you can find a magical opening—an opening through which you can travel down into a magical world. This opening may be through a cave, or through something very surprising, like the roots of a tree, or the bottom of a lake, or even a blade of grass. Trust whatever comes to you.

And imagine that your body is so *fluid and flexible* that it can fit into even the smallest spaces. Because your body feels light and fluid, this might be the perfect moment to realize that you are beginning a *lucid dream*. You are aware that you are dreaming, and now you know that you can change your shape to easily fit into places you would not normally go. Your dream body is fluid and light.

It's comfortable for you to go into the magical opening now. It is large enough for you to travel through easily. You can slide into it with ease. Inside the opening now, you find you are in a tunnel—a tunnel in which it is comfortable and safe for you to travel. You can fly or slide down this tunnel. *Feel* the coolness of the air on your skin as you travel. And notice what is around you in the tunnel. Is there anything special or unusual here?

And as you continue through the tunnel, notice if you *hear* anything now— a whirring sound, bells, or animal sounds? Do you *see* any changes in the light? Do you *sense* a vibration?

And notice how you *feel* as you travel through the tunnel.

And as you get near the entrance to the magical world, you can see its light. Notice if there are any animals waiting for you in the tunnel or on the other side. *(Pause)* When you see your animal, greet it as a friend. Or, if you do not see an animal, invite your animal ally to appear to you now.

You may want to approach your animal, or let it come closer to you. You may want to touch. *(Pause)* And now maybe you can look into your animal's eyes. *(Pause)* Maybe you can sense your animal's special power.

And if you want to, you can let your animal ally show you something special about this magical world it lives in. Let it take you somewhere or do something that will give you some of its knowledge and power. *(Pause)* Maybe there is something your animal ally wants to say to you. *(Pause)* And maybe there is something you want to say to your animal.

Now, you can get ready to say good-bye to your animal. Before you go, you can thank your animal ally for its help. If you want to, you can stroke it or hug it. *(Pause)* And now your animal ally wants to give you a gift. See and feel what it is.

The gift is given with love and wisdom, and you receive it gladly. *(Pause)* Notice that this gift makes tangible the animal's power, so that you can take some of its special ability or energy back with you.

Maybe you want to give your animal ally a gift, too. See and feel what it is, and notice the special quality your gift conveys to your animal ally. You have now created a bond that you can rely on. You can call on your animal ally and feel its energy and wisdom whenever you want to, whenever you need to. And if you can feel the special power of your animal ally inside of you now, you can anchor that good feeling in your body. You can touch your hand to your heart and anchor that special power deep inside.

And now you can get ready to come back through the tunnel to the special place where you started. You can come back quickly through the tunnel...traveling in the light, with your dream body moving fluidly and swiftly, back to where you began...

Emerging at the spot where you started, that special place, where you can rest again for a few moments. And notice how you feel. Notice how your body feels. *(Pause)*

And now bring your awareness back into the room, moving your fingers and toes, feeling refreshed and energized. Bringing the good feeling of meeting your animal ally back with you, as you gently open your eyes, wide awake.

WHAT TO DO: Write down your magical journey while it is fresh.

There are several parts to this journey, and you can write them as distinct sequences or episodes:

- the special place
- the tunnel
- meeting the animal ally
- your interaction with the animal in the magical world
- the gift or gifts

Notice what lucid elements you were able to incorporate into your meditation. Underline the parts of your journey that had a lucid or special energy for you. You might have experienced sensations of falling or flying in the tunnel. You might have seen energy pulses, light, or brilliant colors. You might have sensed the essence of your animal when you looked into its eyes. Maybe you experienced a different state of consciousness when your animal shared with you some of its knowledge and power.

Lastly, do Inner Dialogue on your meditation, speaking as your animal ally and then as yourself. This dialogue will amplify the benefits and insights of your experience. Inner Dialogue, together with this meditation, will help you to incubate a lucid dream.

7

Gifts from the Artist Within

"Playing the Music of My Soul"

"I hear beautiful music playing. I discover it is coming from a medieval lute. I realize that I am playing this wonderful instrument myself. I am playing, not with my hands, but with my entire body, rhythmically brushing across the strings, creating beautiful music.

As I continue to play, the music becomes more and more complex, like a classical opus, with a rich overlay of uplifting melodies and rhythms. Now I am dancing and playing at the same time—playing the music with every movement of my body. The music comes through me, and I am filled with its beauty and joy."

Imagine what it would be like to tap the wellspring of your creativity—shaping your visions, desires and inner music into artistic expressions that you and others could see, hear and feel.

Like the dreamer quoted above, "playing the music of my soul" can symbolize getting fully in touch with your own creative power. Your subconscious can inspire you to express yourself in new and creative ways that involve *your whole being*—conscious and subconscious—so that you can "dance and play at the same time." The lute, as a symbol for the subconscious, conveys a message:

> "The more you play me and let me resonate through you,
> the more beautiful and joyful is the music we make together."

In this chapter, I invite you to discover the artist who resides in the wellspring of all creativity—your subconscious. Everything you see, hear, and feel in Inner Dialogue, Lucid Fantasy and self-hypnosis is a gift from your subconscious. This gift can serve as a source of unique and inspiring artistic ideas, fascinating symbols and stories, and ingenious solutions to problems. You will learn how easy it is to turn a dream or symbol into *art*—a montage, a dream poem, and a dream story.

The idea that we receive gifts of creativity and insight through our dreams and visions is not a new one. For thousands of years, American Indian tribes, as well as many cultures throughout the world, have shared a deep respect for the wisdom and creativity that their "guides" and "allies" give them, both dreaming and awake. Tribal artists use the inspiration of their dreams and visions to create beautiful designs and symbolic images. Young adults go on vision quests seeking a dream that will direct them toward their life's work. Dreams and visions provide songs, ritual, and dances that contribute to the identity and well-being of the individual and community. Even decisions regarding planting crops, finding and using medicinal herbs, and designing villages are influenced by the wisdom of dreams and visions.

HARNESS YOUR CREATIVITY

Like an artist in a tribal culture, you too can use the raw imagery and emotional energy of your subconscious to create beautiful artistic expressions. Whether you think of yourself as artistic or not, when you allow your subconscious to guide you in expressing your deeper self, you will be startled by the extent of your own creativity. You will enjoy a warm sense of satisfaction when you view your own artistic expressions—and you'll be very pleasantly reminded of your inner allies and subconscious resources every time you do.

You will be surprised at how easy and enjoyable creating art from your subconscious resources and symbols can be. And at the same time, you will discover that the process involves a very pleasant hypnotic experience. In fact, art that reflects your subconscious symbols and feelings is very therapeutic, as well as expressive. Because deep emotions and experiences are often condensed into a single image, word or sensation in a dream or hypnotic state, this kind of art often provides healing insights as well as great satisfaction.

The Senoi Tribe of Malaysia, and many other cultures who recognize the importance of dreams, encourage dreamers to *bring back a gift or creative product* that they can share with their community. Many times, this gift is a song, a story, a dance or a visual design. In cultures such as these, every dreamer is regarded as an artist—and every dream gift is given high value. Many tribal songs, dances, prayers and rituals come from dreams and are shared over and over again, with great respect and reverence, because these gifts are regarded as a means of gaining power and wisdom. This custom demonstrates that symbols and dreams are valuable for more than personal healing and expression: they can provide meaning and enjoyment to friends and community as well.

Your creativity can be a source of wonder and inspiration.

For centuries, artists and storytellers in all cultures have sought creative inspiration from their dreams and subconscious. The English poet Samuel Taylor Coleridge dreamed his famous poem *Kubla Khan* and awoke able to write it, in verse, already completed. Another well-known author who used dreams for inspiration is Robert Louis Stevenson. Stevenson imagined his subconscious as filled with creative storytellers whom he called his "Brownies." He credited his subconscious helpers with giving him "better tales than he could fashion for himself."

Many composers have used dreams to inspire their music. Giuseppe Tartini, an Italian violinist and composer, dreamed that he was curious about what kind of a musician the Devil was. He gave his violin to the Devil, and the Devil played a spellbinding solo. Upon awakening, Tartini recreated his dream music. The result was *The Devil's Trill*, one of his best compositions. Ironically, Tartini always regretted that his creation did not nearly recapture the beauty of the *Devil's Trill* in his dream.

Like many well-known artists, you, too, can create poems, stories, and visual art based on your dreams, Inner Dialogues and Lucid Fantasies. Your creative expressions will give you enjoyment and satisfaction for a long time.

ENCOURAGE THE ARTIST WITHIN

In the quick pace of modern life, we often forget to value the artist within us. When it is someone's birthday, we buy a card. As adults we generally do not take the time to make a card, decorate it, and write a personal message on it. Somehow our own art does not seem good enough, so we choose something someone else made instead.

Children do not stop to ask themselves, "Can I create art? Am I an artist?" A child's simple, colorful drawings of trees and flowers, or her playful songs and dances, are a natural, joyful self-expression. As adults, we are charmed by what children express with so much heart and soul. Many times we are awed by the simple beauty that a child can create.

When it is Mommy's or Daddy's birthday, children enjoy making a birthday card to give, perhaps drawing a heart on the cover and writing a simple, loving message. As parents, we treasure these gifts from our children. We recognize them as meaningful expressions of our child's uniqueness and love. And a child who makes such art gains satisfaction and self-esteem from sharing his or her gift.

Like children's art, dream art is a meaningful reflection of your unique self. Every one can harness the creativity of the artist within. Art from your subconscious will provide you with great enjoyment and a meaningful way to share your gift.

VISUAL ART

Like the artist whose pottery design is dream-inspired, the architect whose daydreams suggest plans for buildings and cities, or the painter whose rich subconscious imagery graces her canvas, you can capture the special power of your subconscious and transform it into visual art.

Creating a dream montage is a natural activity for children, but it is also a favorite for adults attending my workshops, and is long-remembered by them. Many say that making a dream montage was one of the most meaningful experiences of their lives—a special time in which they could celebrate their own creativity and subconscious wisdom, giving it a tangible form, as art. People often tell me that this experience was the first time they felt like an artist or realized they could create something beautiful and self-affirming.

Many people begin this project with a lack of confidence in their artistic ability. But within minutes, they are absorbed in the simple and enjoyable process of cutting pictures out of magazines. Soon, they are happily arranging the pictures on a piece of paper and gluing them down. Later, everyone is amazed by the creativity of their dream montage.

Carl came to a workshop firmly believing he had no artistic ability whatsoever. I encouraged him to make a dream montage as an experiment. I assured him that he would not have to draw or paint. All he had to do was look through magazines and choose pictures that "spoke" to him. After a few minutes, Carl was quite involved in this activity, which often becomes an enjoyable meditation. After about an hour, Carl had gathered a sizeable collection of symbolic images.

Next, I asked Carl to place his pictures on a large piece of paper. He could take as much time as he needed, while allowing his subconscious to guide him in choosing the placement of each image.

It didn't take Carl long to place a large picture of a smiling baby at the top left corner. Then he put a picture of a man, looking "cool" in sunglasses, at the top right corner. This picture also contained a few words Carl thought were significant: "Self-deception, a little can help." The man's sunglasses reflected only sky and clouds, seeming to hide him.

In the center of the paper, Carl placed a picture of a young boy with an angry expression and his fist clenched. Nearby, a picture of a beautiful woman emerging naked from the water. Filling the space between the key symbols were pictures of three polar bears swimming in the ocean and a beautiful view of snow-covered mountains.

At the bottom left corner, a picture of an old bearded hermit in his mountain cabin. Near the old man, an image of footprints in the snow. To the right of that, a picture of twin girls playing tug-of-war and another winter scene of an outdoor ice rink crowded with skaters. And lastly, at the bottom right corner, a man Carl's age bodysurfing a wave.

Now Carl's montage was complete: a tableau of imagery that suggested his most personal feelings in a new way—as art. Carl was tremendously proud of his dream montage.

Carl said he did not know, while making his montage, why he chose certain symbols or images. He simply knew that they "felt right." After contemplating his symbols and their relationships, Carl told me that he thought he understood what the montage meant to him.

In his montage, there were many *images of men at different stages in life*, which Carl felt symbolized himself at different ages—past, present and future. He thought there was a strong contrast between the image of the angry boy and the man appearing "cool" in sunglasses; and also between the old man sitting alone and the younger man bodysurfing the wave. These contrasts seemed to suggest questions Carl had about how to live his life. He said that sometimes he felt reluctant to get involved in the unpredictable flow of life (like the angry boy and the man in the wave). He wondered, was it better to remain aloof and separate? (Like the man appearing "cool" and detached, or the old hermit living alone.)

Carl's montage, with its many images of water, trees, and snow, also expressed his love of nature and the outdoors The water, especially, was important to Carl as a symbol for his emotions—and swimming in it (*the woman, the man in the wave, and the three polar bears*) represented his desire for emotional balance.

The beautiful woman emerging from the water was another key symbol, reminding Carl of his need for a satisfying connection with a woman. Her nakedness as she rises from the water suggested to him both sensuality and a timeless, goddess-like quality. Her image, and that of the twin girls playing, also reflected Carl's need to be more in connection with his inner feminine.

The many interrelationships of the symbols in his dream montage were a source of great interest and satisfaction to Carl. He told me that the montage had helped him learn a lot about his symbols and himself. Later, he displayed it prominently in his home, so he could continue to enjoy it and share it with others.

Like Carl, you will find that creating art from your subconscious is both satisfying and therapeutic. As you continue to use Inner Dialogue, Lucid

Fantasy, and self-hypnosis, you will find that your subconscious is continually inspiring art—and your artistic expressions will serve as happy reminders of the confidence and insight you have gained.

As time goes by, you will probably notice and appreciate additional insights and messages in your art. Whether it is a dream montage, dream poem, story, song, or another creative product, you may get fresh inspiration as your art resonates with new experiences and learnings. The same is true of the people with whom you share your creative products. Every person will respond to your art according to their own subconscious, receiving the message they need at that moment.

I encourage you to let your inner artist, as well as your inner child, emerge and revel in the natural, creative artistry within you. *(For further instructions on creating a dream montage, see Exercise 1 in this chapter.)*

DREAM POEMS

Another enjoyable way to create art from your subconscious is through writing a dream poem. *Dream poems* express in lasting form a helpful and healing message you have received from your subconscious—so that it can be enjoyed over and over again.

The subconscious and art have a close relationship: they both speak to you on a condensed, symbolic level—beyond what you can see, say with words, and feel with your senses. For this reason, symbols and dreams translate very naturally into poems.

When you write a dream poem, you turn the lesson of your dream or waking dream into a gift. Writing a dream poem helps you to enjoy and strengthen the bridge between your conscious and subconscious.

Your dream poems can be simple, following no set form—expressing the emotion, action, or insight of a special experience or dream. Or, you can style your dream poems after the Japanese *haiku*. Haikus are special poems in which meaning is condensed into very few words. They are impressionistic, creating bold strokes that evoke strong feelings with an economy of images.

Capture the transforming or healing message of your dream or Lucid Fantasy in your haiku. You can also repeat (or sing) your haiku to yourself, because they make excellent affirmations or mantras.

(See Exercise 2 for further directions on writing a dream haiku or poem.)

FREEDOM RIDES ON STRENGTH

Even a nightmare can be transformed into a powerful dream poem or haiku. You may remember my lucid nightmare *(Chapter 6)*, in which a Woman on Horseback, who looked very much like me, stabbed me in the heart. You might ask, "How could such a nightmare become an enjoyable, artistic poem?"

In my Inner Dialogue, I listened attentively to the Woman's message, delivered now in words, rather than in action:

> "I am trying to *open your heart.* You need to learn to trust the primal, instinctive forces inside you—and let them out. Your pain comes from resisting and fearing me. Trust in what will happen when you let your heart open—and your life force flows freely into the world."

In my Lucid Fantasy:

> I jump up on the horse behind her and ride off to meet her tribe—people who live simply, close to the earth, with open hearts. These are people who express their passion for life every day in their relationships, their work and their art. From them I will learn many things.

Through this dream, my subconscious was pushing me toward more directness and vitality in my life. After I understood the message, I wanted to write a haiku that would capture my dream's startling and passionate energy. Perhaps the most powerful haiku I've written, the message resonates for me every time I read it:

> *Trust heart's fierce pleasure*
> *life pierces limitation*
> *freedom rides on strength*

Another haiku was written by one of my students after she used Inner Dialogue and Lucid Fantasy to explore a relationship as a waking dream. The conflict she experienced with her boyfriend, she discovered, was also being played out *in her own subconscious* between the passionate and spiritual parts of herself. In her haiku, she expressed what she had learned: she could have both passion and spirituality in her life, and in the process be more whole:

> *Love's healing vision*
> *passion and spirit marry*
> *nature's way restored*

The next haiku is based on a dream in which the dreamer is swept up by a tornado—putting him at its mercy. When he did Inner Dialogue, the dreamer discovered that he could negotiate with the terrifying power of the tornado. By joining forces with the tornado, he could make it his ally and put it to work for his benefit. He realized that he could *ride the tornado*—a playful image reminiscent of riding a bronco or a tidal wave. As a result, he was able to experience change, not as a catastrophic force, but as an opportunity to grow:

> *Ride the tornado*
> *realize everything is change*
> *risk free as the wind*

Dream poems capture a moment of powerful insight and healing. Whether your dream poems follow a set form, like a haiku, or follow no form at all, you will discover your own unique style of perception and creative expression. Notice the rich diversity of styles that follow.

A woman reaches for the understanding of what her "dream lover" represents, as a symbol for a part of herself that she is learning to accept:

> *Dream lover—*
> *I love in you*
> *what I struggle to see in myself*
> *You are a reflection of me—*
> *our joyful embrace*
> *makes me whole*

A sense of wonder fills the dreamer when her masculine and feminine symbols, which seemed forever in conflict, make peace. For the first time, these parts of the dreamer come into a friendly alliance:

> *The man is gentle*
> *The woman is whole*
> *The voices are still*
> *sweet sweet sweet sweet sweet*

The next poem begins with the drama and fear of a nightmarish dream, a confrontation between the dreamer and an armed intruder. Even the water faucets in the dream are disturbing—twisted and distorted so they cannot function. After the first few lines, though, the poem takes a surprising turn, revealing the dreamer's Lucid Fantasy:

It was a silver pistol,
gleaming like a mirror.
He took it out of a drawer
where it had lain hidden for years.
He aimed it at me and rather than run,
I said, "Shoot me, please."
The bullet entered me—and dissolved.
It was the silver bullet of Truth
diffusing in me its life-giving light.

And later I found the water taps in my bathroom
were twisted out of shape,
so I put the pistol in their place.
And now I have Truth on tap, whenever I want it!
I turned, and my perfect lover appeared.
We drank Truth together
out of a silver cup,
and when we made love
all of me responded for the first time.
Then, holding me safe and serene in his arms,
he gave me the gift of Clarity.

The magic of a "dream visit" with a loved one who has died is captured by this poem:

The air jumps with rare morning brightness.
Nana sits under a tree at a rough wooden table,
and I realize she is waiting for us.
Around her animals saunter slowly in the meadow
and green tendrils wind around the table's legs.
She, too, seems to have grown out of the earth.
Her face glows youthfully pink, relieved of all cares.
Her youth has returned like another spring.
The table sits atilt on tree roots
and I wonder if she's waited here a long time.
I bring you to her—
this refuge and ally through the years—
sweet giver of blessings.

WEAVING A DREAM STORY

A dream story weaves several dreams (or waking dreams) together into one unified Lucid Fantasy. Another way in which you can enjoy creating art from your subconscious, writing a dream story is a more extensive application of the Lucid Fantasy. There is no limit to how creative you can be.

In my workshops, students find the process of writing their dream stories deeply inspiring. To write a dream story, select three dreams with similar symbols or interrelated themes. To unify these three dreams, look for *key words, common symbols, contrasts, and universal themes.* This process is fascinating in itself—because it reveals the special logic of your subconscious. Paradoxically, you are using your conscious mind to identify the symbols and themes in your subconscious. You are making visible to your conscious mind the amazing logic your subconscious uses to select symbols and create intricate relationships among them.

Three dreams from the same night provide a rewarding opportunity for Weaving a Dream Story. You have as many as five dreams per night, and they are always related to each other—even when they do not appear to be. As though your subconscious is trying out different ways to approach and solve a question or problem, it may use very different symbols in each dream. Often the last dream of the night will clarify or resolve what the earlier dreams have explored.

Writing a dream story is not only an artful expression of your subconscious wisdom. It also serves as a powerful incubation for lucid dreaming. As you gain more lucidity, you will find that the dreams you have in a single night will often blend into one long story. Each scene or episode of the story will be one dream. In your dream story, you will discover the way each successive dream can take you deeper, gradually making the message clearer, and leading you to a specific insight.

To weave her dream story, one of my students, Sylvia, chose three dreams that occurred the same night:

1. Her younger sister gives birth
2. Her grandmother plans to remarry
3. She is dressed in a white gown and preparing
   for a special event

Sylvia followed the Guidelines for Weaving a Dream Story *(described fully in Exercise 3).* She began by recounting her dreams *(Step 1):*

Dream #1: I watch as my younger sister squats near the ground and gives birth. The baby easily drops out of her. As soon as he hits the ground, the baby starts moving with intelligence.

The baby crawls away, as though he has things to do. But he doesn't look at all like a human baby. He looks like a white skeletal being, kind of eerie.

After about an hour, he has grown to be 18 years old. Now he looks human. He is tall, handsome and swarthy. I have a deep feeling for him and he for me.

Dream #2: My 80 year old grandmother is about to remarry. I am surprised, since both she and her fiance' are quite elderly. Her fiance' owns an ancient house where everyone meets to celebrate their engagement. It looks like a 16th century ship—old wood, books, sculpture, bevelled glass windows. It is astonishing. Later I see the ship is almost hidden inside a modern, high-tech shopping center. It is right at the core of the modern buildings.

Dream #3: I am with several other women. Someone uses magic to transform our clothes into gowns. A special event is about to take place. First, I notice my shoes are different—they have brown buckles, like Pilgrims' shoes, which I've always wanted. Then suddenly I'm wearing a stunning white gown. It is like a medieval dress, with flowing veils and a red jewel trim. I feel beautiful. I notice the other young women dressed in white too. I am full of anticipation, waiting for the special event.

If you did not notice any similarities among these dreams at first glance, look again. Recognizing the patterns connecting these dreams will probably involve a different style of perceiving than you normally use.

Sylvia underlined what she considered to be the **key words or symbols** in each of her three dreams *(Step 2):*

> *Birth, white, eerie, deep feeling, marriage,*
> *celebration, anticipation, women, special event.*

The **similar symbols and elements** *(Step 3)* in Sylvia's three dreams would be:

• *White:*

Dream #1: The baby as a white being

Dream #2: The marriage suggests white, as well as the *implied* white-haired grandma

Dream #3: The white gown for the special event

- *Something New Happens:*

  Dream #1: New baby

  Dream #2: New husband

  Dream #3: New dress and a new experience

- *Experiences of Astonishment or Wonder:*

  Dream #1: Unusual birth and unusual baby

  Dream #2: Announcement of plans for marriage

  Dream #3: Anticipation of special event

- *Women:*

  Dream #1: Sister

  Dream #2: Grandma

  Dream #3: Dreamer is in a group of women

- *Eerie Quality, Which Contrasts Old and New:*

  Dream #1: Baby's rapid growth to maturity

  Dream #2: The ancient houseboat contrasted with the modern shopping mall; Grandma's *implied* rejuvenation

  Dream #3: Pilgrim's shoes and medieval gown

Next, contemplating her dreams from a broader perspective, Sylvia looked for **universal or mythic themes** *(Step 4)*. After thinking about it, she realized that each of her dreams seemed to involve a **rite of passage:**

> Dream #1: *Birth*
> Dream #2: *Marriage*
> Dream #3: *Initiation*

Sylvia also noted the **contrasts** in each of her dreams. *(Step 5)*

Dream #1:

> Baby - adult
> Normal awareness - super awareness
> Easy - difficult
> Dependence (baby) - independence (adult)
> Short time - long time
> Male - female

Dream #2:

> Handmade - high-tech
> Ancient - modern
> Core - surface
> Young - old
> Inner - outer
> Male - female

Dream #3:

> New - old
> Utilitarian (pilgrim shoes) - elegant (gown)
> Ordinary - extraordinary (magic)
> Women - men
> Past - present

Sylvia considered how her three separate dreams might be telling *one continuous* story. *(Step 6)* She realized that her dream story would be shaped by the rites of passage which tied her dreams together:

> *Birth and rebirth,*
> *renewal and transformation,*
> *initiation and fertility.*

Now Sylvia was ready for the final step: create a Lucid Fantasy that integrates *all of the dreams* into an empowering adventure. *(Step 7)* This multi-leveled Lucid Fantasy amplifies the benefits of a single Lucid Fantasy many times over.

Sylvia did not know in advance just how her three dreams would become one unified story. She invited her subconscious to suggest the images and actions, spontaneously weaving her dreams into a three-part adventure that overflowed with magic, fantastic images and joy. Afterwards, she gave her story a title:

"THE UNION"

I am in a forest. I squat down, Indian-style, close to the ground. I give birth. The baby comes out easily. I can see immediately that he is very aware and intelligent. He looks at me with acknowledgment—I am important to him, but I've got to let him be independent. He has things to do, and then he will return. I let him go, trusting our bond.

In an hour he returns, a mature young man. He has shed his white cover, and his bronze skin seems to shine and radiate a special energy. His name is Morgan.

He takes me to his place of power, an ancient ship sunken into the earth. We go through a secret subterranean passage to get there.

Inside the ship, I sense the vessel's power and realize that it is charged by the earth's energy. It is a place to meditate and renew ourselves. The ship also has the special ability to move through solid matter and transcend time. In this vessel we can travel in the earth or sky, into the past or future, and into other realities. Together, we will make many journeys of discovery.

Next, I am back on the surface, in the forest. I and several young women are dressed in white. We are about to be initiated in a ceremony that recognizes our coming into power as women, a ceremony that celebrates our fertility. We understand that we can use this energy to bear children as well as to be fertile creatively. We will be helping others to harness their power and fertility, also. We have a great feeling of camaraderie and joy.

After the ceremony, Morgan and I bring the ship to the surface and everyone comes aboard to celebrate. The ship is flying. Everyone is laughing and dancing.

Morgan and I dance together. I look deeply into his blue eyes. He smiles and gives me a ruby ring. The large red stone emanates power. He tells me that his gift acknowledges our deep bond, our likeness, and our love.

I put the ring on my right index finger. I realize that it enables me to feel his strength whenever I need it. I can also use it to call on him for help. I feel a tremendous surge from our combined energies. I am deeply happy that we are allies.

Exercises For
Your Subconscious

EXERCISE 1
Creating a Dream Montage

Begin creating a Dream Montage this week. Look through magazines for images that remind you of your symbols and dreams. Collect these images for a few weeks, until you have ten, twenty or thirty of them.

WHAT TO DO: Place your images randomly on a large piece of paper or posterboard. Enhance your creativity by doing a short self-hypnosis meditation:

> Allow yourself to relax and enter a meditative frame of mind in which you can gain access to your right-brain wisdom and ability to recognize patterns. Now look at the images you have collected. Are you drawn to certain key images? If so, place them in a few different positions on the paper and check with your own intuition as to which positions look or feel "right." Now, select some other images and do the same process—try them in a few different positions, relative to the key images, and notice which positions look or feel "right."
>
> Allow as much time as you need to create your dream montage. Most people take one or two hours to create an arrangement that satisfies them. This process can be deeply enjoyable and rewarding. You may gain many new insights.

When you are fully satisfied with your dream montage arrangement, glue the images into place. Then find a special place to display your dream montage—where you can look at it and meditate on it. Enjoy your dream montage as art—a beautiful expression of your unique creativity and inner wisdom.

Your dream montage creates a bridge between your conscious and subconscious awareness. It is a tangible expression of the helpful guidance you are receiving from your subconscious.

EXERCISE 2
Writing a Dream Poem or Haiku

It is a short step from dreaming to artistic creativity—because both use the vast imaginative resources of your subconscious. Writing a dream poem gives you the chance to appreciate the new awareness and integration your subconscious has provided. Your dream poem also reflects who you are in a very personal and creative way.

After doing Inner Dialogue and Lucid Fantasy, meditate on the symbols and messages your subconscious has sent you. Do a short self-hypnosis meditation and enter into a meditative, relaxed, frame of mind. While writing your poem, be careful not to criticize or edit yourself. You cannot create and judge what you do at the same time! Don't worry about how "good" your poem is or if it makes sense. *It doesn't have to make sense—it's art!*

Style and perfection are not the goals of this exercise. Give yourself permission to write your dream poem in your own way. You may want to capture your dream's lucid understanding, high energy, or healing. Or you may choose to express your dream's special message in terms of a new way of seeing, hearing, or feeling. Often, simply describing the dream will convey the power and poetic beauty of your experience.

WHAT TO DO: In a relaxed and meditative (right-brain) state, you will find this process enjoyable and intriguing. Take a few deep breaths, close your eyes, and get in touch with the enjoyment and healing you felt in your Lucid Fantasy or dream. Now come back and write down the key words that describe your experience. Whether you are writing a free verse poem (without a set form) or a haiku, take your time and experiment with the images, sensations and words, trying several different possibilities before deciding which one may best express the special experience you want to capture in your poem.

Guidelines for Writing a Dream Haiku

1. Write down key words from your Lucid Fantasy or dream—significant symbols, feelings, and actions. Traditionally, haikus use descriptive words that produce a mood and a "picture," often referring to light conditions, the weather and the season. For your dream haiku, you may want to choose words, feelings or images that describe an important ally, as well as any lucid cues you experienced.

2. Arrange your words on three lines. There are only 17 syllables in this poem artform, so you will need to pare your lines down to the barest essentials. The first line is 5 syllables, the second line 7 syllables, and the third line 5 syllables.

3. Since a haiku is only three brief lines, it is best to make your haiku a clear-cut *picture* of a symbol, a feeling, or an insight. Like a Zen ink sketch, your haiku consists only of a few bold strokes—and the rest of the picture is implied.

4. Feel free to experiment and play with your key words, moving them around, even putting words together that are not normally paired or don't make rational sense.

5. Your finished haiku will have a pleasant rhythm when said aloud. It will also evoke the special feeling and new awareness you experienced in your dream or Lucid Fantasy. You can say your haiku as a mantra—and use it to focus your attention and reinforce the insight you have received. Repeating your haiku while in self-hypnosis and meditation is also very enjoyable.

When you are done, give your dream poem or haiku a title. You may want to illustrate it with an image or a montage of images that captures its feeling. Include your dream poems and haikus in your Lucid Storybook.

EXERCISE 3
Weaving Your Dream Story

Weaving a Dream Story will give you an exciting experience of the subconscious logic operating in every symbol.

Mythologist Joseph Campbell has said that stories can teach you how to "follow your bliss." Like the universal myths which Campbell explored and shared, your dream story will liberate deep subconscious resources of creativity, insight, and joy. There is no limit to how creative and fantastic your dream story can be.

WHAT TO DO: Weaving three dreams into one Lucid Fantasy will reveal the special logic of your subconscious. The helpful message encoded in each of your dreams will be enhanced by your Dream Story. Follow these guidelines:

Weaving A Dream Story

1. Choose two or three different dreams or waking dreams which have similar symbols or themes. They may be:

- Three dreams from the same night, even when they seem to have little or no relationship to each other

- Three dreams from different nights
- Three waking dream experiences (Make certain these are experiences you now have a good feeling about, where any conflict has been resolved in an Inner Dialogue and Lucid Fantasy)
- Three Lucid Fantasies

2. Underline what you consider to be the *key words and key symbols in each dream*. (These key symbols may be a person, animal, place, event, color, object, emotion or feeling.) In your journal, list all the words and symbols you have underlined which seem important:

Dream #1:
Dream #2:
Dream #3:

3. What *similar symbols or elements* do these three dreams share? (For instance, a similar person; a sense of anticipation, celebration or newness; or a certain color that appears as a key symbol.) List similar symbols and elements:

Dream #1:
Dream #2:
Dream #3:

4. What *universal or mythic themes* do you notice in your dreams? Is there a *rite of passage* involved? (For example, birth, graduation, coming of age, marriage, or reunion.) Write down any and all themes that may be present:

Dream #1:
Dream #2:
Dream #3:

5. What *contrasts* —such as young and old, male and female, easy or difficult, dependent or independent—stand out to you? List contrasts for each dream:

Dream #1:
Dream #2:
Dream #3:

6. Now try a different perspective: consider your dreams as episodes in *one continuous story.* What is the story being told in these three episodes? What is the thread that ties them together? Ask yourself these questions, but don't try to figure it out with your conscious mind—*let your subconscious provide the answer.*

7. Create a Lucid Fantasy that integrates your dreams into a unified and empowering dream adventure. Remember that your Lucid Fantasy can be magical and fantastic—unlike your everyday experience. This is your chance to do anything you want! Let your subconscious guide you and suggest the dream story to you. Trust what comes, even if it doesn't make sense at first. Write your Dream Story down *as you imagine it,* or speak it aloud to a friend or into a tape recorder.

CONCLUSION

Personal Myths
for Lucid Living

"Lightning is All Around Me"

> *"I'm in a magical room. Lightning is flashing all around me, and I am awestruck as I watch it. The power and light of the flashes are quite beautiful and I don't feel I'm in any danger. Soon, I notice that the lightning is changing. Now it is flashing all around me in an array of brilliant colors! I am filled with rapturous joy and wonder at the beauty of this light. Then I suddenly realize—the lightning is flashing from inside me! All of this beautiful light is coming from my core. The rainbow-colored lightning is really a joyful and powerful part of me."*

There is a story that is told all around the world, in every culture. A Hero goes on a journey of discovery. The Hero's courage and ability are tested by tremendous obstacles and difficulties. In the end, the Hero is victorious. Returning home, the Hero learns that his or her struggles have been a preparation to perform a service in the world that only the Hero can do.

The subconscious connects us intimately with universal stories and myths. We are all myth-makers. According to mythologist Joseph Campbell, we are creating and participating in myth every day of our lives. He defines myth as "the secret opening through which the inexhaustible energies of the cosmos pour into human culture."

Whether dreaming or awake, each of us is like a mythic Hero. Each of us faces challenges, is tested by fear, and is given opportunities to learn lessons that would improve the quality of our lives. Everyone possesses a *personal myth or hero's story* which gives structure and meaning to life events, subconscious blueprints and personal symbols.

Every hero makes a journey of self-discovery. And just as a mythical hero makes his or her journey into the unknown, so your journey through the various challenges of life can be regarded as part of the hero's universal experience. In these terms, *your life is a story,* a myth in the making.

> *You* are the Hero of your own story. Right now your path might be straight and easy—or maybe it is windy and steep. Like a questing knight in search of the elusive grail, perhaps you are uncertain of your direction, as though you are travelling through the thickest and darkest part of a forest. Like the Hero, your courage and determination may waver, but you know you must continue on, with faith that you will find your way.

In mythology, the Hero's struggle always has a higher purpose.

> The tasks you must complete, the fears you need to overcome and even the pain you must endure, are difficulties that are indispensable parts of your Hero's journey. The completion of your journey brings you at last to experience yourself and your world more clearly and compassionately. You discover the unique place in the universe which is yours—and the special contribution you can make to friends, family, and the world at large.

You are on a hero's journey to discover who you are. This journey often leads you to discover *powerful blueprints and symbols* which, like the grail of the Arthurian legend, bring you an awareness that you are much more than you conceived yourself to be.

The lightning symbol in my dream, quoted above, expressed a mythical theme for me—a highly-charged moment in which I realized that much of what I see in the world I see through the lens of *my relationship to myself and my subconscious.* In the dream, I have a Hero's revelation when I realize that the magic, wonder and beauty of the lightning *comes from inside me.*

There is "lightning" inside of *you,* as well. In your subconscious there is tremendous energy, ready to be put to use. You are gifted with a colorful array of talents and abilities, just waiting for a chance to come out.

THE ONE GREAT MYTH

Joseph Campbell sums up the Hero's journey:

> "We have only to follow the thread of the hero-path. And where we had thought to find an abomination, we shall find a god; where we had thought to slay another, we shall slay ourselves; where we had thought to travel outward, we shall come to the center of our own existence; where we had thought to be alone, we shall be with all the world."

By embracing your subconscious, you gain a different way of seeing and experiencing—an expanded perception that opens a doorway, not only to lucid dreams, but also to the mythic dimension. As in lucid dreams, you see yourself or others with new eyes; your senses awaken and grasp an experience more fully than ever before; suddenly, you find your ears are open to hear with a deeper understanding.

> Like the Mythic Hero, you return from your journey with more confidence in your ability and more willingness to meet the challenges that arise. You have gained a stronger sense of self and a clearer perspective of your life. The grand purpose, spiritual mission and meaning of your life has been revealed.

BLACK ELK'S GREAT VISION

Everyone has a different way of seeking, and finding, the mythic or spiritual experience. Many feel it in a church or synagogue, while others sense it in a quiet place at home, under a tree, in the presence of loved ones, at ceremonies and rituals, or alone on a mountain. In every form, the mythic dimension gives us the sense of a grand design and the guidance of an intelligence greater than our conscious identities. We experience a sense of timelessness or eternal time, which endows us with new vision and strength of purpose.

One of the most remarkable records of a mythic or spiritual awakening is told in the great vision of Black Elk, a warrior and medicine man of the Oglala Sioux. At the age of nine, Black Elk became seriously ill and, like many destined to become a shaman or spiritual leader, his near-death experience catapulted him into a vision that revealed to him not only his life's path, but also the future of his tribe for many years to come.

Black Elk's vision incorporates many of the characteristics of lucid dreaming, as well as the mythic quality of "seeing in a sacred manner." The lucid characteristics include flying, changes in the dreambody, vivid and powerful detail, clear understanding, and the lucid awareness that he was experiencing a spiritual revelation.

> In his great vision, Black Elk is summoned out of his sick bed and taken into the sky to a sacred meeting place—a flaming teepee with a rainbow door. He is introduced to the six Grandfathers who preside over the earth. There, a special ceremony takes place in which the Grandfathers give him his spiritual name, as well as gifts to increase his power as a leader. Then Black Elk goes on an amazing and elaborate journey to the "center" of the world—and himself. Along the way, he encounters scenes "so beautiful that nothing anywhere could keep from dancing.
>
> "And while I stood there, I saw more than I can tell and I understood more than I saw; for I was seeing in a sacred manner the shapes of all things in the spirit and the shape of all shapes as they must live together like one being."
>
> Upon awakening, Black Elk knew the role he was to play as a leader of his tribe.

Black Elk and other American Indians, as well as people of many other cultures, are taught to value the mythical and spiritual dimension. Western culture, however, values rational logic more highly than visionary guidance. Most of us are not encouraged to believe in visions and dreams. Nevertheless, we are each capable of having a *big dream*.

BIG DREAMS AND VISIONS

Big dreams encompass a vision and wisdom far beyond our usual dreams. They often seem to arrive at important transitions in life. Like a rite of passage such as coming of age, these dreams point the way to the next stage of growth and development. Big dreams hold a special energy and significance that transcends our normal perceptions and expectations. Although the dreams and visions we have may not be as elaborate as the great vision of Black Elk, they can be just as life-changing.

Black Elk's vision stayed with him his entire life. Even in old age, he pondered its meanings and repercussions, which unfolded slowly to him over many years. As though coming from a timeless source, great visions often picture a reality that is not based in the present. In many cases a vision is of a time that will not come into being for months or years. For example, my dream vision of someone holding a staff on a mountain put me on a new path almost immediately, influencing my decision to become a teacher. But about ten years went by before I understood the dream more clearly—when I found myself standing atop Bell Rock with a staff in my hand.

When you have a big dream, you can capture and express the wisdom of your vision in many ways: by exploring key symbols with Inner Dialogue and Lucid Fantasy; weaving a Dream Story; writing a Dream Haiku; creating a Dream Montage; or creating a personal song, dance, or ritual that captures the energy of your vision. Let the wisdom of your big dream guide your Hero's path and enrich your waking life.

THE ANSWERS JUST COME

Albert Einstein believed that a problem is never solved on the level on which it was created. To find answers to problems, Einstein described his creative process as thinking in images rather than words. He engaged in remarkable fantasies and daydreams, such as imagining what it would be like to ride a light beam into space. Rather than relying solely on logical analysis and the laws of physics as they were understood at the time, Einstein allowed his subconscious and his "illogical" fantasies to help him to formulate the theory of relativity which revolutionized modern physics.

Another scientist, Friedrich Kekulé, was frustrated for many years in his search for the molecular structure of benzene. He could not solve the problem with his conscious mind, on the level it had been created. Then he had a dream in which he saw a snake eating its own tail. Kekulé understood that the visual images of dreams condense knowledge into symbols. His dream image suggested to him the ringlike structure of a closed carbon molecule, a leap in understanding that enabled him to complete the formula for benzene and to revolutionize organic chemistry.

When he later made his report to a scientific conference, Kekulé surprised his colleagues with an account of his dream as the way in which he discovered the benzene formula. He further astounded them with his concluding remark,

"Let us learn to dream, gentlemen, and then
we may perhaps find the truth."

Like Einstein and Kekulé, you need to go beyond the framework within which a problem exists in order to harness the resources which can help you solve it. Your experiences with Inner Dialogue, Lucid Fantasy and self-hypnosis have shown you that your subconscious is always ready to give you a fresh perspective of yourself and your world. As you continue to use these practical tools to embrace your subconscious, you will experience more and more ease in moving beyond the sometimes limited level of rational answers—and you will enjoy the satisfaction of creating a solution that engages both your subconscious and conscious resources.

A LESSON IN HUMOR

Over the years, my symbols and dreams have given me many creative ideas, as well as practical guidance that has helped me to solve real-life problems.

A remarkable example of subconscious help came several years ago when I began to teach dream workshops. During my workshops, I realized that many people were frightened by the idea of getting to know their subconscious. Without realizing it, they were engaged in an inner battle: part of them wanted to know themselves more fully and part of them was afraid of what they might find out.

I was very serious about my subject and committed to teaching people how to understand and use their subconscious. However, something was lacking in my style. I needed to find a way to make a fascinating and useful subject more attractive, even to those who were afraid or skeptical. I mulled this problem over and couldn't solve it consciously. Within a few months, my subconscious responded with the solution. I dreamed:

> I am planning another dream workshop. I go by the meeting place to check that everything is ready. I see an announcement board with my name on it, announcing the workshop as scheduled. Then, I notice that instead of saying "Dream Workshop," the board says "Dream *Comedy* Workshop!" I am rather upset by this mistake, because I know that comedy is not involved in the "serious" subject of dreams.

When I awoke from this dream, it didn't take me long to figure out that I was being *too serious* when I gave presentations on the subconscious and dreams. "Dream Comedy," rather than being a mistake, was absolutely necessary! My subconscious was giving me a clear message: I needed to use humor to help people be more comfortable in learning about subconscious parts of themselves.

After this insight, I made a conscious effort to use humor, and it was as though a huge weight dropped away. Learning about the subconscious immediately became more enjoyable, for both my students and myself. Now, every time I share the humorous way in which symbols can reveal us to ourselves— as with the frantic dreamer whose "Golden Elevator" takes her into outer space—I find that people can laugh while they learn.

Decades after my childhood battle dreams, I was still learning from them: to arm myself with humor when facing difficult situations; and to balance my seriousness with humor—both in dreams and in life.

Significantly, my subconscious continued to teach me about humor in several other dreams. "Dream Comedy" was followed by a new dream theme: I was becoming friends with well-known comedians. In each dream, this relationship with a comedian expressed that I was becoming closer and more comfortable with the playful part of me. In one dream:

> Dudley Moore and I are both dressed in outlandish, comical clothes. We are playing baseball like two circus clowns—complete with jokes and pratfalls.

As a comedian and celebrity, Dudley Moore is a very talented, artistically sensitive, humorous and successful person.

As a *symbol*, Dudley Moore represents the potential to express my own talent, artistic ability, and playfulness. My comedian dreams gave me a chance to recognize and integrate my artistic talents and to see that, like Dudley Moore, I can succeed through an approach to life that incorporates both seriousness and humor.

PRACTICAL GUIDANCE

Symbols and dreams can remind you of unused or forgotten abilities. They offer practical guidance that encourages you toward your goals. A few years after my Dream Comedy revelation, my subconscious gave me guidance again about how to reach my students more effectively. In my dream:

> I am teaching my dream workshop. I give each student a booklet that I've written about the subconscious and dreams. My students are all very happy about it and tell me it is very helpful.

This simple dream inspired me to start writing down my theories about the subconscious. In the year that followed, I began giving my students a short workbook that included the Inner Dialogue and an explanation of the benefits of understanding symbols and dreams. Later, this workbook expanded to one hundred pages. Then it was supplemented by an advanced workbook. My students eagerly awaited each new piece, and I kept writing.

Through other symbols and dreams, my subconscious continued to draw me irresistibly toward my goal, reminding me and encouraging me to write and share my ideas. Then I had another powerful dream, which I titled "Dream Valentines:"

> I am leafing through some letters addressed to me. Many of them are from children who have learned from me how to work with their dreams. The children's notes are on simple little cards, like valentines. Some have a child's simple drawing on them, along with a touching message, saying how much the child liked learning from his or her dreams.
>
> One dream valentine says, "I laughed and cried, and laughed and cried..." Another is a picture a child has drawn, showing her flying in her dream, with the words, "I fly high, hey, ho!"
>
> I feel a profound sense of satisfaction as I continue looking through the notes. I find another card with a wonderful picture drawn on it—several animals, all flying as if in a dream: a raccoon, some other usually non-flying animals, a baby, and even the Gumby character. I lucidly realize that the picture is a wonderful representation of my inner allies, all taking off and joyously expressing themselves. I am very happy.

After "Dream Valentines," I decided to transform my workbook into a full-length book—this one.

Over time, The benefits of communicating with your subconscious will become more and more evident. Solutions to problems will present themselves to you in ways that your subconscious mind never anticipated, leading to a new understanding of yourself and others.

Your inner allies will become like trusted and valued friends, whose counsel you seek regularly, and whose company is always creative and entertaining. Their wise counsel will help you make the decisions, small and large, that take you onto one path or another. Whether you think of this guidance as practical or mythic, coming from a wise part of you or from a greater source, is up to you. What is important is that you take the time to *hear, feel and see* the signals your subconscious sends you, so that you can use its creative wisdom to help you maintain a healthy, satisfying life.

By doing the Exercises for Your Subconscious regularly, you will strengthen your inner resources and create blueprints for success that will give you greater enjoyment, freedom and lucidity—both dreaming and awake.

Embracing Your Subconscious has given you all the tools you need to create a partnership that will increase your vitality, improve your confidence, and help you achieve your goals.

LUCID LIVING

When your conscious and subconscious work together, you will enjoy not only lucid dreaming, but also *lucid living*. A cooperative balance between conscious and subconscious parts of you *(adult and inner child, masculine and feminine, powerful and gentle)* will very naturally lead to the same kind of balance and cooperation in your relationships with others. *Lucid living* means that you can communicate effectively with others, discovering common needs and forging powerful new alliances.

As in lucid dreams and Lucid Fantasies, living lucidly enables you to see the other person, group or country *clearly and compassionately*. You recognize your interdependence with other people and groups and are able to overcome fear of differences and fear of unknowns—this time in the world. Lucid living means that you take an active role, in your waking life, to bring your unique purpose and vision into being.

Just as all of your symbols are part of a larger whole, which is your total personality, so all people are part of a larger whole—part of a family, community, country, and world. We are all indispensable parts of a larger pattern. If you try to discard or ignore a single part, the whole pattern is affected. In world politics, world ecology, and science, this interdependence of all life is becoming more and more apparent.

Several of the recipients of the Nobel Peace Prize can be regarded as people who have *lived lucidly* in the face of difficult social issues—Mother Teresa, Mahatma Gandhi, and Martin Luther King, Jr., among others. These modern heroes have recognized the interdependence of all people and all life. Against great odds, they have followed their vision, living a *lucid waking dream*, helping to create opportunity instead of poverty, unity instead of war, and acceptance instead of oppression. Each of them is like a mythic Hero, struggling to achieve peace, equality and dignity for all people. By living lucidly, they inspire us to try to do the same.

Life presents each of us with a lucid choice: a path that leads to fear and division from ourselves and each other, or a path that leads to acceptance and strong alliances, both within ourselves and with others.

When you resolve your inner conflicts, you can resolve conflicts with others. When you see yourself clearly and compassionately, you can reach out to others with acceptance and love. When you truly embrace your subconscious, you bring the best of who you are into the world.

Readings and Resources

Buber, Martin. *The Way of Man*. Citadel Press, 1966.

Burns, David D. *Feeling Good*. Penguin Books, 1980.

Chopra, Deepak, *Quantum Healing*. Bantam Books, 1989.

Campbell, Joseph. *Hero With A Thousand Faces*. Princeton University Press, 1949.

_____, and Bill Moyers, Ed. *The Power of Myth*. Doubleday, 1988.

Epstein, Gerald. *Healing Visualizations: Creating Health Through Imagery*. Bantam Books, 1989.

Erickson, Milton. *Healing in Hypnosis*. Irvington Publishers, 1983.

_____, and Rossi, Ernest L. *The February Man*. Brunner/Mazel, Inc., 1989.

Faraday, Ann. *The Dream Game*. Harper & Row, 1974.

_____. *Dream Power*. Berkeley Publishing Corp., 1972.

Feldenkrais, Moshe. *Awareness Through Movement*. Harper & Row, 1977.

_____. *Body and Mature Behavior*. International Universities Press, Inc., 1975.

Gardner, Howard. *Creating Minds*. BasicBooks, 1993.

Garfield, Patricia. *Creative Dreaming*. Ballantine Books, 1974.

_____. *Pathway to Ecstasy*. Holt, Rinehart, Winston, 1979.

_____. *Your Child's Dreams*. Ballantine Books, 1984.

Gilligan, Stephen G. *Therapeutic Trances*. Brunner/Mazel, Inc., 1987.

Harner, Michael. *The Way of the Shaman*. Harper & Row, 1980.

Hilgard, Ernest R., and Hilgard, Josephine R. *Hypnosis in the Relief of Pain*. Kaufmann, 1983.

Horney, Karen. *Our Inner Conflicts*. W.W. Norton & Co., 1945.

_____. *Neurosis and Human Growth*. W.W. Norton & Co., 1950.

Jung, Carl G. *Man and His Symbols*. Dell, 1968.

_____. *Memories, Dreams, Reflections*. Random House, 1965.

_____. *Mandala Symbolism*. Princeton University Press, 1972.

Keirsey, David, and Bates, Marilyn. *Please Understand Me (Character and Temperament Types)*. Prometheus Nemesis Book Co., 1978.

Korn, Errol R., and Johnson, Karen. *Visualization: The Uses of Imagery in the Health Professions*. Dow Jones-Irwin, 1983.

LaBerge, Stephen. *Lucid Dreaming*. Ballantine, 1986.

Lame Deer, John, and Erdoes, Richard. *Lame Deer, Seeker of Visions*. Simon & Schuster, 1972.

Lowen, Alexander. *The Language of the Body*. Collier Books, 1971.

_____. *The Betrayal of the Body*. Collier Books, 1967.

Lyon, Bret. *Personal Power Program*. Medallion Books/Tidal Wave Press, 1986.

May, Rollo. *Love and Will*. W.W. Norton & Co., 1969.

McMullin, Rian E. *Handbook of Cognitive Therapy Techiques*. Penguin Books, 1986.

Mead, Margaret. *Male and Female: A Study of the Sexes in a Changing World*. William Morrow & Co., 1967.

Mills, Joyce, and Crowley, Richard, with Ryan, Margaret O. *Therapeutic Metaphors for Children and the Child Within*. Brunner/Mazel, Inc., 1986.

Moyers, Bill; Flowers, Betty Sue, Ed., and Grubin, David, Executive Ed. *Healing and the Mind, Conversations with Bill Moyers*. Doubleday, 1993.

Neihardt, John G. *Black Elk Speaks*. Simon & Schuster, Inc., 1959.

Paul, Jordan, and Paul, Margaret. *Do I Have to Give Up Me to be Loved By You?* CompCare, 1983.

Perls, Frederick. *Gestalt Therapy Verbatim*. Real People Press, 1969.

Restak, Richard. *The Brain*. Bantam Books, 1984.

Robbins, Anthony. *Unlimited Power*. Fawcett Columbine, 1987.

Rossi, Ernest L., and Cheek, David B. *Mind-Body Therapy*. W.W. Norton & Co., 1988.

Sacks, Oliver. *Awakenings*. E.P. Dutton, 1973.

_____. *The Man Who Mistook His Wife for A Hat*. Perennial Library, 1992.

Satir, Virginia. *Peoplemaking*. Science & Behavior Books, Inc., 1972.

Silva, Jose', and Goldman, Burt. *Silva Method of Mental Dynamics*. Simon & Schuster, Inc. 1988.

Simonton, O. Carl, and Simonton, Stephanie. *Getting Well Again*. Bantam Books, 1978.

Steiner, Claude. *Scripts People Live*. Bantam Books, 1974.

Steinem, Gloria. *Revolution From Within*. Little, Brown & Co., 1992.

Taylor, Jeremy. *Dream Work*. Paulist Press, 1983.

Tubesing, Donald A. *Kicking Your Stress Habits*. Whole Person Assoc., Inc., 1981.

Yankura, Joseph, and Dryden, Windy. *Doing RET: Albert Ellis in Action*. Springer Publishing Co., 1990.

Zdenek, Marilee. *The Right-Brain Experience*. MacGraw-Hill, 1983.

THE INNER DIALOGUE

Tear-out page

A process developed by Jenny Davidow, M.A. © 1982

Excerpted from *Embracing Your Subconscious*

1. Choose a dream, waking dream, or individual symbol *(one that inspires, puzzles or haunts you)*. We'll call this your "dream."
   a. Write the dream in your journal, in the present tense.
   b. List the main symbols, as well as unusual symbols.
   c. List the contrasts you notice: i.e., dark-light, big-small, confident-afraid, masculine-feminine, child-adult, etc. *(See Exercise 2.)*

2. Speak as the first symbol. (Begin with a symbol that is not you, the dreamer.) Say: "I am...(name of the symbol)" and describe yourself physically.

3. As the first symbol, complete these phrases:
   a. **"My job or function is..."**
   b. **"My unique qualities are..."**
   c. **"I am different from _____** *(another person, animal, object of the same category)* in that..."

Remember that in dreams, real people whom you know in waking life often symbolize aspects of your consciousness. If your symbol is a person, speak as that person in your Inner Dialogue. In addition, ask: **How do I characterize myself as a person? What is my personality like?** For example, "I'm the kind of person that never gives up," "I'm a terrific business person," "I'm very artistic," "I thrive on adventure," etc.

4. As the first symbol, **"What is happening from my point of view is..."**

5. As the first symbol, **"How I feel as this is happening is..."**

6. Repeat Steps 2 - 5 for another symbol in the dream. *(If you choose yourself as the second symbol, and if you are your "usual self" in the dream, skip this step and go on to Steps 7 & 8.)*

7. & 8. Let each symbol say, in turn, to the other symbol:
   a. **"How I feel about you is..."**
   b. **"My gripes toward you are..."**
   c. **"What I want to say to you is..."**

9. Develop a spontaneous dialogue between the symbols. Some suggestions:
   a. *Identify the Conflict:*
   > **"What I don't like about you is..."**
   > **"If it weren't for you I could..."**

   b. *Negotiate an Alliance:*
   > **"It would be easier to trust you/accept you if..."**
   > **"It would be easier for me to get closer to you if..."**
   > **"It would be easier to let you come closer to me if..."**
   > **"If you could be less _____(overpowering, etc.),**
   > **I could be more _____(friendly, etc.)"**

   c. *Define the Terms of Your Alliance:*
   > **"Let's make a deal: I will...**(do something specific for you) if **you will...**(do something specific for me)." Now check in with the other symbol to see if the "deal" is acceptable. Make certain the deal benefits *both* symbols.

Keep negotiating until you get specific agreement. If it is difficult to imagine a symbol's energy as valuable, try negotiating to *accept one molecule at a time*; **i.e., "By using one molecule of your energy or strength, I will be able to..."**
When you do not know how to begin to make a deal with a difficult symbol, or if you reach an impasse in your negotiations, it is helpful to go on to step 9-d before finishing with the "let's make a deal" step.

   d. *Resolution and Integration:*
   > **"What I like or value about you is..."**
   > **"I need you in order to..."**
   > **"If we could be allies and work together, we could..."**
   > **"By joining forces and using your _____(special quality or**
   > *strength)* **in my life, I can..."**

10. At this point or earlier, think about the ways in which your negotiation and alliance with your symbol can help you to resolve an inner conflict and be more effective with others. Notice in what ways your symbol(s) may picture, give voice to, or give you a grasp of specific situations and feelings in your waking life.

Think about the message or insight you have received on as many levels as possible, such as relationships, career, creativity, spirituality, health, and inner child.

(A process developed by Jenny Davidow, M.A. © 1982)

HYPNOTHERAPY AUDIOTAPES

by Jenny Davidow, M.A.

Hypnotic Meditations—guide you through experiences similar to those described in *Embracing Your Subconscious*. You will want to listen to these therapeutic tapes again and again. Each time you do, you will enjoy a comfortable, creative partnership with your subconscious.

1. Comfortable and Capable. *(Side A)* A deeply satisfying hypnotic meditation that will increase your energy and creativity. Helps you to relax, build confidence, and improve well-being.

Sweet Dreams. *(Side B)* A relaxing meditation to help you unwind just before bed, sleep restfully, and have pleasant dreams.

2. Meet Your Inner Child. *(Side A)* Visit the child part of you in a safe and comfortable place. Helps you to create a playful, loving, healing bond with your inner child.

Meet Your Future Self. *(Side B)* Meet the best possible "you," someone who has already accomplished many of your goals. Let your future self show you how to harness more confidence and improve any area of your life.

3. Taking Off With Lucid Fantasy. *(Side A)* Enjoy a Lucid Fantasy meditation that helps you transform any dream into a confident, creative adventure.

Meet Your Animal Ally. *(Side B)* Let this special helper or guide give you its instinctive wisdom and natural strength. Ask your ally a question, receive a message, and experience it helping you to achieve a goal.

4. Rhythms: Achieving Inner Balance. *(Side A)* A soothing, centering meditation when you are in the midst of changes or feeling unbalanced. Works on many levels at once to promote the natural rhythms and healing forces of the body, encouraging positive mental and emotional attitudes. Especially useful when you need to balance a busy schedule with rest and time for yourself.

Climbing Jacob's Ladder. *(Side B)* Travel through the "rungs of awareness" on the ladder inside you—your chakras. Connect more deeply with yourself, meet a loving inner guide and receive a healing message.

5. A Meditation for Weight Loss. *(Side A)* A comfortable meditation to help you achieve and maintain your ideal weight.

Negotiate with Your Inner Saboteur. *(Side B)* This guided exercise will help you to meet the hidden part of you that resists losing weight. You will discover its reasons and enlist its cooperation.

6. Achieve Your Goal. *(Side A)* Change a subconscious obstacle into an inner resource that will motivate, energize and inspire you to achieve your goal.

Hypnosis for Performance. *(Side B)* Feel confident and calm while speaking to groups. Prepare yourself mentally for a challenging situation or presentation. Bring added energy and inner resources with you—to get the results you want.

II. Seminars. Further explains many of the topics described in *Embracing Your Subconscious,* helping you to utilize the techniques more fully.

7. The Creative and Healing Power of Your Dreams. A dynamic introduction to the power of your dreams and subconscious. Includes a visualization and exercise that will help you increase dream recall and gain special insight from your dreams and meditations. Exciting live seminar. *One hour.*

8. Dream Visualizations. Increase access to your right brain and creativity. Includes three meditations and exercises that will encourage your dreams to be more vivid and lucid. Dialogue with your symbols and gain insight. *One hour.*

9. How to Do Inner Dialogue. Understand any symbol, from dreams or waking dreams. Learn practical steps to transform symbols into allies and resources that increase your energy and confidence. An exciting live-seminar demonstration. *One hour.*

10. How to Do Lucid Fantasy. Learn how to give healing and empowering alternatives to your subconscious. Create a Blueprint for Success that gives you more confidence, creativity and inner balance. Works as mental first-aid on both dreams and waking dreams. A dynamic live-seminar demonstration. *One hour.*

Hypnotherapy Audiotapes, $15 each.

Any three audiotapes for $40, six for $75.
All ten audiotapes for $110.

Please add $2.90 shipping per order.
California residents, please add CA sales tax.

Make checks payable to Jenny Davidow and mail to address below.
Indicate tape title and number.
Please include your name, address and phone number.
Allow 2-4 weeks for delivery.

Please write for a current list of Jenny Davidow's audiotapes
and a schedule of her workshops and speaking engagements
in Santa Cruz and the San Francisco Bay area.

Tidal Wave Press
Attention: Jenny Davidow

PATHWAYS TO INNER PEACE
336 36th St., #232
Bellingham, WA 98225
www.JennyDavidow.com

About the Author

Jenny Davidow has kept a daily and dream journal for twenty-five years. For more than fifteen years, she has offered workshops to help people use the creative power of the subconscious. Her unique approach—combining methods from Gestalt and Jungian psychology, hypnotherapy, shamanism, and lucid dreaming—quickly gained attention. She has been featured nationally on television and radio, as well as at health conventions and the Whole Life Expo.

Her interest in the subconscious began as a child, when Jenny had frequent nightmares. She was a soldier on a battlefield—with cannons firing, the enemy advancing, and little hope for survival. This dream plagued her for many years, and she could not figure out why.

At the time, Jenny could not have guessed that her nightmares were leading her into an area so exciting and creative that her career would be devoted to the subconscious.

While earning a Masters Degree in Psychology, Jenny developed specific steps to help herself and others to identify and understand the messages given in every symbol and dream. These steps became the *Inner Dialogue.*

In her workshops and with individual clients, Jenny observed that we are being influenced by the subconscious twenty-four hours a day, both dreaming and awake. Certain patterns and behaviors repeat again and again, often without our knowing why or how to change them. This realization led her to apply the Inner Dialogue to real-life events or *waking dreams*, as well as to the spontaneous lessons the subconscious gives us every night in dreams.

Born in Los Angeles, Jenny Davidow now lives in Santa Cruz, California, with her husband, Bret Lyon. She maintains a private practice, helping people of all ages to embrace their subconscious. She holds a Masters Degree in Psychology and a Doctorate in Clinical Hypnotherapy.

Living in a peaceful forest with a beautiful country garden, Jenny continues to plant seeds, write and fulfill her dreams.

Additional copies of *Embracing Your Subconscious* can be
purchased at any bookstore or directly from the publisher at:

Tidal Wave Press

PATHWAYS TO INNER PEACE
336 36th St., #232
Bellingham, WA 98225
www.JennyDavidow.com

Single copy , . shipping.
Make checks payable to Jenny Davidow.
CA residents, please add sales tax.
Please enclose your name, address and phone number.